UNFREE MARKETS

COLUMBIA STUDIES IN THE HISTORY OF U.S. CAPITALISM

COLUMBIA STUDIES IN THE HISTORY OF U.S. CAPITALISM

Series Editors: Devin Fergus, Louis Hyman, Bethany Moreton, and Julia Ott

Capitalism has served as an engine of growth, a source of inequality, and a catalyst for conflict in American history. While remaking our material world, capitalism's myriad forms have altered—and been shaped by—our most fundamental experiences of race, gender, sexuality, nation, and citizenship. This series takes the full measure of the complexity and significance of capitalism, placing it squarely back at the center of the American experience. By drawing insight and inspiration from a range of disciplines and alloying novel methods of social and cultural analysis with the traditions of labor and business history, our authors take history "from the bottom up" all the way to the top.

For a complete list of title, see page 271.

UNFREE MARKETS

THE SLAVES' ECONOMY AND THE RISE OF CAPITALISM IN SOUTH CAROLINA

JUSTENE HILL EDWARDS

Columbia University Press

New York

Columbia University Press
Publishers Since 1893
New York Chichester, West Sussex
cup.columbia.edu

Library of Congress Cataloging-in-Publication Data
Names: Hill Edwards, Justene, author.
Title: Unfree markets : the slaves' economy and the rise of capitalism in South Carolina / Justene Hill Edwards.
Other titles: Columbia studies in the history of U.S. capitalism.
Description: New York : Columbia University Press, [2021] | Series: Columbia studies in the history of U.S. capitalism | Includes bibliographical references and index.
Identifiers: LCCN 2020038704 (print) | LCCN 2020038705 (ebook) | ISBN 9780231191128 (hardback) | ISBN 9780231191135 (trade paperback) | ISBN 9780231549264 (ebook)
Subjects: LCSH: Slaves—South Carolina—Economic conditions. | Capitalism—South Carolina—History. | South Carolina—Economic conditions—18th century. | South Carolina—Economic conditions—19th century.
Classification: LCC E445.S7 H55 2021 (print) | LCC E445.S7 (ebook) | DDC 306.3/6209757—dc23
LC record available at https://lccn.loc.gov/2020038704
LC ebook record available at https://lccn.loc.gov/2020038705

Columbia University Press books are printed on permanent and durable acid-free paper.
Printed in the United States of America

Cover image: National Numismatics Collection, National Museum of American History, Smithsonian Institution
Cover design: Elliott S. Cairns

CONTENTS

ACKNOWLEDGMENTS

I've been writing this book for a long time; in fact, for most of my adult life. This book has taken up space in my mind, startling me awake at night, following me like a shadow. Over the past twelve years, I have thought about this project almost every day. But I did not finish this book by myself. I feel so grateful and privileged to express gratitude to everyone who has helped me along the way. As much as I have been working on this project—and sometimes it has felt like a solitary endeavor—without the support of my network of friends and family, this book would not be out in the world.

First and foremost, I must thank my mother. Deborah Bryan has been my most vocal supporter from the beginning of this journey. She has been my steadfast cheerleader from the moment she brought me into this world. She instilled in me a confidence that has stayed with me from the moment I stepped into my first classroom as a child. From the beginning, she has believed in my talents as a writer, a historian, a professor, and as a scholar. My mother somehow divined that I would be a professor. She tells a story of observing me as a child arranging my dolls and stuffed animals, preparing to give them a lesson. So maybe it's no surprise that she has been guiding me on this path. From the marching band performances and her faith that I would excel in boarding school, to supporting me in navigating the rough patches of academia, my mother has listened to my cries of frustration during the process of finishing a PhD, finding and securing a job, obtaining a book contract, and finishing this project. She had confidence in me when mine was waning. I would not be where I am today without her unyielding support of my hopes, goals, and dreams. Her unconditional love pushed me to the finish line. We did it, Mom!

My husband, Kenneth, has been by my side from the early years of the research process, through the terrifying times in the hospital, to seeing this book in its current form. He has been my partner as I researched and completed my dissertation, through the stresses of looking for and starting an academic job, and the pressures of finishing this book. He has encouraged me though the writing blocks and offered me glasses of wine when my eyes could no longer stare at the words on the computer screen. He has persuaded me to think more broadly about the impact of my work, pushing me to speak to people outside of my field and outside of academia. We have gotten into hours-long conversations about the history of race, slavery, and economic inequality in America. He has been my companion in life, his words of encouragement and love pulling me through and illuminating the darkest of times. His influence on this book and my life are indelible. I love you.

My daughter Kenadie came into my life at an auspicious moment, as I was making the transition from student to professor. She has only known me as I worked on this book. I'm sure she has wondered why I could not devote more time to her as I finished this project. She, in many ways, has been my partner in crime as I finished this book. She accompanied me on research trips, sat in my classes when she had days off from school as I lectured about slavery, and witnessed me present conference papers. In many ways, she has observed this project evolve from a dissertation to a book. I hope she understands that this book is not only for me, but for us. And I promise to tear myself away from my work more often to bake, to watch TV, and to play Fortnite.

I first met Ernest Stewart when I was in third grade. In the first interaction that I can remember, he jokingly chastised me for my grades (which were stellar). Throughout the years, he bought me my first clarinet, made sure I had everything that I needed to succeed when I went away to school (including chopped wood), called me early on weekend mornings during my years at Swarthmore to make sure that I was getting my work done, and was enthusiastic when I decided to pursue a career in academia. He traveled with me on research trips, an ever-encouraging research assistant, from Newport, Rhode Island to Bridgetown, Barbados. Over the past several years, he encouraged me to relax more and enjoy all that I had accomplished. He always called asking two questions: How are you? Are you finishing the book? Now, Stu, the book is done.

I am blessed to have a supportive network of family who have provided love and inspiration. Stephanie Bryan, Terence Bryan, Alan Hill, Ashely Hill, Lorenzo Hill, Theda Edwards LaBome, and the Bryan and Plunkett families have been consistent sources of support. I am deeply grateful to my extended family: Teddy Coney, Bob and Lori Grady, Joe and Peri Kelly, David Lozada, and Denise Saddler.

I am beyond thankful to have a wonderful group of friends. Jennifer D. Jones, Ava Purkiss, Valeria Escauriaza López Fadul, and Creston Higgins are the best friends I could ever ask for. Each in your individual ways have provided me with support, love, friendship, and a sisterhood through the darkest and happiest of times. To Audrey Dorélien and Neferterneken Francis, I remember so clearly our freshman-year quad at Swarthmore. The stars aligned that made us not only roommates, but the best of friends. Even though we have been scattered around the world, we always find our way back to one another. I look forward to growing together for the next twenty years!

Corinne Field and Sarah Milov continue to be my accountability partners and my good friends. They have fielded my rants about the frustrations of finishing a book at such an unpredictable time and have encouraged me to be both productive and easy on myself during difficult parts of this process. I have come to rely on our check-ins and I would not have made it through this process in one piece without their steadfast friendship and support.

Along the way, I have developed friendships with a dynamic group of scholars. Tikia Hamilton, Jayanti Owens, Amanda Gibson, and Kelly Kean Sharp are brilliant scholars and friends. Sarah Haley and Erica Armstrong Dunbar are rock stars, and I am so fortunate to have had the chance to get to know them. I was fortunate to have worked with Amanda Moniz at the American Historical Association when I was not sure where my career was headed.

I am fortunate to be surrounded by wonderful colleagues at the University of Virginia. There are times when I cannot believe that I get to work with such brilliant and amazing scholars. From the moment that I arrived on the grounds, I have been welcomed by a dynamic group of historians who have been enthusiastic not only about my place among the faculty, but of my book's potential. Liz Varon, Carrie Janney, Max Edelson, and Olivier Zunz read and workshopped the manuscript at a critical point in the revision process. Gary Gallagher read an early version of the book proposal, and he swiftly told me that I needed to be a bolder and more audacious writer. I had the honor of receiving words of encouragement and feedback on chapter 5 from the late Joseph Miller. Fahad Bishara, Kevin Gaines, Grace Hale, Andrew Kahrl, John Mason, Christina Mobley, Penny Von Eshen, Jennifer Sessions, and Alan Taylor all gave me advice on not just how to shape the work, but also on how to navigate finishing a book while on the tenure track. Deborah McDowell has been an advocate from the very beginning of my time at UVA. Claudrena Harold is a force. I am stunned by her brilliance and empathy and I am so fortunate to have her as a friend. Kathleen Miller radiates so much positive energy and I am so grateful to have her as a colleague and friend. Whitney Yancey, Kelly Robeson, and Scott Roberts kept the wheels turning in the Corcoran Department of History. I am fortunate to have worked with an amazing group of undergraduate and graduate research assistants. Deanna Cook, Brian Neumann, Alisia Simmons, and Molly Wilson served as diligent research assistants, helping me with discrete tasks in the process of finishing this book.

My years at Princeton proved to be a turning point in my life. After working with wonderful professors at Florida International University as a master's student, I made the leap to a doctoral program. I first spoke to Tera Hunter in the fall of 2007 and I was immediately awed by her willingness to chat with me about my scholarly interests and the possibility of working together. Reading her scholarship was a revelation and I knew that I wanted to follow in her footsteps. I could not have imagined the influence that she would have on me and my scholarship. I offer her my sincerest thanks for her patience and support as I developed into an historian, teacher, and a scholar. Hendrik Hartog, Sean Wilentz, and Seth Rockman played pivotal roles as committee members, from the very beginning of the research process to the very end of the program.

The archivists at the South Carolina Department of Archives and History, the South Caroliniana Library at the University of South Carolina, the South Carolina Historical Society, and the Southern Historical Collection at the University of North Carolina-Chapel Hill supported this project when I wasn't sure how it would turn out. They showed me innovative ways to understand the lives of enslaved people in South Carolina.

I first began to entertain the idea of studying African American history at Swarthmore College. Though I was not a history major, I followed Allison Dorsey, taking her classes, as one of her acolytes. Over the years she has kept track of my progress, encouraging me along the way. First, Allison was my professor, then she became my mentor, and now I consider her a friend.

The following institutions offered financial support for this project: the McNeil Center for Early American Studies at the University of Pennsylvania, the Program in American Studies at Princeton University, the Program in African-American Studies at Princeton University, and the College of Arts and Sciences at the University of Virginia. I have had the pleasure of presenting chapters and sections of this manuscript in a variety of venues including the American Society for Legal History, Brown University, Cornell University, the Business History Conference, Midland School, the Organization of American Historians, the Society for Historians of the Early American Republic, the Southern Historical Association, the University of Delaware, the University of Nottingham, and the University of Pennsylvania.

I could not have asked for a more amazing set of publishing partners than the people with whom I have worked at Columbia University Press in the History of U.S. Capitalism series. I began working with Bridget Flannery-McCoy after a great conversation at the Business History Conference in 2017. I think every new history PhD is a little worried that no one will think that their recently defended dissertation could be turned into a book. I certainly had this concern. Bridget shared my enthusiasm about the project, supported my vision, and encouraged me to think more ambitiously about what this book could be. When Bridget left for a wonderful position at another university press, I began working with Stephen Wesley, who has offered me consistent support, feedback, and encouragement. He has fielded my random (and sometimes frantic) emails with an unparalleled level of patience. He has ushered this book through the publication process and I could not be more thankful that I had an opportunity to work with him. I also appreciate the work of Christian Winting in providing editorial assistance. Calvin Schermerhorn and the anonymous reviewers helped me make this a better book at a pivotal juncture in the revision process. The series editors for the History of U.S. Capitalism series provided me with timely comments that helped me strengthen my arguments and interventions. I worked with Cecelia Cancellaro as I began to revise my dissertation and she provided me with the type of feedback that only a skilled editor could.

I would be remiss if I did not acknowledge that this book almost did not come to fruition. On March 19, 2019, I suffered a major heart attack that almost ended my life. The doctors and medical staff at the University of Virginia Medical Center treated my case with urgency and a care that I fear I might not have received at any other hospital. I am ever grateful to have received outstanding medical care from the doctors, nurses, physical therapists, and medical staff who helped me recover physically and emotionally.

I owe a debt that I can only begin to repay. Thank you to all of the people who have helped me complete this project. Importantly, I am grateful to the enslaved people of South Carolina who have, over the past many years, amazed me. I am so honored to have had the opportunity to explore their epic journeys of survival.

UNFREE MARKETS

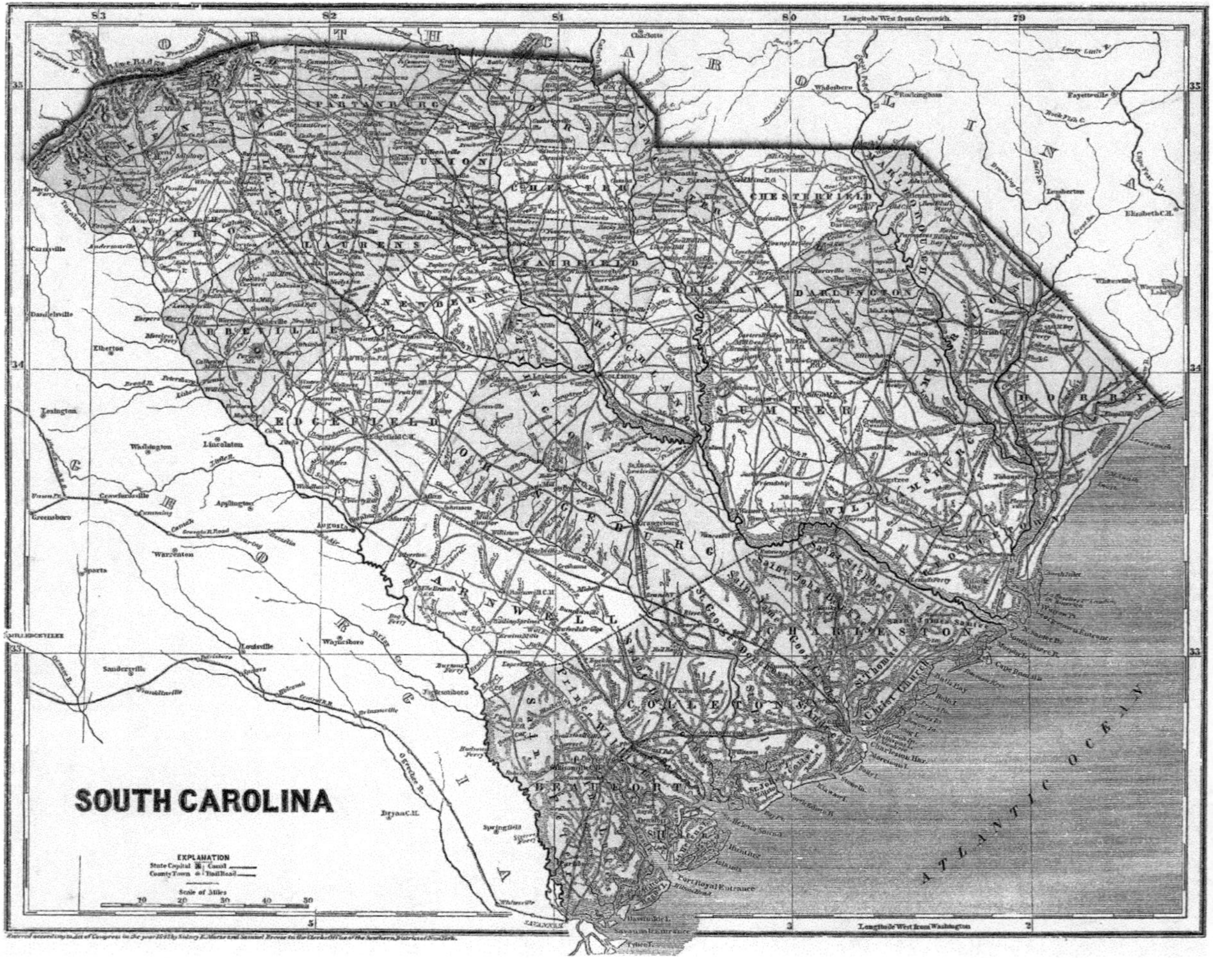

FIGURE 0.1 Map of South Carolina

INTRODUCTION

Capitalism in the Economic Lives of Enslaved People

Gus Feaster was a young man on the cusp of adulthood at the outbreak of the American Civil War. He had no information about when or where he was born, which meant that he did not know his exact age. Nor did he have a clear memory of his early childhood in Union, South Carolina. But when the ninety-something-year-old man was interviewed by Caldwell Sims, a fieldworker with the Federal Writers' Project, on June 28, 1937, the one aspect of his youth that he did recall, in stunning clarity, was of work, specifically his early years enslaved on a South Carolina plantation. "The furs' work dat I done was drapping peas," he began, as he chronicled for Sims his responsibilities as an enslaved child. But Feaster's memories were not relegated to work that his enslaver compelled him to complete. His recollection also included work for which he received compensation—work that he did for himself. Feaster earned money "by gathering blackberries to sell at Goshen Hill to a lady dat made wine frum them."[1] Then, he did what any young person would do with a bit of money in their pocket and the freedom to buy whatever their heart desired. "I bought candy wit de money," he revealed. The money that he earned from picking and selling blackberries satisfied not only his sweet tooth, but also his sense of youthful independence. That was the reason, he joked, "I ain't got no toofies [teeth] now."[2] Not only did Feaster remember how work shaped his life as an enslaved boy, but he also articulated how his experience as a young bondsperson included work for money.[3]

It may appear as though Gus Feaster's experience earning money was an anomaly, but it was not. The historical record is flush with examples of enslaved people figuring out how to make use of their time and their labor to earn wages, buy goods, accumulate property and, in general, participate in the economic lives of their communities. Enslaved men and women with not only money, but also the purchasing power of their labor, were ever-present. They traded on plantations and in city centers, along riverways and in ports. Enslaved people bought items that they desired and sold goods to anyone willing to engage economically with them. They hustled and haggled with travelers on country roads, earned wages for their labor, negotiated with their enslavers and white employers for money, and occupied public markets selling food and other handmade goods. All of these economic pursuits comprise what historians call "the slaves' economy."[4]

Enslaved people thought about their own economic enterprises in a variety of ways, especially in South Carolina. Charlie Grant, a former bondsman from Florence, described that his mother "had a big garden" and planted "collards en everything like dat you want to eat."[5] But the only time that she could tend to her garden was at night, "especially moonlight nights," because enslaved people "had to work in de field all day till sundown."[6] If she decided to not eat the food that she grew, she probably traded it among other enslaved people, sold it to her enslaver, or found whites who were willing to buy the goods from her. Though Grant does not reveal if his mother used the produce that she grew to obtain other items, she certainly relied on her gardening efforts to provide for herself and her family. Former bondswoman Sylvia Cannon offers another perspective, one in which she described the slaves' trade in a positive light. She believed that African Americans fared better in slavery than in freedom because whites "looked out for" them and they had "time off to work every Saturday."[7] All the extra crops that Cannon and her fellow enslaved people grew they could keep for themselves—to consume, to trade, or to sell. Yet after the Civil War, Cannon witnessed former slaves struggling to support themselves and their families.[8]

The recollections of Gus Feaster, Charlie Grant, and Sylvia Cannon cast enslaved peoples' economic enterprise in a sobering light. While

Feaster conveys a sense of youthful enthusiasm about earning money to buy candy, Cannon and Grant do not discuss how they and other enslaved people felt about having limited free time not to rest or spend time with family, but to work. At the end of the day, who benefitted from enslaved peoples' dedication to their own economic interests? Other than earning a bit of money to buy pieces of clothing or candy, what could the purchasing power of enslaved peoples' extra labor get them? Could Gus Feaster, for example, have turned his small-scale enterprise into something more significant, perhaps earning enough money to buy more autonomy or perhaps his own liberation?

On the surface, it may appear as though enslaved peoples' experiences in the American economy can be distilled to their experiences as property, as capital investments. After all, enslavers and slave traders viewed bondspeople as movable assets.[9] And enslaved peoples' labor helped to catapult the American economy into global prominence in the nineteenth century. The historical record, however, shows a more complex story. Embedded in the archive emerges the inner workings of enslaved peoples' economic lives. Documentary accounts illustrate that enslaved women and men cultivated an economic culture of their own as a material and emotional shield against the traumas of their enslavement.[10] Their economic lives were not always dictated by enslavers who believed that they were mere commodities, or by slave traders who placed pecuniary value on their bodies.[11] Instead, enslaved people made decisions, whenever possible, about where they would work, the wages they would accept, and with whom they would trade. They were compelled by their need to survive, and encouraged by the opportunities around them, to pursue their own entrepreneurial endeavors. All of this means that enslaved people with access to money, wages, and goods were everywhere. In fact, there was no aspect of slaveholding life that was not influenced in some way by enslaved peoples' economic aspirations.

But just because slaves' commercial pursuits were ubiquitous does not mean that bondspeople benefitted fully from their own economic activities. What happens when we explore the limits of economic and capitalist enterprise in enslaved peoples' lives? What if enslaved peoples' investment in capitalism undermined their pursuit of freedom?

This book foregrounds a radical idea. There were moments when enslaved people acted as capitalists. They were engaged in the types of economic activities that characterized capitalism during the period of legal slavery in America, especially in the nineteenth century. But for enslaved people, capitalist enterprise did not equal freedom.[12] Though enslaved people developed their own economic networks under the violence and trauma of slavery, they remained enslaved. These two ideas, that bondspeople pursued a measure of economic autonomy while living in bondage, were not anathema. And these activities *did not* upend the institution of slavery. Rather, enslaved peoples' economic enterprises reinforced it.

Moving chronologically from the early colonial period to the outbreak of the Civil War, I show that while enslavers in South Carolina embraced capitalist enterprise, which helped them build wealth and secure their economic status, for enslaved people, capitalism did not equal economic self-determination in the same way. Instead, it meant a continuation of the violent and exploitative regime that shaped their lives. By interrogating how slaves' entrepreneurial behavior evolved in South Carolina, this book maintains that enslaved people missed out on the promise of capitalism. It is true that enslaved individuals created avenues through which to act as economic agents within their local communities. Moreover, these pursuits helped them to weather the horrors of slavery.[13] Though bondspeople endeavored to deploy all the economic tools at their disposal to survive, economic enterprise alone did not help them achieve their ultimate goal: freedom. I argue that enslaved peoples' investments in their own economic lives only entrenched them even more deeply within the institution of slavery.

Unfree Markets asserts that the economic networks that enslaved people created were not always informal, internal, independent, or underground. Nor was the slaves' economy always relegated to the shadows or a marginal piece of the formal economy of slavery. Enslaved peoples' networks of enterprise were certainly not always illicit or extralegal. Indeed, enslaved peoples' economic activities were all of those things and more, from illicit and underground, to visible and legal.[14] Enslaved people were economic innovators in their own right, often pushing against social and legal boundaries to profit from their labor in as many ways as possible. Though the wages they earned, commodities they traded, and goods they acquired were not large in scale, enslaved people innovated their own brand of economic enterprise. And these ventures were ever-present. Gus Feaster's purchase of candy, for example, could be considered a minor occurrence. The episode, however, made an impact on him. Not only did he remember the incident in his old age, but he also connected the act of purchasing candy to wages that he earned. Though he did not earn a large sum of money, he did relish the ability to purchase something that he desired. And Feaster's experience was not singular; it shows that bondspeople were not only workers, but also enterprising economic actors invested in their own small-scale networks of commerce within an increasingly capitalist economy.[15] Ultimately, they were enterprising and they were entrepreneurs.

The experiences of an enslaved woman named Venus serve as a particularly poignant example. Venus's first appearance in the historical record occurs in November 1755, when her enslaver, John Bruce, described her as a "little negro girl" with "an iron on each leg."[16] Bruce called attention to young Venus because she ran away and he wanted to have her apprehended and brought to Charleston's workhouse to retrieve her. But this would not be Venus's final attempt to escape. Less than a year later, in August 1756, young Venus left Bruce's plantation again, and he assumed she was being harbored by a free woman of color named Judith.[17] Venus may have returned to Bruce of her own volition or was captured, because she fled for a final time in 1758.

On the lam for seven years, Venus lived under various pseudonyms including "free Hannah" and "free Mary" to disguise her true identity.[18] During her seven-year absence, she had three children and created a home for herself near Charleston. To provide for family, she worked as a washerwoman, employed illicitly by white families in the city. It was not uncommon for bondswomen to find work as washerwomen in colonial Charleston. Enslaved women created economic niches in urban centers during the colonial era, using their entrepreneurial skills to support themselves and their families.[19] Venus counted herself among this group. It is possible that she cultivated relationships with other free and enslaved blacks in the city during her various attempts to live free. In the summer of 1765, the executors of the recently deceased John Bruce wanted to include her, and presumably her enslaved children, in the sale of Bruce's lands and property holdings—holdings that including Bruce's enslaved property. And where did they believe she sought refuge? They believed that Venus "was lately seen in [Charleston's] lower market," a place where enslaved people frequently bartered, traded, and haggled with any customer who wanted to purchase their goods.[20]

Venus must have understood both the power and the limitations of her economic endeavors, and their connections to her pursuit of freedom. On the one hand, she fled, living as a semifree woman for seven years, providing for her family and taking advantage of every economic opportunity at her fingertips, through her own courage and enterprise. On the other hand, her persistence could not secure what she must have desired most for herself and her three children: their legal freedom, a goal that she pursued for herself from childhood. She must have lived under the constant fear of being captured and taken back to Bruce. The historical record does not reveal if Venus gained her freedom or if she and her family were caught, only to be returned and included in Bruce's list of assets. Nevertheless, Venus's experience illuminates the complexities of and inherent dangers in enslaved Africans' quest for liberty. While she surely understood that cultivating economic literacy was crucial to her survival, she must have quickly realized that her participation in her local marketplace of labor could not provide her—or her family—with full freedom or security.

While *Unfree Markets* offers an analysis of the economic strategies that enslaved people used to make their lives better, it does not offer a triumphant story of bondswomen and bondsmen unshackling themselves from the violent chains of slavery through economic ingenuity and enterprise. Viewed through the lens of capitalism's rise in the United States, enslaved peoples' entrepreneurial activities take on a more potentially destructive significance in the history of American slavery. Though it was true, as the historian Juliet E. K. Walker has proposed, that American economic growth in the decades before the Civil War "indirectly encouraged the entrepreneurial participation of blacks," enslaved entrepreneurship did not undermine the institution of slavery. Instead, enslaved entrepreneurship reinforced it.[21]

The pages that follow will reveal the ways in which capitalism proved to be an obstacle in enslaved peoples' lives. The tools of capitalist development that emerged during the period of legal slavery—adopted by enslavers and capitalists more generally—exploited the labor and the economic potential of enslaved people. Even though bondspeople had access to material goods, they continued to live in impoverished circumstances. Furthermore, though enslaved people took advantage of opportunities to profit from their labor to purchase their own freedom, these instances were few and far between. A small percentage of people of African descent in South Carolina were able to earn and save enough money to buy their freedom, especially in the three decades after the end of the American Revolution. But they were exceptions, not the rule.[22] Consequently, while enslaved people strategized to pursue their own financial goals, hoping to transform their work into freedom, capitalists—especially enslavers—controlled the mechanisms of economic influence and enslaved peoples' potential for economic advancement. Capitalists who invested in slavery and slave labor used their economic influence to extract as much labor and capital from enslaved people as possible.

Ultimately, enslaved people were not only bonded laborers, living under the brutalities of racial slavery. They were forced by enslavers, coerced by merchants, and compelled by their own deprivation to work as capitalist actors within an increasingly capitalist economy. As slaveholding capitalists invested more capital and resources into the successful proliferation of the slavery-based economy, so too did enslaved people. But enslaved peoples' investment in capitalism was not always a choice. Though their participation in local market economies began as a means of survival, in the beginning of the nineteenth century enslaved people were being *forced to* engage as capitalist actors more frequently within their local communities. It was at this time when the slaves' economy became part and parcel of South Carolina's increasingly capitalist economy of slavery. They were obligated to adopt a capitalist mindset in order to survive the increased economic burdens placed on them by their enslavers to survive. Though they earned small amounts of money and received the purchasing power of their labor to buy goods such as clothing and shoes, their enslavers forced them to work longer and harder to acquire these necessary items. Enslaved peoples' economic activities, therefore, were not outside the capitalist transformations that occurred at the larger levels of the economy. Bondsmen and bondswomen were fully part of an increasingly capitalist economy.[23]

South Carolina is the setting for this story. Examples of enslaved Africans navigating their local communities in search of economic opportunities abound in almost every region of the slaveholding Atlantic world.[24] But the culture of slavery and slaves' economic activities in South Carolina was as distinctive as it was unique. First, it was the original colony in what would become the United States that English colonists established for the development of slavery. Slavery shaped every social, economic, legal, and cultural development in South Carolina from its very inception. Moreover, enslaved African entrepreneurship had always been a part of South Carolina's culture of slavery. From the moment English colonists from Barbados established Carolina as a permanent colony in 1670, African slaves found ways to trade with anyone willing to trade with them. They even engaged in commodity exchange with their enslavers. In South Carolina, slaves' economic activities revolved around their access to two things: free time and land. By necessity, enslaved Africans used whatever free time they had to grow their own food. They used land allocated to them by their masters to plant gardens filled with corn, potatoes, and pumpkins. African slaves also used their land to tend their own livestock such as hogs and fowl. They would then seek out trading partners, both black and white, in an attempt to earn money or purchasing power from their independent work.

Second, South Carolina was distinctive from a demographic standpoint. Enslaved people quickly became a "black majority" early in South Carolina's history as a colony.[25] South Carolina's enslaved majority shaped how enslaved peoples' commercial practices evolved and survived, a trend that began in the colonial era and continued through the nineteenth century. South Carolina also had the highest percentage of enslaved people of any state in 1860. Enslaved people comprised 57 percent of the state's population on the eve of the Civil War, higher than any other state in the Union.[26]

Third, slave owners and politicians in South Carolina were in a unique political position, situating themselves at the forefront of deliberations about the future of the United States. They were often outspoken advocates for slavery and the federal government's protection of slaveholding interests. Indeed, during the 1787 Constitutional Convention in Philadelphia, South Carolina's delegates defended their proslavery agendas and fought vehemently to ensure that their right to own human property would be constitutionally protected.[27] During the first half of the nineteenth century, slaveholding politicians such as John C. Calhoun and James Henry Hammond were in the vanguard of legislative debates at the federal level about preserving slavery as an institution.[28] And South Carolina was the first state to declare its exodus from the Union in December 1860, upon the election of Abraham Lincoln. South Carolina's departure triggered the Civil War, with slavery as the state's rallying cry. South Carolina's political, economic, and social history make it the perfect setting for this study.

Though the slaves' economy in South Carolina is the focus of this book, enslaved people in the American colonies and in the United States adopted similar types of economic behavior. The culture of slavery varied based on time and place, but the slaves' economy remained a visible force within slave communities in the United States, and even the Atlantic world more broadly.[29] As the nineteenth century's capitalist fervor influenced how enslavers and slave traders exploited enslaved peoples' bodies and their labor, so too did enslaved people seek to make money and buy goods throughout the slaveholding South.

The economic lives of enslaved people have remained at the margins of broader conversations about the rise of American capitalism and slavery. If enslaved people bought and sold their own goods *and* received compensation for their labor, how do we evaluate their contributions to the growth of economic enterprise in the United States? More directly, how did capitalism work in the lives of slaves? This book connects enslaved enterprise, entrepreneurship, and enslaved peoples' investment in small-scale economic endeavors to emerging forms of capitalism in late eighteenth- and nineteenth-century America.[30]

A full quantitative accounting of the slaves' economy is impossible. Yet a surprisingly robust archive for enslaved peoples' networks of enterprise in South Carolina can be found in account books, slave narratives, and travelers' accounts. Enslaved people could not often reveal the inner workings of their lives and experiences; they did not leave behind a full archive of their own. Also, much of what we know about enslaved peoples' relationship to money and property comes through the words of whites, especially in the late seventeenth and eighteenth centuries. Not until the nineteenth century do the words of African Americans, both enslaved and free, emerge through narratives. So a project like this—one that seeks to unearth what was at times visible and invisible *and* existed in the space between what was legal and illegal—posed an immediate challenge. Exploring the narratives of runaway slaves, legislative records, and slave owners' and merchants' account books illuminated how enslaved people adapted their enterprising skills to South Carolina's increasingly capitalist culture of slavery.

Furthermore, the inner workings of enslaved enterprises were also revealed in a surprising place: the law. By its very nature, much of the slaves' economy straddled the boundaries between what was legal and illegal.[31] Historians understand that contingency defined the legal culture of slavery from the seventeenth to the nineteenth centuries. That is to say, slave laws were enforced in arbitrary ways. When legal administrators deemed the slaves' trade illicit, enslaved individuals who earned money and traded for goods materialized in the legal record. The legal archive demonstrated unequivocally that bondspeople were always involved in their own networks of exchange during the entire period of slavery in South Carolina. There were hundreds of court cases, from incidences of illicit trade handled by magistrates in district courts to larger questions about the role of the slaves' trade in South Carolina society writ large debated by state Supreme Court justices. Lawmakers began creating laws to address slaves' trading early in South Carolina history, in the late seventeenth century. It became increasingly clear that one of the reasons why slaves' economic activities continued to exist in the legal record of slavery in South Carolina was because legal administrators—specifically lawmakers, justices of the peace, judges, and members of slave patrols—could not fully rationalize whether they should eliminate the slaves' trade or allow it. Lawmakers ultimately created laws to regulate the slaves' economy. But in practice, the relationship between enslaved people and the law was messy and complex.[32] This complexity extends to how enslaved entrepreneurship appeared in South Carolina's legal culture of slavery.

The archival records reveal that as bondspeople stood at the center of larger trade networks, enslaved peoples' networks of economic enterprise did not flourish only because of their labor. In South Carolina, the economies of the enslaved could not have remained as visible as they were without the contributions of whites. This is not to say that white South Carolinians acted as selfless economic partners who ensured that enslaved people participated in economic networks unencumbered. To believe this idea would be to misunderstand the real ways in which slavery shaped market economics, race, and even capitalism during the period of slavery in South Carolina and in the United States more broadly. The reality of slaves' market activities, however, was that they involved whites at every rung of the social and economic hierarchy, from those at the bottom of the economic ladder to those at the top. Moreover, because most enslaved people were not literate and did not have access to the tools necessary to communicate in written form, much of the archival record comes from people who held power over them: enslavers, magistrates, merchants, and middling whites. This book pays attention as much to how bondspeople strove to maintain their own economies as it does to the white South Carolinians who participated in, attempted to profit from, and ultimately controlled enslaved peoples' investments in their own enterprises.

This book begins in the colonial period, and chapter 1 examines how enslaved enterprises became an important component of South Carolina's culture of slavery in the early colonial era. Beginning in 1670 with South Carolina's founding, enslaved Africans took advantage of opportunities to develop their own informal networks of trade. Shaped by the structure of slave labor organization on Lowcountry plantations, enslaved entrepreneurship quickly became an unmistakable feature of slavery in the colony—but not without controversy. Though colonial administrators ratified the first statute to regulate the slaves' trade in 1686, the law did not produce its intended effect. African slaves, and the white colonists with whom they traded, ignored this and future legislative attempts to interfere in slaves' entrepreneurial activities. In the late seventeenth and eighteenth centuries, as enslaved African labor bolstered South Carolina's rice economy, enslaved people innovated strategies to wedge themselves even more directly into the colony's economic life as buyers and sellers of goods. Enslaved men skilled in a trade found paying job opportunities as shoemakers and blacksmiths and enslaved African women sold foodstuffs they grew in their provision gardens to travelers in the Charleston marketplace. They took advantage of the task system, which structured their work lives on Lowcountry rice plantations, to cultivate individual garden plots, make foodstuff to sell in local marketplaces, and find employment opportunities when possible outside their plantation homes. Yet a threat to the slaves' economy loomed on the horizon.

Chapter 2 considers the slaves' trade in late eighteenth-century South Carolina and shows that during the American Revolution, enslaved Africans did not abandon their economic pursuits in the midst of war. Disrupted but not eliminated by wartime instabilities, enslaved peoples' networks of economic enterprise continued. Bondspeople sold goods such as firewood and food to Loyalist and Patriot soldiers alike and maintained their independent cultivation, all in an effort to survive the unpredictability of war. After the Revolutionary War ended in 1783, a new frontier of enslaved labor emerged as a wedge that drove apart slaveholders and poor whites: slave hiring. While enslaved people cultivated a measure of commercial savvy to profit from slave hiring, equally skilled whites saw this practice as a threat to their economic survival. Political debates ensued among nonpropertied whites and whites of the working classes about the place of slave hire in the new nation. They rejected not just the value of skilled slaves who earned money from their labor, but they also objected to white employers, merchants, and even enslavers who propped up the practice. The fissures that slave hiring caused between white citizens occurred concurrently with two of the most important developments in the history of American slavery: the invention of the cotton gin and the rise of short-staple cotton.

The advent of the cotton gin in 1793 and the popularity of short-staple cotton had a dramatic effect on the role of enslaved enterprises in the larger South Carolina economy. Chapter 3 explores how short-staple cotton production in the Upcountry regions of the state quickly eclipsed the state's rice economy in the early nineteenth century. This development altered the nature of the slaves' economy. What was once informal and underground became more visible. Enslaved peoples' trading networks expanded as bondspeople gained access to a wider variety of consumer goods and people with whom to trade. Therefore, as the economy of slavery grew, so too did the economies of the enslaved. But even though enslaved people had access to a wider array of material goods, their lives in slavery did not improve. Instead, they continued to grapple with the unyielding burden of their enslavement in the midst of an economic boom powered by the cotton that they cultivated.

White South Carolinians' fears of enslaved people with money fueled their concerns about the rapid growth of slaves' commercial endeavors. Increasingly in the first two decades of the nineteenth century, whites relegated to work as artisans and mechanics complained that neither slaveholders, nor merchants or lawmakers, protected them from equally skilled slaves. These white South Carolinians took their grievances to local and state lawmakers. Though state legislators often protected slave-owning interests in their responses to many of these concerns, their tone shifted in the aftermath of one of the biggest slave insurrection conspiracies in American history: the Denmark Vesey insurrection plot of 1822. Chapter 4 places the enslaved economy at the center of the Vesey plot. By recounting the aftermath of the Vesey conspiracy, it is clear that even though white South Carolinians feared the destructive potential of rebellious slaves, and of even free blacks, their fear did not stop them from participating in slaves' economic networks. At a pivotal moment when the specter of black violence reached its peak, neither enslaved people nor their white trading partners wanted their economic relationships to collapse.

As the American cotton economy continued to expand, enslavers, slave traders, and merchants found new ways to profit from their investments in slavery. New technologies infiltrated the lives of enterprising enslaved people. Chapter 5 explores the ways in which innovations in plantation management changed the ways that enslaved people approached their entrepreneurial pursuits. Instead of dictating with whom they would trade and negotiating the price at which they would sell their goods or labor, enslaved people began to lose this economic autonomy to their enslavers. In the aftermath of economic panics in 1819 and 1837, enslavers (including slaveholding politicians such as James Henry Hammond and Whitemarsh Seabrook) seized control of and extracted more value from enslaved peoples' expanding trade. Slaveholding capitalists invested in the cotton economy recognized that they could profit not only from slaves' labor, but also from enslaved peoples' investment in trade as well. Though the trade between enslavers and the enslaved was not new, enslavers in the mid-nineteenth century had more urgent motivations: money and profits. They exploited enslaved peoples' economic interests and they forced their slaves to take on more responsibilities to make their plantation enterprises more self-sufficient. Slaveholders also began tracking, in account books, the profitability of their slaves' independent cultivation. Enslavers introduced business practices such as accounting to their economic interactions with enslaved people. All of this meant that enslavers in the antebellum era innovated new ways to exploit enslaved peoples' capitalist ambitions.

By the 1840s and 1850s, it was clear to enslaved people that their economic enterprises may have afforded them the psychic and emotional uplift to withstand the increasingly exploitative structure of slavery, but their economic ambitions would not provide them with the means to dramatically alter their enslaved status. Chapter 6 shows that while slaveholding capitalists within South Carolina slaveholding society exploited all the economic tools at their disposal to profit from their investments in slavery, enslaved people who invested in their own ventures missed out on the larger benefits of capitalist enterprise. In addition to enduring the brutal labor regimes characteristic of plantation slavery, enslaved people were forced by their enslavers to grow their own food, tend their own livestock, and clothe themselves. Though enslavers argued that these activities fell under the guise of benevolent mastery, in reality slaveholders demanded that enslaved people increase their work output to boost their own profits. At the same time, the slaves' trade further exposed class divisions between white South Carolinians—a division that had been simmering since the late eighteenth century and had the potential to derail white solidarity around secession in 1860. The proliferation of enslaved enterprise and entrepreneurship brought the animus between nonelite whites and propertied whites to the surface. Though slaveholding capitalists in the three decades before the outbreak of the Civil War more willingly encouraged enslaved enterprise, which fanned the flames of class conflict between propertied and nonpropertied whites, this push ultimately supported enslavers' profit motives—not enslaved peoples' quest for freedom.

It is well-known that work shaped enslaved peoples' lives in the United States. But there is another aspect of enslaved peoples' lived experiences that deserves equal attention: the work that they did for themselves. While enslaved peoples' lives necessarily revolved around the brutalizing and violent labor regimes under which they worked, they carved out networks of trade for themselves. In essence, they were active participants in America's burgeoning capitalist and consumerist culture of the nineteenth century.[33] Enslaved peoples' commercial networks, however informal or illicit, were as dynamic as the formal economy of slavery. Their economic innovations may have afforded them a modicum of independence and provided a material and psychological buffer against the deprivation and violence inherent in American slavery. But the wages and purchasing power that slaves earned represented more than just episodes of agency. Enslaved people built their own economic networks, often in response to their enslavers' efforts to control them.[34]

However, the reality that enslaved people could earn money, purchase goods, and accumulate property does not mean that their participation in local market economies secured them physical or psychological freedom. The relationship between economic activity and freedom was fraught. Enslaved people understood this very clearly.[35] Bondspeople may have gained the psychological benefits of buying goods that they desired, but they could not fully enjoy the economic benefits of working for themselves because, ultimately, they remained enslaved. The historian Dylan Penningroth, in particular, contends that "owning property does not, by itself, make a person free."[36] For enslaved people, freedom did not come from economic activity or capitalist enterprise.

Even though enslaved people accumulated other forms of capital—social capital, for example—building their reputations as reliable economic agents with whom whites traded frequently, social capital alone did not elevate them out of slavery. Instead, enslaved people became even more tethered to the institution of slavery and the shackles of their enslavement. Bondspeople in South Carolina were important contributors to their local economies, not as property or capital, but as participants. Yet enslaved peoples' efforts to earn money could not secure what they desired most: their freedom.

1

"NEGROES PUBLICKLY CABALING IN THE STREETS"

The Enslaved Economy and the Culture of Slavery in Colonial South Carolina

On November 30, 1765, Henry Laurens, one of the colonial era's wealthiest merchants and slaveholders, wrote to Frederick Wiggins, the overseer of Ashepoo, a Lowcountry rice plantation outside of Charleston. An infirmity, Laurens wrote, forced him to remain in Charleston, spoiling his travel plans to Ashepoo to check on his late brother-in-law's plantation. He requested that Wiggins continue managing the estate, and the labor of the African slaves, in his stead. In addition to giving Wiggins a set of instructions about preparing the upcoming batch of rice for export, Laurens explained to Wiggins that if he were to run low on provisions, then there were other ways for him to obtain food. He could purchase food from the plantation's enslaved people. "If you apprehend a want of Provision," Laurens informed, "it will be proper to purchase of your own Negroes all that you know *Lawfully* belongs to themselves at the lowest price that they will sell for it."[1]

Though the correspondence was relatively short in length, its significance cannot be overstated. Laurens gave Wiggins permission to engage economically with the enslaved people on Ashepoo. It would have been easy for Wiggins to have helped himself to the slaves' independently grown products—goods such as corn and potatoes. Instead, Laurens encouraged Wiggins to think of the enslaved people as trading partners. He was conveying to Wiggins that he recognized enslaved peoples' rights to the food that they cultivated, including the right to sell their own goods at the price at which they determined.[2] Admittedly, Laurens may have believed that Wiggins needed to be apprised that it was not entirely uncommon for bondspeople on Ashepoo to appropriate or steal foodstuff that did not belong to them, only to turn around and sell the goods to willing customers. For this reason, he directs Wiggins to be cognizant of the difference between enslaved peoples' goods—items that "*Lawfully* belongs to themselves"—versus goods that belonged to Laurens. He knew that the enslaved people would not hesitate to steal his products to sell as their own if the opportunity presented itself. Nevertheless, enslaved Africans' entrepreneurial endeavors, and the informal economic networks that grew out of them, had become a visible feature of plantation life on Ashepoo for both Laurens and the bondspeople enslaved there.

The potential trade between the enslaved Africans and Wiggins on Ashepoo was not unusual. Indeed, the circumstance that Laurens described—that of enslaved people acting on their entrepreneurial ambitions and the enslaver recognizing slaves' property rights—reflected a tradition embedded deep within the culture of slavery in colonial South Carolina. Perhaps Laurens understood that respecting slaves' investment in trade was necessary not just for the management of the plantation, but by extension, to the stability of slavery in South Carolina writ large. The visibility of economic exchange that involved enslaved people not as property, but as economic agents with their own agendas and motivations, shaped South Carolina's culture of slavery from the earliest of colonial moments. This brief 1765 letter captures the ways in which enslaved Africans' customary right to sell their own goods fit into the social architecture of the South Carolina Lowcountry during the colonial period.

Enslaved peoples' entrepreneurial activities became an extension of the types of negotiations that occurred between enslavers and the enslaved in the colonial era.[3] African slaves' commodity exchange and independent work fulfilled their own subsistence needs *and* those of white colonists. Thus, enslaved peoples' entrepreneurial activities became an indelible aspect of South Carolina's culture of slavery early in its colonial history. It was not only enslaved people, but white colonists, enslavers in particular, who ensured that slaves' colonial-era networks of entrepreneurship and enterprise could flourish. The tradition of the enslaved economy found its roots in the late seventeenth and eighteenth centuries and shaped the ways in which white and black South Carolinians interacted economically far into the future.[4]

A closer interrogation of African slaves' economic innovations in a location such as the colonial South Carolina Lowcountry, however, reveals something more. Enslaved Africans' marketing pursuits were not always ancillary or informal. Bondswomen and bondsmen did not always have to hide their economic ambitions during the first generations of slavery in South Carolina. Rather, enslaved peoples' entrepreneurship was a common feature of colonial South Carolina milieu from its inception. Enterprising slaves navigated the colony's culture of slavery to capitalize on their own interest in purchasing goods and selling their products for any exchangeable commodity. But this is only part of a larger story. Slaveholders, in an effort to control enslaved peoples' investment of time and labor, protected slaves' economic ventures because they realized that these commercial practices helped to safeguard their investments in slavery.[5]

The economic interests of enslaved people, enslavers, and even non-propertied white colonists were not always mutually exclusive. While enslavers relieved themselves of the financial burden of providing slaves with subsistence, and while nonpropertied whites had access to relatively affordable foodstuff, enslaved Africans worked to make their lives better materially. If the correspondence between Laurens and Wiggins proves anything, it is that the slaves' trade fit into the Lowcountry's burgeoning culture of slavery. All South Carolinians were interested, in some way, in the slaves' trade during the colonial period.

By reconstructing the landscapes in which black and white residents of colonial South Carolina operated to cultivate enslaved peoples' marketing pursuits, this chapter connects enslaved peoples' entrepreneurial activities to the colony's culture of slavery.[6] White residents, slaveholding and nonslaveholding alike, quickly realized the importance of enslaved peoples' commercial networks. Enslaved Africans maintained economic arrangements that involved not only other enslaved people, but increasingly white colonists, travelers, and even enslavers. Slave owners, in particular, attempted to control the economic pursuits of their slaves, using enslaved peoples' commodity exchange as a boon for their investments in plantation slavery and slave labor. Enslaved peoples' trading strategies grew more important to a wider swath of the Lowcountry's white residents, as white colonists increasingly relied on the slaves' trade for a variety of goods. The transactions that occurred amongst a multiclassed and multiracial group of Lowcountry residents, with enslaved Africans at the center, became a valuable component of slaveholding life. Ultimately, slave-generated networks of exchange proved integral to South Carolina's culture of slavery in the colonial period. As enslavers strove to establish a regime of slave control, enslaved people endeavored to cultivate economic networks of their own. The struggle between slave owners' and enslaved peoples' economic interests played out in the development of slavery in colonial South Carolina.

Colonists and enslaved people in the Lowcountry adopted much of the culture of slavery from Barbados, including early residents' outlook on enslaved entrepreneurship. The tradition of enslaved people marketing and trading was well-established in Barbados when colonists from the island officially founded Carolina in 1670. Enslaved people quickly developed patterns of buying and selling, with enslavers recognizing this practice, in particular how enslaved people connected trade to growing their own food. Enslaved Africans and white colonists imported the tradition of slaves trading and provisioning themselves to Carolina.[7] According to the historian Jack Greene, more than half of the enslaved people and approximately half of the white colonists who inhabited Carolina during its first two years were from Barbados. The demographic breakdown continued for two decades.[8] The Barbadian influence was embedded in the development of slavery in the Lowcountry from its inception.

Enslaved people created economic networks in Barbados, as they would in Carolina, out of necessity. Trading with white free people and servants whenever possible, African slaves in seventeenth-century Barbados took advantage of opportunities to develop networks of trade with anyone willing to engage economically with them. The numbers of enterprising slaves increased as enslaved Africans quickly began to replace the numbers of white indentured servants. In 1661, the Assembly of Barbados, the island colony's legislative body, created a robust set of regulations designed to not only delineate the rights of white laborers from those of enslaved Africans, but to control what they surely believed was rebellious slave behavior. The island's slaveholders, who populated the legislative assembly and designed the laws, sought to prevent slave mobility and economic activity, making white free people subject to a fine if they were caught selling to servants or slaves. The statute targeted any "freeman or trader" who "presume[d] to buy or sell any commodities whatsoever, with any Servant or Slave . . . without the consent of the Master."[9] The Assembly of Barbados developed regulations in hopes of controlling African slaves' assertion of economic independence and to prevent enslaved people from trafficking in stolen goods, all while attempting to curtail economic interactions between indentured servants and bondspeople.

In the Barbadian 1661 slave code, slaveholding lawmakers recognized the growth of enslaved Africans' networks of trade. The code reflected the ways in which enslaved people lived and behaved during the first three decades of English settlement and African slavery in Barbados. The enterprising mindset of enslaved Africans in Barbados—and slave owners' perception of slaves' economic interests—influenced how the first group of white settlers and enslaved people in the colony of Carolina thought about networks of enslaved entrepreneurship.[10]

Against the backdrop of the Barbadian culture of slavery, enslaved women and men adapted their enterprising skills to the violent labor regime that characterized not only Barbados, but early colonial Carolina. From the late seventeenth century to the first two decades of the eighteenth century, enslaved Africans and white colonists in Carolina toiled in the dangerous work of establishing Carolina's plantation economy.[11] They cleared swamps and marshes and felled trees. They prepared land that would subsequently be used to plant and cultivate rice, the commodity that catapulted Carolina to prominence in the Atlantic world at the beginning of the eighteenth century. It was harrowing work for enslavers and other bonded white workers. It was even more violent for enslaved Africans, as they surely struggled to adjust to the brutal and unpredictable working conditions.

Yet enslaved Africans searched for ways to improve their immediate material conditions. They used the land that enslavers allocated to them to grow food for themselves in provision gardens. They used the little time they had at their disposal to create their own insular networks of trade, selling or bartering anything that they could grow in their gardens to anyone willing to exchange goods with them. But these small-scale pursuits did not shield them from enslavers' violence. In addition to implementing a system of cruel punishments, slaveholders understood that they could profit from enslaved peoples' investment in independent cultivation.[12] "For if they do not work they make mischief," one visitor revealed, "and do damage." For this reason, enslavers gave enslaved Africans "as much land as they can handle."[13]

The first generations of enslaved people sought out opportunities to make their daily lives better through trade and exchange from the moment that they reached the shores of the Carolina Lowcountry. But it may have been enslavers who created the environment for enslaved peoples' entrepreneurship to flourish. The historian Peter Wood has argued that before 1700, enslavers required enslaved Africans to raise their own crops because of the limited stores of subsistence in the Lowcountry during the early colonial era.[14] An early traveler to the colony observed that after enslaved people had finished their day's work, "They sell their crops and buy necessary things."[15] African slaves, therefore, transitioned into the economic life of early Carolina, not merely as bondspeople, but as independent economic actors. This first generation of enslaved Africans, by necessity, dedicated whatever free time and spare energy they had to the cultivation of their own goods, sometimes as a way to transform their commodity production into purchasing power to acquire other items such as clothing and shoes. One traveler revealed, "But in Carolina many have to plant their own food and have to earn their few clothes by Sunday work."[16] Despite the additional labor that planting and cultivating food required, enslaved Africans protected these traditions. Their survival depended on it. For enslaved people, therefore, provisioning themselves soon became not only a means of survival, but also a way to monetize their food cultivation. The legislative record reveals that bondspeople took the surplus of their independent cultivation outside the plantation, selling to anyone willing to buy from them.[17]

The documentary evidence for the period between 1670 and 1700 is relatively sparse in terms of locating the scope of enslaved peoples' networks of trade. Though the archival base is scarce, it is possible to hypothesize that enslaved people and enslavers came to informal agreements about the role of slaves' independent cultivation within Carolina's architecture of slavery. Enslaved Africans could, on occasion and with enslaver permission, transform their independent cultivation into the purchasing power to obtain merchandise or goods that they wanted.[18] Yet incidents of enslaved people finding trading partners without permission and participating in commodity exchange with stolen goods must have become prevalent enough for enslavers to push for and support legislative mechanisms to control such activities.

The most readily available sources that uncover the extent to which enslaved people transitioned into the marketplace as economic actors, and the problems that such activities might have caused, are legal records. That is to say, the best gauge of how enslaved people acted on their material and economic interests in the late seventeenth century exists in slave laws. This legislative effort began in 1686. In "An Act Inhibiting the Trading with Servants or Slaves," ratified in 1686, lawmakers attempted to allay enslavers' concerns about enslaved Africans' economic engagements in Charleston and the city's surrounding Lowcountry communities.[19] With the statute's ratification, enslavers sought to rein in enslaved peoples' and servants' participation in "indirect bargaines" with white colonists, meaning illegal commodity exchange that involved enslaved people. It outlined that no "freeman or free woman, servant or slave" was allowed "to buy, sell, barter, contract, bargain, or exchange any manner of goods or commodities whatsoever, of, for, to, or with any servant or slave" during their time of servitude.[20] Ultimately, the statute recognized the prevalence of enslaved peoples' entrepreneurialism. Lawmakers, acting on behalf of enslavers, argued that enslaved people "adventured privately to embezzle . . . their master's goods" and were responsible for "nourishing and introducing" vice to the young colony.[21] To curb the diffusion of this behavior, the 1686 Act targeted not only African slaves, but also white servants and other free white people who were caught trading illegally with the colony's enslaved population.

Slave laws, in general, and the 1686 statute in particular, reflected enslavers' beliefs about acceptable slave behavior. Enslavers embedded their ideas about enslaved peoples' investment in trade within laws and regulations. The 1686 statute proved that the slaves' trade was not a major concern for slave owners. In fact, the idea that enslaved people exercised a modicum of economic agency did not alarm enslavers because they believed that such activities kept enslaved Africans out of trouble—and enslaved people economic enterprise proved to be an economic benefit to them. Instead, slaveholders were concerned when bondspeople stole goods from them and then sold those goods to other consumers. They wanted an end to instances when bondspeople "embezzle, wast, and sell . . . their master's goods."[22] Slaveholders did not want to upend the entire system of enslaved peoples' commodity exchange, a system that benefited them.

For this reason, lawmakers included a clause to protect not only slaves' economic enterprise, but also enslavers' involvement in it. Slave owners' concerns did not revolve around entrepreneurial slaves; they were focused on enslaved people stealing goods that did not belong to them, a worry that Henry Laurens expressed seventy-nine years later. Enslaved Africans could legally trade with free people—or with one another—with the "consent of the master or mistress."[23] Enslaver consent recognized their dominion over enslaved people—a recognition that would remain codified until the end of legal slavery in 1865—and became a pillar on which enslaved peoples' networks of trade would have some form of legal standing in South Carolina. Lawmakers reinforced enslavers' interests because, by and large, they were one in the same. The laws, therefore, upheld enslavers' discretionary power over their slaves, including enslavers' freedom to permit the slaves' trade.

Despite slave owners' anxieties about stealing, enslaved Africans endeavored to use their own networks of trade as a way to meet their own survival needs. Indeed, they began to protect their customary right to entrepreneurship as a way to weather the insecurity of their lives as bondspeople and to obtain goods that their enslavers were not providing for them. The ubiquity of the slaves' trade must have garnered a heightened amount of attention and acceptance from white colonists who were benefitting from buying foodstuff from bondspeople. Enslaved people, therefore, became accustomed to navigating Carolina's legal and social architecture. They understood that as long as their enslavers approved of their entrepreneurial pursuits, then they could engage in commodity exchange relatively unencumbered. Though African slaves may have recognized the dubious legality of their commercial activities, they encountered willing parties—both black and white—who eagerly traded for and purchased their products.[24]

What the 1686 statute reveals is clear: enslaved people sought out opportunities to trade and market independently. The legal code is clear about where lawmakers and enslavers stood on enslaved Africans marketing efforts. Their perspective on enslaved peoples' networks of economic enterprise was one of acceptance, within bounds. After all, enslavers compelled enslaved Africans to grow their own subsistence, goods such as melons, pumpkins, peanuts, corn, and potatoes. Therefore, while enslaved people were finding ways to resist the bonds of their enslavement, not only through stealing from their enslavers but trading stolen goods for items that they desired, enslavers relied on the law to keep slaves' economic activities in check. Enslavers wanted to ensure that enslaved people did not regularly use stolen goods in their independent marketing.

In this respect, the legal instruments created by slave-owning legislators to protect their own property rights were not an outlier. In slaveholding colonial societies around the Atlantic world, enslavers increasingly allocated spare land they had at their disposal to their slaves.[25] This typically occurred when slaveholders' dedication to staple production, such as rice in the Carolina Lowcountry, were nascent. It would be a mistake, however, to believe that enslavers acted out of altruistic concern for enslaved peoples' well-being. Enslaved Africans involvement in both the cultivation of their own food, and also their own networks of trade, revolved around their access to land and free time.[26] The land that slave owners allocated to enslaved people was land on which enslaved Africans planted gardens and grew food that they then consumed. These lands, and the provision gardens that enslaved people planted therein, formed the basis for enslaved Africans' independent production.[27]

Despite the concerns expressed by slave owners about enslaved people stealing and reselling their goods, enslavers did not ban black enterprises entirely. While African slaves made participation in their own commercial activities an essential aspect of their lives, enslavers attempted to use enslaved peoples' investment in economic enterprise as a form of control to buttress their investments in slave labor. It was not uncommon for enslavers to allow enslaved people to "sell their own crops and buy some necessary things" as a way to ensure that slaves kept themselves busy during periods of nonplantation work.[28]

Bondspeoples' economic autonomy required constant negotiation between themselves and their enslavers. But the 1686 statute protected not only slaveholders' acceptance of enslaved peoples' marketing pursuits; it ultimately protected enslaved peoples' system of enterprise itself. It established a precedent to which enslaved people and slaveholders would refer when they defended bondspeoples' economic pursuits. It created space for enslaved entrepreneurship in South Carolina to be legal.

It is difficult to quantify the extent of the slaves' trade in the colonial era. However, if the documentary record and enslaved population growth are any indication, enslaved peoples' networks of commodity production and trade proliferated in the Lowcountry during the late seventeenth and early eighteenth centuries.[29] It is possible that the influx of more enslaved Africans to labor on Lowcountry rice plantations contributed to the rising numbers of not only trading partners, but willing enslaved participants in slaves' entrepreneurial ventures. The enslaved African population increased steadily in the late seventeenth century, from 200 people of African descent in 1680 to 1,500 in 1690, a jump of 16 percent of the colony's population to 38 percent in a decade. By 1700, African slaves comprised approximately 42.8 percent of the colony's population.[30] It is also probable that as the population increased, from 200 in 1670 to 2,444 in 1700, that enslaved people were exposed to more potential trading partners.

The frequency with which the slaves' trade arose in the public discourse indicates that enslaved people, and the people with whom they were trading, became more visible. It also suggests that enslavers were not opposing enslaved peoples' public demonstration of their investments of time and resources in entrepreneurship. In fact, African slaves' presence as marketers in Charleston was so prominent that it spurred colonial legislators to revise the 1686 statute in 1712, and again in 1722.[31] As the number of enslaved Africans in the colony increased to over

70 percent of the colony's inhabitants in 1720, African slaves' networks of commerce became even more public facing as well.[32] The consistent public attention that bondspeople attracted, however, does not suggest that all white colonists strove to curtail enslaved peoples' networks of entrepreneurship. Indeed, it meant that white colonists were attempting to stymie the illegal slaves' trade, specifically enslaved people marketing goods stolen from their enslavers.

In the midst of amplified legislative interference in the early eighteenth century, enslaved Africans attempted to take advantage of the access that they had to both land and their labor. The historian Philip D. Morgan reminds us that the evolution of enslaved peoples' entrepreneurship in colonial South Carolina was directly related to slave owners' adoption of the task system.[33] A task measured the specific amount of work that an enslaver or overseer expected an enslaved person to complete in a day. If a bondsperson completed the day's task, he or she could have "free time" to engage in other, often productive, activities. Despite the structure of the task system, and the customary rights that enslaved people attempted to protect, overseers and enslavers did not hesitate to use violence to punish slaves who failed to complete their day's tasks. According to the historian S. Max Edelson, as much as enslaved Africans tried to take advantage of their free time to invest in profitmaking activities, enslavers and overseers found ways to extract more labor out of them.[34] In the process, enslaved people were consistently attempting to extract as much free time as possible under increasing workloads. Nevertheless, without the task system, enslaved peoples' networks of commerce would not have taken such a strong foothold in the culture of Lowcountry slavery. Though it is unclear when the task system came to define labor organization in the Lowcountry, enslaved people were certainly working by task by the first half of the eighteenth century.

Enslaved people used their free time to put in extra work, tending their provision gardens for example. Sometimes they even spent their free time maintaining livestock, such as hogs and chickens. In 1728 two enslaved people, Abraham and Marcia, received remuneration from their enslaver Elias Ball: Abraham for raising fowls and Marcia for hogs. Abraham earned £1 and 10s in the sale. In 1736, twenty-two people sold Ball food that they had grown in their provision gardens and collectively they earned £50. The historian Edward Ball has argued that for enslavers, "a thin system of wages was a means to buy cooperation."[35] Thus, slaveholders were beginning to implement systems of compensation for enslaved Africans as a way to compel slave compliance without the use of overt violence. The establishment of the task system was a tool in this effort.

Though the task system provided enslaved people with the opportunity to invest their free time in local economic networks, it was in Charleston where enslaved Africans sought to make the most of their nonworking time. Charleston, the colony's economic hub and colonial America's most prosperous port city, became the center of enslaved peoples' networks of economic enterprise. One such instance in 1732 involved enslaved Africans owned by enslaver J. Townsend. The bondspeople had been earning money, perhaps by hiring out their time in the city, and keeping the money for themselves instead paying their earnings to Townsend.[36] Consequently, Townsend published a note in the *South Carolina Gazette* alerting all white Lowcountry residents that if anyone had conducted any financial transactions with him through his slaves, then they had to pay him directly. He warned every person "not to pay any sum or sums of Money to any of the Negroes" and concluded that if they did not comply with his order, then he would sue them for the funds.[37] The enslaved people clearly disregarded regulations established by both their enslaver and lawmakers by keeping their earnings. Yet in spite of the law and Townsend's directives, the bondspeople understood the economic and legal landscape of Charleston and took advantage of the availability of willing employers. The conspicuousness of their economic pursuits threatened Townsend enough that he appealed to the public to help him recover the money that he believed his slaves had stolen from him.

Perhaps the enslaved Africans owned by Townsend were members of the enslaved contingent who regularly congregated to sell goods or engage in self-hire in Charleston in the early 1730s. In 1733, the numbers of enslaved people assembling in the city increased to the point where white colonists issued complaints to the colonial assembly about their boisterousness and visibility in the port city, saying that enslaved Africans were causing "great Noise and Disturbance."[38] Not only did bondspeople travel to Charleston to sell their goods, but they also made voyages to the city to hire themselves out, with enslavers allowing enslaved people to find employment on their own. With their wages in hand, hired out slaves purchased a variety of goods, including alcohol. Enslaved peoples' consumer habits elicited strong responses from white city residents in 1734, when they accused hired out enslaved Africans of "Idleness, drunkenness, and other Enormities."[39]

It was not always the desire to buy goods that drove enslaved people to practice self-hire in the city. Enslaved Africans also made the excursion to Charleston to fellowship with one another. These trips often took place on Sundays, when they enjoyed free time, and enslaved Africans relished their time in the city so much that they were accused of "endangering the Safety of the Inhabitants" with their exuberance.[40]

The practice of slave hire, in particular, allowed enslaved people a small degree of autonomy to seek employment on their own, particularly in Charleston, which had grown in the eighteenth century to be a bustling entrepôt that brimmed with economic opportunities. The plethora of odd jobs led enslaved people to the city, but the increasing numbers of other enslaved Africans kept them there. Carolina, an enslaved man who was described as "a tall Gambia negro man," ran away from his enslaver in October 1737. His distinguishing markers were both his stature and that he spoke "broken English." Carolina also "used to attend the market," an indicator of where he may have spent the majority of his free time.[41] In the early eighteenth century Charleston began to serve as a communal space for African slaves, where they combined their economic pursuits with the opportunity to congregate with one another. The ways in which enslaved Africans used Charleston as a social and economic hub proved bothersome for the city's white colonists. Perhaps the complaints about the prevalence of enslaved Africans came from colonists who were not directly benefitting economically from trading with or hiring out enslaved people.

The ubiquity of enslaved peoples' entrepreneurship in Charleston prompted lawmakers to revise slave laws in 1734 and again in 1738. Enslaved people had been more bold in taking on opportunities to "go wither and work where they please," both with and without their enslavers' permission.[42] At times, bondspeople and slave owners would negotiate the amount of money the enslaved person needed to bring back to their enslavers in order to go in search of their own employment. Yet enslaved people often attempted to profit from these pursuits, earning more from their employment than the amount required from their enslavers. Bondspeople would then save the profits from their self-hire, profits that they could use to buy cloth, clothing, shoes, or other necessities.[43]

The existing legal instruments of control had little effect on enslaved Africans and the white colonists with whom they were trading. It is not surprising then that between 1712 and 1738, enslaved peoples' entrepreneurial activities had become more visible. African slaves' networks of enterprise expanded so quickly, and so conspicuously, that even on Sundays they were found "publickly [*sic*] cabaling in the Streets."[44] In this period, in addition to selling their goods to customers on the streets of Charleston, enslaved vendors targeted their energies to the city's wharf. One account reveals that African slaves would consistently purchase goods such as corn, peas, and chickens at low prices and then take these goods to the Charleston wharf and sell them at exorbitant prices to anyone willing to pay their rates.[45] Enslaved Africans also adroitly navigated the rivers, streams, and roadways between South Carolina's rice plantations and Charleston. They took advantage of the flow into and out of the port for their own benefit. One enslaved man, Jack, a ship carpenter, pretended to be free in order to earn his own wages. In 1737, he ran away from his master, with both his knowledge of ship-building and navigation, and also with the money he earned from his independent work.[46]

The visibility of enslaved Africans trading and hiring themselves out did not compel colonial administrators and enslavers to re-evaluate increasing the penalties for bondspeoples' engagement in economic activities. But the fear of violent slave insurrection surely did. On Sunday, September 9, 1739, a group of African slaves congregated near the Stono River in St. Paul's Parish, approximately twenty miles south of Charleston. On this day the enslaved rebels burglarized a store, stole munitions, and ransacked the surrounding area in hopes of seeking refuge—and freedom—in Spanish Florida.[47] Together, they killed thirty-nine colonists. The Stono Rebellion was one of the first major slave revolts in British North America. White colonists' fear of rebellious and violent enslaved Africans increasingly revolved around slaves' ability to move freely around cities and their ability to earn money and act as consumers.

The Stono Rebellion revealed that enslaved people desired one thing above all: their freedom. Though many enslaved men and women in the

Lowcountry protected their customary privileges to trade and engage in commodity exchange, their economic activities in many instances did not provide them with what they really wanted, which was their emancipation. They may have inched toward a semblance of freedom, through self-hire and marketing, but few bondspeople earned enough money to emancipate themselves. It is for this reason, as the historian Cynthia Kennedy has shown, that enslaved people defined liberty on their own terms.[48] Some ran away and sought shelter among the small population of free blacks. Others took up arms, pledging to die in their fight for freedom. Despite the proliferation of slaves' networks of trade, and despite enslavers' sanctioning their trading pursuits, enslaved people did not earn the purchasing power to buy their way out of slavery. The Stono uprising did destabilize the foundations of slavery in South Carolina for a brief period of time, with enslavers and lawmakers paying particular attention to the economic habits the region's bondspeople. But the rebellion did not destroy enslaved peoples' networks of trade, nor the system of slavery.

The upheaval caused by the violent event at Stono, and perhaps white colonists' complaints to a lesser extent, compelled lawmakers to revisit the efficacy of laws that they created to regulate black slaves' and whites' participation in enslaved Africans' economic networks. Therefore, in 1740, members of the colonial Assembly overhauled the colony's statutes. This revision proved to be the most substantive of the colonial period. In the additional amendments, legislators added addendums that included implementing a stronger ticketing system, wherein bondspeople were required to possess a ticket from their masters if they worked outside their master's household or property. The ticket had to stipulate the slaves' destination, the travel date, and if the enslaved person had permission to purchase or sell goods.[49]

Despite the legislative overhaul in 1740, which continued through the 1740s into the 1750s, enslaved people found eager customers—white and black, enslaved and free.[50] They also continued to "openly buy and sell sundry sorts of Wares" and "hire themselves to work, without a Ticket from their respective Masters and Mistresses." Enslaved women, in particular, used the earnings made from their marketing to upgrade their clothing. White Charlestonians, in 1744, complained that enslaved women did "not restrain themselves in their clothing" and outfitted themselves instead in "Apparel quite gay and beyond their condition." The complainants argued that bondspeople did not earn money for themselves outright, but resorted to stealing from their masters and mistresses. White colonists believed that bondspeople, and bondswomen in particular, could not have leveraged their enterprising skills to receive the financial benefits of their hard work, despite their conspicuousness as vendors in the streets of Charleston. Though enslaved people made visible their economic actions, some white Charlestonians were eager to ensure that enslaved people could use their economic power. White vendors, including "Retailers of strong Liquors," were selling rum to city's enslaved people.[51] It is clear that the statute meant to curtail what had become an important aspect of life in the Lowcountry. Instead, the enslaved economy continued as it had, benefitting white colonists as well as enslaved people themselves.

It is not surprising, therefore, that even in the midst of social turmoil in the wake of Stono, enslaved Africans traded often out of necessity, with enslavers continuing to support and sometimes turning a blind eye toward these activities. In October 1742, one visitor to Charleston remarked with astonishment that enslaved people had been "turn[ing] their crops into money and buy[ing] themselves some old rags."[52] While this visitor recognized that the bondspeople had not received adequate clothing from their enslavers, he highlighted the connection between enslaved people working for themselves, selling their own crops on Sundays, and enslavers' approval of the slaves' trade.

It is possible that this traveler did not fully understand the reciprocal economic arrangements that dictated how enslavers and enslaved people interacted. While enslavers instituted strategies hoping that their slaves would be compliant and not run away, some enslaved people realized that they could direct their trading interests toward their enslavers. Enslaved Africans on Henry Ravenel's Hanover plantation in the Berkeley District had been selling goods to and buying goods from Ravenel throughout the 1760s. Two enslaved people, Pompey and Amey, were the most frequent of Ravenel's enslaved trading partners. Pompey regularly sold Ravenel independently grown corn and fowls while Amey was compensated for her hogs, fowls, and corn.[53] Between 1764 and 1771, twenty-seven enslaved Africans sold goods to Ravenel. This plantation-based system of exchange perhaps reflected an understanding between enslaved people and Ravenel, one that required the buy-in of both parties. While Ravenel allowed the slaves on his plantation to work for compensation, surely as a form of control, the enslaved people used the economic arrangement with Ravenel to profit off of their labor.

Yet even after the Stono Rebellion, enslaved people consistently tested the boundaries and limits of their enslavers' permission to trade. In October 1746, Bella ran away from her enslaver, John Stanyarne. She had been a frequent presence in the Charleston marketplace, "being every day at Market selling divers things."[54] There is no information about whether or not Bella had Stanyarne's permission to sell her goods in Charleston. It is possible that Stanyarne acknowledged her daily attendance to the city's market as an extension of her negotiated privileges. Perhaps Bella's independent marketing only became a problem for Stanyarne once she made the choice to abscond. Bella decided to deprive Stanyarne of not only her labor, but also the profits of her commodity exchange.[55] It was in this way that Bella not just tested, but undermined, what may have been an agreement between herself and her enslaver. Ultimately, Bella wanted her freedom and she understood that she could use her knowledge of the marketplace to take it.

Bella's experience also suggests the extent to which enslaved people used the actual marketplace as a safe haven. A runaway slave ad in 1767 identified an elderly enslaved man, Noko, not only by the "remarkable large wart on one of his shoulders," but also for his association with Lowcountry slaves who frequented the public marketplace.[56] In 1770, an enslaved woman, Lizette, was suspected of having stolen six bills of credit. The owner of the bills offered a reward to anyone with information about the crime and noted that Lizette attended "the Lower Market, and frequently has Things to dispose of there."[57]

The phenomenon of runaway slaves absconding to seek safety in the marketplace was particularly prevalent among enslaved women, in what historian Shauna Sweeney calls "market marronage."[58] Bella ran to the marketplace, seeing it as a place to shield herself from the grips of her enslaver. She may not have only stolen goods to sell to willing buyers, but she stole what was most valuable to her enslaver: herself. Bella took a calculated gamble with her future, hiding herself within the hustle-and-bustle that characterized Charleston's colonial marketplace. It is possible that Bella recognized that in order to ensure her survival, she had to blend in with the other enslaved black women who had become centerpieces of Lowcountry marketplaces as vendors.

The presence of enslaved African women—also known as "market women"—selling their merchandise was not unusual in regions of the slaveholding Atlantic world during the eighteenth century. According to historian the Hilary Beckles, in his study of enslaved African women in Barbados, black women's roles as traders and sellers in the public marketplace mimicked West African cultural traditions of women controlling their family's economic lives. Because women had been responsible for representing their family's economic interests at the market, enslaved women in West Indian slave colonies such as Jamaica and Barbados adapted marketing activities into their lives as bondswomen. Despite the legal regulations created by colonial administrators to control enslaved women's economic autonomy, bondswomens' marketing activities thrived during the seventeenth and eighteenth centuries. Enslaved women used the marketplace as both a space and an economic mindset, to hide themselves in plain sight, using their trading activities to earn wages as a way to shield themselves from their enslavers.[59]

Enslaved women were singled out for their positions as hucksters in the Charleston marketplace, a phenomenon common in cities of the Atlantic world. The historian Robert Olwell has argued that enslaved African women took seriously their positions as marketers in the Lowcountry. The presence of enslaved African women in the Charleston marketplace, therefore, was an extension of a tradition that had existed—and had been developing—in marketplaces around the Atlantic world.[60] Marketing bondswomen took up space in public markets, selling their wares and haggling with buyers, and their visibility only increased after the formal establishment of Charleston's central marketplace in 1739.[61] Enslaved women who worked as vendors were called "insolent," "loose," and "disorderly" by colonists who dismissed their enterprising interests as foul behavior.[62] Despite these slurs, marketing bondswomen maintained their place in the landscape of urban life in the Lowcountry, often expanding their plantation roles to incorporate the selling of commodities that they and their families produced.[63] The marketplace was one venue in which enslaved women could wield power and influence.

Yet market women in Charleston represented the fundamental conundrum of enslaved enterprise during the colonial era. They received the brunt of public scrutiny about their marketing ambitions while being the main purveyors of food in and around the Lowcountry. They brought much-needed produce to the city's Lower Market, goods such as "poultry, fruit, eggs," and other food that fed the Lowcountry's black and white residents.[64] They populated the marketplace "from morn til night," sometimes privileging their black customers over white ones.[65] One observer even detailed that market women did not hesitate to "*wrest* things out of the hands of white people" in order to sell their goods to other enslaved people instead of white customers. Despite the prominent role that enslaved marketing women occupied in the Lowcountry's landscape of provisioning, where market women sold the food that fed the region's residents, they could not escape the critical eye of whites who relied on them for food while criticizing them for their raucous behavior.

Even though white colonists complained about "idle negro wenches, selling dry goods, cakes, rice" in public marketing spaces, slave traders sometimes used enslaved women's roles in the market as a selling point.[66] On August 16, 1771, three bondswomen were sold at a public auction near Charleston. One woman, described as "middle-aged," was accustomed to "attend[ing] the market."[67] A similar ad noted that three young enslaved women were being sold "for no Fault," which meant that they were being sold for no perceived character flaws or bad behavior. In addition to one of the enslaved women being a skilled seamstress, the two other women were "used to Marketing."[68] Enslaved African women in the Lowcountry had established themselves as worthy economic agents, visible in the local marketplace. Enslavers quickly understood that they could capitalize off of enslaved women's economic acumen.

Enslaved women and men were forced by their circumstances to innovate ways both inside and outside the marketplace to ensure their survival during the colonial period. Enterprising enslaved Africans in the Lowcountry did not relegate their economic pursuits to just trade with their enslavers or trade in the marketplace. African slaves did not hesitate to take advantage of any opportunity that presented itself to ameliorate their material conditions. This was the case in the aftermath of the Great Hurricane of 1752. In mid-September 1752 a major storm swept through South Carolina's Lowcountry, with gale-force winds decimating rice plantations and the sea swell flooding the streets of Charleston.[69] In response to the general upending of life both in the city and on surrounding plantations, enslaved Africans looked for opportunity. They scoured hurricane-damaged neighborhoods in search of items that they could put to good use. Soon after the winds died down and the hurricane swells subsided, the Charleston council forbade any enslaved person from pillaging the hurricane-ravaged region of "Goods, Wares or Merchandize, Houshold [*sic*] Furniture, Sails, Rigging, Timber, Boards, Shingles, or other Things," with the penalty being time spent in the local work house.[70] Members of the city council recognized that enslaved Africans took advantage of the natural disaster to procure goods that they could either use for themselves or sell whenever the opportunity presented itself. After all, bondspeople in and around Charleston were prepared to sell anything for a profit.

During the 1760s and the early 1770s, as enslaved Africans became even more active participants in the colony's economic culture, they provided important foodstuff for Lowcountry residents in a more substantive way. Enslaved people had been so public with their marketing that they had been raising the prices of "almost every necessary of life."[71] The enslaved sellers were accused of being engaged in "various other acts of extortion," to the detriment of primarily white buyers who relied on purchasing necessary goods from bondspeople.[72] Enslaved people, though, continued to face pushback in the form of stronger regulations on their networks of commodity exchange, especially within the Charleston marketplace. In April 1760 and again in March 1761, the commissioners of the Charleston marketplace tried to enforce a fine of two shillings and six pence for each enslaved person who attempted to sell their provisions in the market without a valid ticket from their master.[73]

Enslaved people openly disregarded the regulations that attempted to restrict their sale of goods in public marketplaces. They understood that with enslaver support they could continue—perhaps even expand—their investments of labor and time into their marketing pursuits. In a vehement rebuke of not only enslaved traders, but also their customers and the slaveholders who allowed such economic pursuits, four commissioners of the Charleston market (Daniel Cannon, William Bampfield, Benjamin Baker, and Robert Deans) made a public supplication. Their complaint suggested that the market's enslaved sellers had been taking advantage of their economic opportunities, and exploiting the economic principles of supply and demand. They argued that enslaved marketers were in the habit of shifting the prices at which they would sell their goods to Charleston inhabitants to make the largest profits possible from their sales. The complaint also reveals the importance of enslaved sellers in providing necessary foodstuff to Charleston residents. Even though the commissioners argued that the enslaved traders were spreading "idleness, drunkenness and dishonesty" among themselves, they clearly understood enslaved peoples' roles as suppliers of essential goods to Lowcountry populations. Enslaved people had found a way to exploit their economic niches.[74]

Moreover, there was a strong contingent of white colonists with political power and economic influence who continued to economically benefit from slaves' commodity exchange: enslavers. Some Lowcountry slaveholders preyed on enslaved peoples' interest in earning money to obtain goods. The experiences of enslaved Africans on several Lowcountry rice plantations exemplify slaveholders' embrace of the slaves' trade. In 1766, enslaved Africans owned by Henry Laurens had the opportunity to buy eating utensils from him. But he noted that the slaves had to pay for the goods, specifically bowls and mugs, "according to the Planter's custom or remitted as I shall think proper."[75] Enslavers' largely supported enslaved peoples' enterprising within reason and regulations had little impact on the expansion of enslaved peoples' networks of trade.

Not only were enslaved Africans selling the profits of their garden plots, but they also used their purchasing and bartering power to obtain a wide variety of goods, not the least of which included alcohol.[76] Enslaved peoples' presence as consumers in Lowcountry taverns became so widespread that in April 1767, colonial lawmakers passed a regulation directed at local taverns and "punch houses." The "Act for regulating Taverns and Punch [*sic*] Houses" fined tavern keepers who sold "beer, cyder, wine, rum, brandy, or other spirituous liquors, or strong liquors whatsoever" to enslaved people without their owner's consent. Violators were subject to a five-pound fine for the first offense and a ten-pound fine for the second offense.[77] But what does this statute reveal about the legality of enslaved people using their purchasing power to acquire goods, even "spirituous liquors"? Enslaved Africans frequented these locations enough to arouse suspicions. But their presence—and in particular, their patronage—did not make tavern owners, legislators, nor slaveholders concerned enough to fully outlaw such activities. In fact, the act gave tavern owners a bit of leeway. The act included three rounds of increasing fines, which suggests that lawmakers did not seek to discourage tavern owners immediately from selling to slaves. Perhaps they were aware that a significant portion of tavern owners' revenue came from selling liquor to enslaved patrons.

Moreover, in November 1770, the Commissioners of the Work House and Markets approved stronger punishments for slaves being "riotous and disorderly" in Charleston's public market. Specifically, enslaved people who were repeatedly caught buying or selling goods illegally in the market would be whipped, not exceeding thirty-nine lashes, near the market. It is possible that the commissioners wanted the whippings to be put on public display to warn other slaves against the same fate.[78] Yet other than attempting to create more regulations on the slaves' trade, the commissioners did not intervene in any substantive way, which led some colonists to flag shortcomings in both the regulations and enforcement.

Enslaved Africans' marketing endeavors elicited a variety of complaints from whites as the colony's economy of slavery expanded. White freeholders most commonly protested, particularly in and around Charleston, where enslaved people used the public marketplaces to deal in stolen goods, threaten the "regular trade," and market to white Charlestonians and visitors who were buying slaves' stolen goods.[79] One group of colonists in 1770 even blamed local magistrates, accusing them of "supineness and inactivity" for failing to "carry the Negro Acts into execution."[80] Their complaint focused singularly on slaves who used the "public markets and streets of Charles-Town" to "cook, bake, sell fruits, dry goods, and other ways traffic, [and] barter."[81] Enslaved people, and bondswomen specifically, had been using the public marketplace and the city streets to sell their baked and dry goods with little or no intervention from the magistrates who colonial lawmakers had empowered to regulate such slave activity.[82] Though freeholders took to airing their grievances to lawmakers, there is little evidence to suggest that lawmakers intervened to ameliorate what had become a conspicuous facet of life for both black and white people in colonial Charleston.

Enslaved peoples' networks of trade had become widespread in the Lowcountry for several reasons. First, enslavers did not want to curtail them. Second, enslaved Africans were serving an important contingent of colonists who relied on them for foodstuff. It is possible that colonial lawmakers did not intervene, and local policing forces could not contain, the expansion of slaves' economic networks because these systems of trade were so widespread. Enslaved people were not only trading with one another, but they were also trading with white Charleston residents and visitors, and this interracial trade intersected with the city's formal economy. In December 1761, John Marley, a white Charlestonian in the business of selling timber to ship captains in the port, published a notice in the *South Carolina Gazette*.[83] "Whereas there are people in *Charles-Town*," Marley announced, "who are of the practice of purchasing stolen firewood from Negroes, by which I have been a great suffer."[84] Marley offered a fifty-pound reward to anyone with valid information about the enslaved Africans who were trafficking in firewood and the whites who were purchasing the purloined wood. Marley attempted to secure his lucrative firewood business by eliminating his potential competitors, slaves. He maligned enslaved vendors, arguing that their trade in wood was fraudulent, and he criticized whites who purchased such slave goods. Ultimately, he believed that he was carrying out the work of local patrols and magistrates who failed to enforce the laws. Marley was trying to intervene publicly in the policing work that local administrators failed to do.

Enslaved Africans' marketing skills became a tool for enslavers and slave traders to fetch higher prices for them from interested purchasers. Some enslaved people were so visible as vendors and hucksters in the colonial Charleston marketplace that their public identities were connected to their marketing activities. Slave auction advertisements sometimes included bits of information about enslaved peoples' economic acuity. Perhaps enslavers and slave traders surmised that enslaved people with skills in trade and commerce would be more valuable to potential buyers. A 1771 slave ad noted that of the seven enslaved people being sold, some were "well acquainted with raising of Poultry and Marketing."[85] Similarly, in 1773, one enslaved man was described in a slave auction ad as being a "valuable butcher" and "used to attend the markets."[86] On another occasion, sixty-five enslaved Africans, so-called valuable Negroes, were being auctioned off on February 23, 1775, in a location outside of Charleston. The slave men and women were trained at various skilled trades, including coopers, cooks, and seamstresses. There were also "market men" in the group to be auctioned off to the highest bidder.[87] Some enslaved people were so visible in the colonial Charleston marketplace that the value placed on them was connected directly to their marketing activities.

Enslaved peoples' direct involvement as consumers and sellers of goods occurred in concert with the expansion of South Carolina's economy of slavery. The colony grew demographically and economically in the 1760s as rice production expanded, from approximately 35 million pounds of rice exported in 1760 to more than 83 million pounds exported in 1770.[88] The historian Gregory E. O'Malley has maintained that the slave trade stood at the center of all economic activity in colonial Charleston.[89] Perhaps it was not only the slave trade, but also enslaved peoples' networks of trade, that emerged as a component of the city's economic culture of slavery. Their marketing fit into the architecture of life in the burgeoning city of Charleston and the Lowcountry as a region.

The dynamic nature of the slaves' trade in the Lowcountry during the colonial era shaped the ways in which enslaved people conceptualized of their market activities. Enslaved people held tightly onto their hard-fought traditions, making sure that they could continue to make their lives—at least materially—better by working on their own to trade, barter, and buy goods for themselves. At the same time, it is clear that enslaved Africans were not the only economic actors benefiting from the networks of trade in which they were invested. Entire communities of white colonists, enslavers in particular, relied on the marketing activities of enslaved people to secure goods that they could not or did not cultivate themselves.

For enslavers, enslaved peoples' networks of economic enterprise proved to be an aspect of their investments in the success of plantation slavery. Slaveholders such as Henry Laurens understood that if enslaved Africans dedicated their free time toward activities that relieved him of the sole responsibility of provisioning his slaves, then enslaved Africans' commodity exchange could exist in tandem with other forms of slave control.

But not all white colonists believed that the slaves' trade was beneficial. Enslaved peoples' marketing made some colonists anxious. If the historical record shows anything, it is that the presence of entrepreneurial enslaved people challenged what some lawmakers, enslavers, and other white colonists believed should have been available to them. But such fear did not stop whites from trading with slaves. Nor did it stop enslaved Africans from finding customers for their goods anywhere they could find them.

Enslaved Africans' networks of economic enterprise became imbricated in the fabric of life in colonial South Carolina. African slaves, poor whites, merchants, enslavers, and even colonial lawmakers recognized (and some even accepted) the place of the slaves' trade within colonial South Carolina society. Ultimately, enslaved entrepreneurship characterized the Lowcountry way of life during the colonial period as much as did the rice economy or the influx of African slaves. The traditions that enslaved people and enslavers established during the colonial period became an enduring aspect of slavery for not only enslaved, but also slaveholding and nonslaveholding whites. The conspicuousness of slaves' economic interests became emblematic of social relations in South Carolina that the vision of slaves trading and marketing was not uncommon. Indeed, enslaved peoples' networks of enterprise structured, even in small ways, the relationships and power dynamics between enslaved people and all other colonists. By the end of South Carolina's colonial era, enslaved Africans' systems of economic innovation became tethered to the growth and prosperity of slavery in the colony.

2

"THIS INFAMOUS TRAFFICK"

The Slaves' Trade in the Age of Revolution

Maybe Fortune always looked to exploit opportunities to escape the Snee Farm plantation on which he was enslaved. Freedom from bondage and from the privations of slave life on a Lowcountry indigo plantation was perhaps his long-held goal. It is possible that he saw his chance at freedom materialize when British soldiers invaded Charleston in May 1780. The British occupation could have provided Fortune with a glimmer of hope, a rare opportunity to make his escape during the increasing volatilities of war.[1] After all, his enslaver, Patriot colonel Charles Cotesworth Pinckney, had been captured by members of the British militia during their siege of the city. Four months into Pinckney's forced detention, Fortune made his escape. In a desperate move, Pinckney reached out to his mother, asking her to relay a message to him. He wrote, "I am told Fortune has run away from his Mistress; if so, tell the Negroes to let him know that if he will come over here to me immediately I will pardon him."[2] It is possible that Fortune entertained the idea of escaping to live with the increasing numbers of runaway slaves in maroon communities in the Lowcountry's swampy and secluded areas.[3] Or maybe he fled to Charleston to seek refuge with the enslaved marketers and hucksters that inhabited the city. Even still, he might have joined the enslaved people owned by Eliza Pinckney who she believed had "robbd and deserted" her.[4]

Fortune was swept up in the political conflict between American colonists and British military forces, catalyzed by the first shots in Lexington and Concord, Massachusetts, in April 1775. He must have weighed important decisions during his absence—decisions that could have changed the course of his life. Could he hide himself among Charleston's enterprising slaves? For how long? Would he join the bondspeople owned by Eliza Pinckney, mirroring their insolence toward their enslaver? Would he risk his life for freedom?

Fortune made his decision, opting to make his leave short-lived. Perhaps he did not want to ruin the good will that he had cultivated with Pinckney during this period of social instability. Instead, he returned to Charles Cotesworth Pinckney's service— we do not know if by his own volition or by force—perhaps because he was only seeking a short respite from enslaved life. Fortune subsequently proved to be Pinckney's honorable ally. In turn, Pinckney did not question Fortune's loyalty to him because in the fall of 1780, Fortune carried out numerous errands for Pinckney during his time as a British prisoner of war. These errands included Fortune travelling to Pinckney's "Estate in the Country" with "orders to the overseer to send me down Six Sheep and four hogs for my family use."[5] In later years, Fortune even accompanied Pinckney to the Constitutional Convention in Philadelphia.

Though the first battles of the American Revolution occurred in New England, residents of South Carolina geared up for a fight of their own. For white South Carolinians, the military clashes between Patriots and Loyalists ushered in an era of instability, where colonists' allegiances were put to the test. But for enslaved people, the war signified something very different. They sought liberation, not from the shackles of British tyranny, but from their enslavers' chains.

Amidst the military rivalries that began between the patriot and British factions, bondspeople more fully embraced their own economic practices during the Revolutionary conflict of the 1770s and 1780s. Bondspeople such as Fortune exploited opportunities to exercise all forms of autonomy during the American Revolution. From living without direct white oversight and fleeing their homes in search of real freedom, to investing time and energy into their own economic enterprises, enslaved people attempted to take advantage of the instabilities that came with persevering within a society at war.

But enslaved people also faced the challenges of wartime survival. Some fought on the front lines, situating themselves on both sides of the conflict, making the calculated gamble to enter the war not for American colonists or the British, but for themselves. These freedom fighters sought, above all, to make their dreams of emancipation a reality. Others attempted to steer clear of British soldiers. Between 1780 and 1782, British commanders decided to ship captured Lowcountry slaves to other coastal locations up the Atlantic seaboard or to regions of the British West Indies in an effort to secure Patriot loyalty. British military strategies involved the use enslaved people as tools in an attempt to guarantee allegiance from Loyalists and to threaten Southern Patriots.[6] Enslaved Africans in South Carolina were aware of the real threat that capture by British soldiers posed to them. In addition to the risks introduced by the military and political battles, enslaved people faced an epidemiological threat as well. A smallpox epidemic swept through the Lowcountry in the late 1770s, which further undermined enslaved Africans' attempts to survive the tumult of war.[7]

Yet once the war ended in 1783, enslaved people found themselves within a new nation, but not members of it. While white Americans established the foundations of the republic and solidified slavery's place in it, enslaved people were subjected to the political whims of white founders who debated their status within the fabric of the new American republic.[8] Nevertheless, bondspeople forged ahead with their entrepreneurial pursuits. They continued investing time, energy, and resources into their own economic networks to survive the unpredictability of enslaved life in the young nation. But in a departure from the colonial era, entrepreneurial slaves faced new resistance from poor and working-class whites, who themselves became more vocal advocates for their own economic survival.

By exploring the revolutionary and early national eras, this chapter examines the ways in which enslaved people such as Fortune carved out spaces to make the best use of their enterprising skills. During and after the war, enterprising slaves traded and bartered, hired out their time for compensation, and established themselves even more firmly as entrepreneurial agents within their communities. Enslaved peoples' public displays of entrepreneurship in the late eighteenth and early nineteenth centuries sparked strong reactions from whites, especially poor whites, during this period of economic and political redevelopment.

But the expansion of slaves' economic practices in the Revolutionary era also fomented tensions between white South Carolinians. The economies of slave hiring, in particular, angered white South Carolinians who were in competition with equally skilled slaves. Members of the white laboring class increasingly argued that enslaved peoples' moneymaking ventures threatened their economic futures. This economic clash—between enterprising slaves and laboring whites—fanned the flames of class conflict between elite slaveholding whites and members of the white working class. Among the economic practices that flourished during and after the war—practices that became a facet of enslaved peoples' moneymaking ventures—was slave hiring. Ultimately, slaves' networks of enterprise not only survived the Revolutionary era; they thrived. In the process, enslaved peoples' entrepreneurial pursuits challenged how some white South Carolinians believed slaves' economic practices fit into the architecture of slavery during the early national period.

Beginning in the mid-1770s, bondspeople took advantage of the British threat in the Lowcountry, a threat that undermined how enslaved people and enslavers interacted as the British military campaign transitioned southward from New England and the mid-Atlantic colonies to South Carolina and Georgia. The social volatilities triggered by the outbreak of war in the late 1770s caused enslaved men and enslaved women to deduce quickly that they did not have to respond in one way to the Revolution. Enslaved people situated themselves on both sides of the war for continental independence, fighting for opportunities to leverage military service and allegiance for freedom from both the Patriots and the Loyalists alike.

Some fled. Though the exact numbers are difficult to determine, historians suggest that 25,000 enslaved people—or a quarter of bondspeople in South Carolina—absconded between 1775 and 1783.[9] Enslaved people who escaped their enslavement during the war even sought refuge with maroon communities, which were established by runaway slaves in the mountains and swamps in the Lowcountry outside the reach of white colonists. These communities were increasing in size during the Revolutionary War, as enslaved people absconded to live free lives.[10]

Other enslaved Africans began to escape in droves to Charleston in search of British ships and vessels where they could offer their loyalty in exchange for freedom. They served as guides or informants for British soldiers, hoping to earn freedom by the war's end.[11] In 1777, enslaved people on one rice plantation were "continually deserting," seeking sanctuary and freedom in Charleston instead of remaining enslaved on the plantation.[12] Others still served alongside their masters fighting on both sides of the conflict.[13]

Throughout the realignment of political allegiances and the military instabilities that characterized South Carolina during the 1770s and early 1780s, enslaved people had two goals: survival and freedom. African slaves took advantage of the war's precariousness to challenge their enslavers and take more control over their own lives and livelihoods, including their economic pursuits. Compelled to hold onto their own economic networks, enslaved people saw their market activities as a key component of their survival and their claims to freedom. Amidst the military rivalries between Patriots and Loyalists over the independence of the American colonies, enslaved Africans more fully embraced their own economic endeavors because, in the end, these activities helped them survive.

However, as slaves innovated ways to maintain their moneymaking and marketing pursuits, seeking to trade with Patriots and Loyalists alike, they became swept up in the political and economic transformations that characterized Revolutionary-era South Carolina. Enslaved people rejected, as much as possible, attempts by both Patriots and Loyalists to use them as pawns to sway the momentum of the war in their direction. Instead, bondspeople had their own agendas. They used the insecurity that characterized life in the colony for white South Carolinians during the war to their advantage.

Enslaved women situated themselves at the forefront of enslaved peoples' trading networks, sustaining their market activities during the war. In Charleston alone, they deployed a mixture of enterprise, ingenuity, and courage to maintain their investments in economic exchange as the war intensified. Undeterred, bondswomen continued to attend Lowcountry marketplaces intending to sell their goods. An observer in February 1778 recounted that sixty-four enslaved women had been occupying various parts of Charleston "selling cakes, nuts, and so forth."[14] This was a drop in the number of enslaved women that typically marketed in Charleston throughout the eighteenth century. The historian Robert Olwell has argued that in the mid-eighteenth century, several hundred enslaved women could be found selling their goods in the Charleston marketplace at any one time.[15] Perhaps the outbreak of war in the northern colonies caused both bondspeople and white buyers to be more careful about their presence in Lowcountry marketplaces. Nevertheless, these bondswomen saw an opportunity to bring their goods to eager customers and they profited from the influx of new buyers for their merchandise.[16] They witnessed more soldiers patronizing the marketplaces looking for cheap and readily available food. And enterprising enslaved women sought to fill that niche.

Bondswomen took advantage of the wartime environment, and their accepted visibility in the marketplace, to not only put their enterprising skills to good use selling to both Patriot and Loyalist soldiers, but to emancipate themselves. An enslaved woman named Sarah fled her enslaver in 1780 and sought refuge among the enslaved women in Charleston. Her enslaver suspected that she had been working independently, hiring herself out to willing employers and keeping the profits for herself. Sarah did not possess a ticket verifying her enslavers' permission to find waged work. Instead, she used her knowledge of the employment landscape for enslaved women in the city to take her freedom and find ways to provide for herself economically.[17] The visibility of enslaved women working in Charleston on their own provided bondswomen such as Sarah with the opportunity to use their labor to escape from their enslavers and from slavery during the Revolution.

While slaves in Charleston and on Lowcountry plantations fiercely defended their right to stay on plantations or run for their freedom, white families fled South Carolina in droves, in chaotic anticipation of the British siege on the area.[18] In June 1779, Sir Henry Clinton, Commander-in-Chief of the British army in America, issued the Philipsburg Proclamation, intending to subvert Patriot forces in the war's Southern theater. Using a similar strategy to that of Lord Dunmore in

Virginia in 1775, Clinton sought to "use slaves as a weapon against their masters," by offering enslaved people freedom for leaving their owners.[19] With the proclamation, Clinton put captured or escaped slaves to work for the British military, allowed Southern Loyalists to maintain their enslaved property, and awarded bondspeople as prizes to British officers. Clinton used slaves as a component of his military strategy. He believed that deploying enslaved people as tools of war would ensure British military dominance by weakening rebellious Patriot factions in the Southern colonies. News of Clinton's march to Charleston reached colonists in South Carolina quickly in late 1779. Residents, both white and black, had been fleeing the Lowcountry in anticipation of the British arrival. However, when colonists heard about Clinton's impending raid, they vacated the Lowcountry en masse. One slaveholding woman observed that when she arrived in Charleston in February 1780, "People go out of town very fast," referring to the exodus of white residents from the region.[20] In May 1780, British military forces, led by Clinton, invaded and subsequently captured Charleston.

Enslaved people embraced and attempted to utilize the small moments of autonomy that they experienced during the war, particularly during the British occupation of Charleston. Some enslaved people, abandoned by their enslavers, lived autonomously, deciding to remain on plantations in the midst of the revolutionary fracas.[21] With the absence of their enslavers, bondspeople worked for themselves, by their own designs and desires, largely free of white masters, mistresses, and overseers.[22] Continuing to invest their time and energies into practices that helped to ensure their survival, enslaved men and women cultivated goods that only they needed to subsist. Enslaved people on John F. Grimké's Lowcountry plantation had been growing a limited supply of foodstuff and long-staple cotton—all for themselves. At the war's end in the winter of 1782, South Carolina militiaman and Georgetown rice planter Peter Horry returned to his plantation, which neighbored Grimké's, and he remarked that not only had the enslaved people been providing for only themselves, but they subsequently ran away, presumably to take advantage of the final throes of war to liberate themselves.[23] Of the bondspeople who remained on plantations during the war, many worked by their own design, acting as "their own masters."[24]

Without steady white supervision from enslavers or overseers, enslaved people configured their own schedules, working only when necessary. They even resorted to stealing from military encampments to augment their own subsistence needs and to maintain networks of commerce in which they had invested before the war began. In 1782, enslaved people in the Lowcountry had been conducting nightly raids for horses and cattle housed in Patriot encampments. On August 29, 1782, General John Matthews expressed his frustration, wanting to "put a stop to this infamous traffic."[25] Enslaved people had been making daily trips to his encampment, carrying off livestock and other goods they desired, then subsequently selling the purloined items in the Charleston marketplace. General Matthews implored fellow Patriot General Francis Marion to "form some plan which will be most effectual to stop such a shameful commerce."[26]

What General Marion deemed a "shameful commerce" served as a means of survival for enslaved people. Slaves saw opportunity in the military conflict to continue capitalizing off of their entrepreneurial skills with anyone who would trade with them, which included stealing goods from soldiers and selling those goods for a profit. In the process of transforming stolen goods into personal financial gains, bondspeople strengthened their commitments to their own economic activities, a move that continued after the war's end.[27]

The conclusion of the war, made official by the Treaty of Paris in September 1783, ushered South Carolina into a new era of economic activity. The war upended South Carolina's plantation economy, slowing the exportation of rice and the importation of African slaves to a startling halt. In 1783, for example, approximately 65,000 barrels of rice were exported from South Carolina. For comparison, at the zenith of South Carolina's eighteenth-century rice trade in 1763, over 100,000 barrels of rice was exported from Charleston alone.[28] Nevertheless, South Carolina's economy rebounded slowly in the mid-1780s, with enslaved peoples' labor reemerging as the hinge around which the economy revolved and grew. As historian Peter Coclanis has shown, the economy of Charleston experienced sustained growth in the last quarter of the eighteenth century.[29]

Enslaved people, however, did not abdicate the autonomy by which they had lived and worked during the war without a struggle. In fact, in the post-Revolutionary years, enslaved men and women rebuffed attempts by slave owners to re-establish the same systems of labor and exploitation that had existed before the Revolution began. One Lowcountry slaveholder complained that during the Revolution, bondsmen and bondswomen lived "perfectly free" lives, ignoring disempowered white overseers and helping themselves to "the best produce of the plantation."[30] The enslaved people felt so emboldened that they "paid no attention" to the overseer's order.[31] While slaves strove to maintain the privileges by which they lived, enslavers endeavored to strip the remaining slaves of their autonomy in an attempt to re-establish control. In fact, according to a 1784 case before the Privy Council, enslaved people on one plantation had, for ten years, usurped their enslaver's property and "planted for themselves a little field on the same land."[32] As the slaveholding regime sought to re-establish the foundations of mastery in the years after the Revolution, bondspeople strove to maintain networks of enterprise and autonomy that benefitted them during the war years.

As a consequence, enterprising bondspeople attempted to capitalize as much as possible on rebuilding efforts in the 1780s. Slave hiring, in particular, grew into a more public and more lucrative venture for enslavers, as they benefited financially from hiring out their slaves. Enslaved people proved integral to the construction efforts that got underway after the British departed the Lowcountry in 1783, as historian Ryan Quintana has shown.[33] Bondspeople hired out in Charleston, for example, were co-opted by the postwar legislature into the "public works," labor that benefitted the public good. In the process, some enslaved laborers pocketed the wages that they were supposed to pay to their enslavers. In 1783, two enslaved women and two enslaved men had been "working out in town" and keeping their wages instead of handing over their earnings to their owner, Eliza Lucas Pinckney. Pinckney in turn believed that the enslaved people had "robd [*sic*]" her before she even received their earnings.[34] Even before the outbreak of the war, skilled slaves hired by white employers was a common sight, especially in Charleston.

During the rebuilding phase in the late eighteenth century, slave hiring became more significant for enslaved people. They were eager to engage in slave hiring *if* they could gain some material or economic benefits from their work. Not only did hired slaves have the potential to enjoy relatively higher levels of autonomy and mobility than their plantation-bound counterparts, but slave hiring during the post-Revolutionary era afforded a very small subset of enslaved people the opportunity to buy their freedom. The historian Larry Koger argues that during the post-Revolutionary era, it was not uncommon for hired slaves to get permission from their enslavers to both hire themselves out and earn enough money to negotiate the price of their emancipation. The connection between slave hire and manumission in the decades after the Revolution is reflected in the increased free black population in the state. Between 1790 and 1800, the free black population grew by 76.8 percent, increasing from 1,801 to 3,185.[35]

Yet even though slave hiring may have placed the real prospect of freedom within slaves reach, the experiences of hired slaves was rife with violence and exploitation. One historian notes that enslaved peoples' experiences ran the gamut, from "nearly full autonomy to harsh exploitation."[36] Though they had the opportunity to earn small sums of money for themselves, perhaps even the chance to earn enough money to negotiate the terms of their emancipation, these experiences were not without the specter of violence and abuse at the hands of white hirers.[37]

After the war, enslaved people, white employers, and enslavers became even more tightly bound in an economic relationship structured around slave hire. When bondspeople worked to earn wages to keep for themselves, white employers used enslaved labor to complete work at competitive prices. But it was enslavers who reaped the largest economic benefits from slave hire after the Revolution.[38] For enslavers, the economy of slave hire represented one of the enduring benefits of their investments in enslaved labor. Enslaved men who possessed skills in the mechanical trades were "to their owners an interest-bearing capital," meaning an investment that generated a continuous stream of profits.[39] One traveler to South Carolina in the post-Revolutionary era observed that slave owners were unrepentant in their reliance on income from slave hiring. Johann David Schoepf, a German physician and botanist, traveled to Charleston in 1784 and witnessed that slaveholders who sought to maintain steady incomes "place[d] their capital in negroes, and in the strict sense, are by them supported, living careless on the bitter sweat of the hired."[40] Therefore, the new frontier of slavery in the late eighteenth century revolved around slave hiring.

Enslaved hiring in the late eighteenth century proved to be so lucrative for hirers, enslavers, and sometimes for enslaved people, that the practice drew the ire of whites who belonged neither to the slaveholding class nor to the emerging merchant classes who were hiring skilled bondspeople. In the mid-1780s, members of the white laboring class began to express the belief that enslaved peoples' eagerness to earn money from their labor thwarted their own employment prospects. In February 1783, thirty-six white carpenters and bricklayers from Charleston appealed to city lawmakers, protesting the competition they faced from equally skilled enslaved men. "Jobbing Negro Tradesmen," they criticized, were hiring out their own labor, to the detriment of Charleston's skilled white labor community. Such competition, they argued, deprived white workers "of the Means of gaining a Livelihood from their Industry."[41] The carpenters and bricklayers petitioned lawmakers to enact a law that would restrict "Negroes from undertaking Work on their own Account."[42] To them, the visibility of enslaved skilled workers—blacksmiths, bricklayers, carpenters, tailors, master coopers, and washerwomen—challenged the structure of a racialized slaveholding society. More directly, they argued that the economy of skilled enslaved workers undermined the economic security of white South Carolinians who lived outside the rarefied class of elite slaveholders or even the increasing class of wealthy merchants. A new labor market was emerging, pitting poor whites and skilled slaves against one another. Ultimately, enslaved people, wanting to earn their own wages, and enslavers who wanted to profit even more from the labor of their skilled slaves, challenged the skilled white workers' economic prospects.

Charleston's city council responded to the calls for legislative reform in November 1783 by approving its first post-Revolutionary ordinance aimed at reining in all economic activities in which enslaved people participated. "For the Better Ordering and Governing of Negroes and other slaves, and of Free Negroes, Mulattoes and Mustizos, within the City of Charleston" was a comprehensive set of regulations ratified by lawmakers to control a variety of slaves' extra-plantation work. Lawmakers approved the regulation to control slaves' working as independent vendors in the Charleston public marketplace, slaves renting their own homes within city limits, and enslaved people working as apprentices.[43] Above all, the ordinance was designed to standardize and regulate slave hiring.

The city council's solution included a system of slave badges to control which slaves could be legally eligible to engage in slave hire. Under this arrangement, enslavers would purchase officially recognized badges for their enslaved laborers, and the badges would be valid for up to a year.[44] The ordinance detailed a fee schedule for slave badges and outlined the varying rates for badges as well. The most expensive badges, costing forty shillings, were designated for skilled slaves, a group that included black carpenters, blacksmiths, fishermen, and gold/silversmiths. The second tier of badges, priced at fifteen shillings, went to tailors and tanners, and the ten-shilling badges went to mariners and ropemakers. All other badges, to be purchased for five shillings, were allocated to slaves who hired out as washerwomen, cooks, or maids, occupations dominated by enslaved women.[45]

The 1783 ordinance, like its colonial predecessors, did not only apply to enslaved people, but to whites as well. To deter whites from illicitly trading with, purchasing goods from, and illegally hiring slaves, the city council enacted more strict fines and penalties against them. Specifically, the ordinance fined whites between five shillings and forty pounds if they were caught illegally employing slave laborers, renting rooms to slaves, or selling "spirituous liquors" to bondsmen and bondswomen in taverns or "other houses of entertainment."[46] Not even slaveholders could escape the council's oversight. Slave owners could be fined twenty shillings for each day that their slaves were illegally hiring themselves out as mechanics or in any other skilled occupation.

On the surface, the 1783 ordinance appeared to be an effort by city lawmakers to re-establish the boundaries of slavery after the instability of the Revolution. In particular, it is possible that members of the white working class hoped that lawmakers would sympathize with their efforts to compete with the increasing numbers of skilled enslaved laborers. Unfortunately, they did not receive the sympathy from legislators, enslavers, nor slave hirers that they hoped would have come. The white laboring-class men and women learned quickly that legislative intervention did little to stymie the proliferation of slave hiring, and therefore the dwindling of their economic prospects. In fact, enslaved people, enslavers, slave hirers, and whites who regularly traded in goods with slaves ignored the laws completely. Just as the economy of slave hiring and slaves' independent marketing relied on the cooperation of enslavers and white hirers, compliance with the laws required equal amounts of cooperation from the same groups of people. For this reason, the regulations failed to be effective, to the frustration and disappointment of Charleston's working-class whites.

Not only did enslaved people find employers eager to hire them; enslavers and slave traders even advertised the skills of enslaved tradesmen as an economic benefit to potential slave purchasers. In October 1783, nine months after the white Charleston tradesmen complained about equally skilled enslaved black workers, a "gang of fourteen very valuable slaves" were put up for private sale, including "house wenches," "field negroes," and importantly, "tradesmen," meaning enslaved men trained in a skilled trade.[47] Despite the existence of laws created to control slave hiring, and despite the vocal grievances of skilled white workers, slave traders promoted the value of enslaved people with marketable skills. Slave owners understood that slave hiring was a profitable investment. And the market for skilled slaves continued to grow in the late eighteenth century, even as a cadre of laboring whites sought to curtail the economic practice.

It is not surprising, therefore, that the economic activities of enslaved people did not decline in Charleston after the city council ratified the ordinance of 1783. In fact, enslaved women and men simply ignored the regulation, which suggests that they were successful in finding economic partners who continued to express an interest in their networks of enterprise during the post-Revolutionary era. The historian Philip D. Morgan has maintained that life for enslaved people in the Lowcountry immediately after the Revolution remained relatively static.[48] Yet if the quickness with which the Charleston City Council revised and ratified the city's set of slave regulations is indicative of anything, it is that enslaved people perhaps became even more devoted to trading, marketing their own goods, and self-hire. The 1783 ordinance was in effect for three years before Charleston officials revisited its effectiveness in 1786. It had done little to mitigate the increasingly visible economic networks that revolved around slaves' marketing activities and self-hire. Enslaved people ignored the ordinance by "sitting in and about the markets, selling sundry articles," patronizing drinking establishments (called grog shops, dram shops, or tippling houses), and gambling in public.[49] Yet the responsibility did not fall solely on enslaved people. City officials failed to enforce the fines mandated by the regulations. Also, white merchants continued to eagerly accept enslaved customers.[50] For these reasons, Charleston's City Council amended the ordinance in 1786 because, first and foremost, black and white residents publicly rejected the city's regulations.

In addition to the unsuccessful restrictions that legislators attempted to place on enslaved peoples' marketing and slave hiring, the revised slave badge system did not have the effect that Charleston administrators desired. The City Council argued that Charleston residents had "neglected to take out the annual badge, of permission to hire out their Negroes for work."[51] While the 1783 ordinance did not limit the number of slaves that could hire themselves, the 1786 revision limited the number of slaves that a slaveholder could hire in Charleston to two. City administrators also attempted to address enslaved hucksters in the public marketplace. The ordinance specified that slaves had to possess a valid ticket from a master or mistress to be allowed to sell "any kind of provision or fruit" in the Charleston marketplace, a mandate that failed when colonial lawmakers made similar attempts.[52] But in June 1789, Charleston's city council swiftly reversed their policies. The revision did not mention badges, nor did city administrators outline a fee structure for slave owners to purchase badges for their hired out slaves. Instead, the ordinance reverted back to pre-Revolutionary habits, requiring slaves hiring out their own time, or selling goods in the public marketplace, simply to possess written permission from their enslavers, customs by which many Charlestonians did not abide. The city council temporarily eliminated the slave badge system and repealed the 1783 and 1786 ordinances.[53]

The practice of slave hire forced Charleston's city council into an almost decade-long struggle to create new mechanisms to stabilize interactions between black slaves and whites. This struggle exemplified the post-Revolutionary era's legislative and economic environment. Most visibly, enslaved people, enslavers, and hirers were successful at finding ways to circumvent the city's ordinances, which ultimately failed to reduce illicit slave hiring or curtail instances of enslaved people selling their goods in the Charleston marketplace. Enslaved peoples' prominence as marketers and as skilled workers angered groups of white Charlestonians who were infuriated by both the city ordinances' ineffectiveness and the lack of local apparatuses to regulate the increasing competitiveness of skilled enslaved laborers. Skilled white Charlestonians consequently turned to state legislators and vented their concerns about local failures to regulate slaves and the whites who buttressed their moneymaking endeavors. In August 1791, these white Charlestonians made their complaints official. In a grievance not to city administrators but to state lawmakers, the small group of white Charleston residents condemned "negroes . . . keeping a public market, to the disturbance of their owners, and to the disturbance of the good citizens in that part of the city."[54] Though this complaint contained various criticisms, enslaved peoples' economic activities stood out as their most important concern.

In the 1780s and 1790s, as enslaved peoples' networks of trade and commerce expanded, some white residents appealed to state lawmakers more frequently, petitioning them to do what local administrators could not do to regulate enslaved peoples' economic behavior more effectively. Between 1783 and 1800, white residents made almost yearly complaints to lawmakers pleading for legislative relief from slaves who they believed threatened their economic prospects. Enslaved people had been receiving small sums of money for their labor from hirers (with and without valid tickets); occupying public marketplaces hawking their own good; using waterways to trade illicitly with white patrons; and buying liquor and other commodities. Enslaved peoples' economic and consumer behavior had become so public that white residents from the Lowcountry to the expanding Upcountry began using the power of petitioning to urge lawmakers to better regulate enslaved peoples' economic pursuits, be it making money or spending it.[55]

Throughout the eighteenth century, enslaved entrepreneurship drew the most scrutiny in Charleston, but enslaved peoples' marketing activities were not relegated to the city. Bondspeoples' networks of trade garnered increased legislative attention in the last two decades of the eighteenth century from white residents, specifically in Georgetown, Charleston's

Lowcountry neighbor to the north. As in other regions of the Lowcountry during the colonial era, Georgetown's economy revolved around rice. The historian Joyce Chaplin has shown that Lowcountry planters turned to new rice cultivation techniques before the Revolution, and they made a dedicated effort in the 1780s to revitalize plantation agriculture using newly developed rice cultivation techniques.[56] Though these methods—including tidal cultivation—introduced innovative rice cultivation technology, enslavers' push for agricultural modernization had the potential to undermine the customary privileges that enslaved people fought for under the task system in the first half of the eighteenth century. Despite the new challenges, enslaved people in Georgetown made the most of planters' adoption of tidal cultivation.[57] In many ways, the transition to tidal irrigation in the late eighteenth century facilitated the growth of enslaved peoples' independent economies in Georgetown.

With the free time that they gained, enslaved people sold their own goods at public marketplaces on a scale that rivaled slaves' marketing in Charleston.[58] The Georgetown marketplace was established in 1787 and the city's residents initially wanted the space free of market women and enslaved hucksters hawking their merchandise, a sight many visitors to neighboring Charleston witnessed.[59] Georgetown residents established that if enslaved vendors sold "rice, corn, poultry or other provisions" without a ticket from his or her master, mistress, overseer, or employer, then any white person could legally "seize such articles" for themselves.[60] Bondspeople ignored the mandate and flooded the Georgetown marketplace shortly after its creation. As Georgetown's economy matured, the city's commercial hub welcomed the influx of rice merchants. Enterprising enslaved marketers followed suit. In 1789 and 1790, the conspicuousness of enslaved marketers prompted white residents to make formal complaints to state lawmakers, this time arguing that the laws regulating the town and the marketplace were "defective" and expressing concerns about instances in which whites traded with enslaved people and sold them "spirituous" liquors. They requested that "every person be prevented from trading with Negroes and other Slaves within the Rivers of the said District."[61] Enslaved entrepreneurs made themselves visible actors in Georgetown's burgeoning economic life, and their independent economic engagements coincided with the expansion of Georgetown's post-Revolutionary economy.

The complaints reveal that the increased visibility of enterprising slaves again put enslavers and nonslaveholding whites at odds. Slaves' entrepreneurial pursuits emerged as a political wedge between groups of white South Carolinians. Enslaved people were adept at finding willing white trading partners who would engage economically with them and hire them with and without proper documentation. Though some whites, often members of the skilled nonslaveholding and laboring classes, objected to enslaved peoples' status as independent economic actors, prominent members of South Carolina's slaveholding society explicitly supported enslaved peoples' pursuit of their own material and economic interests. Bondspeoples' involvement in local commercial networks would not have occurred on such a public stage if not for the cooperation from members of the slaveholding and economically influential classes. It was clear that slaves' economic endeavors required not only enslavers' buy-in, but also larger white support.[62] Slaveholders, merchants, and nonpropertied whites did not hesitate to participate in and support potentially lucrative economic dealings with enslaved people. The commercial activities of enterprising slaves were part and parcel of South Carolina's early national economy. Despite fears of labor market insecurity expressed by members of the white laboring class, white businesspeople understood that slaves' economic practices comprised an important aspect of their own economic enterprises.

Even though white South Carolinians benefitted from enslaved peoples' investments in economic activities, these interactions in the late eighteenth century did not occur without legal consequences. The social and legal quandaries presented by enslaved peoples' commodity exchange in general, and slave hiring in particular, is exemplified in a 1792 case before South Carolina's Supreme Court. In this case an enslaved woman hired herself out, with her master's permission, to a white man, Mr. Beaty, for an unspecified number of years. During her years of hire, she "acquired a considerable sum of money, over and above what she stipulated to pay for her monthly wages to her master."[63] This bondswoman—her name was never revealed in the court record—developed "an affection" for Sally, a young enslaved woman owned by Beaty. The bond that developed between the enslaved woman and Sally over the years of the woman's hire was strong enough that it inspired the woman to use the money that she had accumulated over several years to purchase Sally's freedom from Beaty. After the enslaved woman paid Beaty for Sally's emancipation, Beaty made no formal claims to Sally. He had not paid yearly taxes on Sally after the enslaved woman paid for Sally's freedom, and Beaty even "acknowledged he had no property in her." The problem arose when Beaty was "called upon to deliver up the girl as free." He refused to honor the arrangement, however informal, that he made with the enslaved woman for Sally's freedom.[64]

The opinion, drafted by Chief Justice John Rutledge, recognized the unconventional nature of the issues presented in the case. Surprisingly, Rutledge even admitted, "the Court found no difficulty whatever, in forming an opinion on it."[65] The jury ruled that Sally could keep the wages she earned after paying her owner the agreed upon sum of money. Judge Rutledge's opinion made no reference to statutes or common law. Instead, he directed the jury to consider the circumstances of the case and the generous gift of freedom that the enslaved woman gave to Sally. He declared that since the enslaved woman "chose to appropriate the savings of her extra labor, to the purchase of this girl, in order afterwards to set her free—would a jury of the country say no?"[66] He asserted that the jurors should not penalize such a benevolent act. The jury, he said, was "too humane and upright" to allow such an "extraordinary" act to be overturned. Without retreating from the courtroom to deliberate on a verdict, the jury found in favor of the plaintiff, and Sally gained her freedom.[67]

The Guardian of Sally, a Negro, v. Beaty is significant for several reasons. First, the case established a judicial precedent regarding the legality of enslaved peoples' possession of property in South Carolina. This was the first case before the state's appellate court in the early republican period on which legal authorities discussed an enslaved woman's claim to money that she earned. Second, Rutledge recognized the prevalence and the acceptance of enslaved people negotiating with their owners to save a portion of their earnings for themselves. He not only legitimized the practice of enslaved people earning money for themselves, but he suggested that slaves earning and keeping wages for themselves was in line with the foundations of racial slavery. The practice did not undermine slavery, nor did it thwart enslavers' authority over their slaves. Moreover, the enslaved woman who purchased Sally's freedom challenged the constraints of her enslaved status in very specific ways. As a woman, she worked outside the confines of her enslaver's home. As a bondswoman, she earned money and participated actively in her local labor market. Despite the uncharted characteristics of the case, Rutledge revealed that the case's novelty did not hinder him, nor the jury, from considering what hung in the balance: Sally's claim to her freedom. Ultimately, the court upheld the reciprocal legal obligation between the enslaved woman and Beaty.

The legal questions introduced in the case—slave hiring and enslaved people earning money—illuminated inconsistencies between state statutes as written and the ways in which such laws were applied practically.[68] The unwillingness of lawmakers and local administrators to make enslaved peoples' efforts to earn money for themselves illegal underscored the permanence of slaves' economic pursuits in South Carolina slaveholding society—and the political and legal power of the slaveholding class. The case also highlights ambiguities in South Carolina slave law. Meanwhile, the legitimacy of slave hiring forecasted the challenges that lawmakers would continue to face with not only regulating enslaved men's and enslaved women's engagement in their own money-making efforts, but what enslaved people did with their earnings. Above all, glaring discrepancies existed in South Carolina slave law. Such varying ideas about the role of state regulation in the lives of South Carolinians influenced the ways in which whites and blacks in the late eighteenth century understood how laws would be applied, or not applied, to them.

The issues presented in the case are suggestive of why white skilled laborers in particular, but some white residents more broadly, in the late eighteenth century began challenging legislators to create statutes that would regulate slave hire and slave marketing more effectively. White workers took issue with slave hiring because they believed that it undermined the social and legal advantages that whites held over blacks in Southern slave society. As much as white laborers felt threatened by emancipated slaves, they were also suspicious of enslaved people with even a modicum of economic control. This was especially true when local customs protected bondspeoples' right to challenge white workers in the labor marketplace and when enslaved people tested state and local statutes in public ways.

White tension around enslaved enterprise only increased in the 1790s, with white residents becoming more active in the public performance of citizenship through serving on grand juries and signing onto petitions to state lawmakers. In 1792, for example, grand jurors in Charleston deliberated on several local matters that plagued their community, the most prominent of which was "the number of Dram shops around the City."[69] The jurors, however, were not concerned merely with the presence of drams shops, or drinking establishments. They were concerned, instead, with the shops' clientele. According to the grand jurors, comprised of white Charleston freeholders, enslaved people had been patronizing dram shops with increased frequency. The jurors proposed "that the laws against retailing spirituous liquors to Negroes without permission from their Masters be strictly enforced."[70]

Grand juries submitted an official record, called presentments, in which they expressed residents' grievances—large and small. One historian has asserted that grand juries in colonial and early national South Carolina functioned as "communal sounding boards," making presentments official records of a community's grievances.[71] White citizens relied on these legislative processes in hopes that lawmakers would consider their appeals and make the requisite legislative changes recommended in their formally submitted requests. Petitioning was a longstanding form of popular legislative participation, with antecedents in English constitutionalism.[72] White male petitioners embraced the legislative process as a right to which they were entitled; they understood participation not as a legal act, but as an exercise in political agency. Often, white citizens' grievances were circumscribed and parochial in nature. But in South Carolina, enslaved peoples' behavior was often the topic of these complaints. Many white South Carolinians used the system of petitioning and grand jury service to publicize their criticisms about not only enslaved people and their public displays of economic autonomy, but also the slave owners who directly and indirectly protected enslaved entrepreneurship and enterprise.

In 1793, for example, a group of white master coopers from Charleston sent an official letter to state lawmakers expressing their frustrations with a "growing evil" in their community. The coopers had been witnessing violations of the 1740 statute, later revised in 1783, which forbade slaveholders from allowing their slaves to carry on a skilled trade and engage in marketing for themselves. They stated that enslaved people residing in and around Charleston had been "privileged, although illegally to traffick [*sic*] and barter, as well as to carry on difference trades and occupations."[73] And, they argued, slaves engaged in such activities independently—that is to say, outside a white person's supervision. The white Charleston coopers insisted that such enslaved activity undermined white laborers trained in the "mechanical trades" in particular. Enslaved people were "selling their Commodities, and working at their trades much lower and at much cheaper rates than those persons who are privileged by their citizenship."[74] In opposing bondspeople working as vendors in Charleston and slaves earning money through selling their goods, the coopers condemned, above all, the economic competition posed by equally skilled black mechanics. Though white Charlestonians had been criticizing enslaved peoples' participation in local market activities since the colonial period, white skilled laborers had not formally expressed their rejection of enslaved people as skilled in the mechanical trades until the late eighteenth century, specifically in the period after the Revolution. It is possible that white artisans' consistent outrage reflected their understanding of their newly endowed citizenship rights in the new republic. They certainly believed that the privileges of citizenship meant that their economic prospects should have been protected from enslaved competitors. Ultimately, the Charleston master coopers' petitioned lawmakers to officially recognize "The Society of Master Coopers of Charleston." In this request, the coopers sought recognition for their organization so that they could, with state support, enforce existing statutes that forbade slaves from hiring their own time and engaging in trade in their local marketplaces. They argued that they wanted lawmakers' approval to maintain "good order and decorum" among enslaved people in and around Charleston.[75]

Enslaved people challenged white laborers in the "mechanical trades," competing with white working men and women for a variety of skilled and semiskilled work. Skilled bondspeople were employed as coopers and mechanics, as well as jobs such as hairdressers. Bondspeoples' success as hairdressers thwarted the economic viability of white hairdressers' business in post-Revolutionary Charleston. In November 1793, four white Charleston hairdressers appealed to the city's slaveholders in Charleston's *City Gazette and Daily Advertiser*, issuing a public notice drawing attention to a city ordinance that outlined the trades in which enslaved people could pursue, with slaveholder permission. They declared that hairdressing was not a trade in which enslaved people should work. Enslaved people had been intervening in their business and they entreated slaveholders to better manage slaves' employment prospects.[76]

The master coopers' and the hair dressers' arguments epitomize the claims against slave hire that permeated communities of white skilled laborers in the late eighteenth century. They directed their criticism toward the legal system and social customs that accepted enslaved employment. Skilled white workers observed that employers increasingly used skilled slaves to complete short-term or long-term work projects because they were a cheaper source of labor. In response to being challenged by enslaved people in the labor marketplace, white workingmen's groups banded together in an effort to protect their employment opportunities. They began a crusade of sorts, that included lobbying for stronger laws that would better regulate enslaved people and petitioned lawmakers to penalize people more consistently who hired slave workers over competent whites. In their appeals, members of the white laboring class called for increased intervention from state lawmakers. Nonelite whites vocalized their hostility toward ineffective laws that failed to curtail what they believed was a menacing threat to the state's social and racial stability.[77]

Enslaved peoples' increased visibility in the mechanical and handicraft trades in Charleston's labor marketplace once again caught the attention of city administrators during the summer of 1796. Meanwhile, white laborers expressed their discontent with enslaved people with whom they were in competition and enslavers who they believed failed to properly regulate skilled enslaved workers. Led by Charleston's mayor, John Edwards, the city council passed an ordinance in August 17, 1796 to allay the concerns of the white laboring classes in the city. The ordinance was primarily directed at slaveholders, believed by members of the city council to control the labor competition posed by skilled enslaved workers in the city. It imposed steep fines of up to $85 on slaveholders who allowed enslaved people to seek out opportunities to earn money while being employed in "any mechanical or handicraft trades of themselves, in any shop, or otherwise" within the city of Charleston.[78] Though city administrators expressed concerns about enslaved people learning and apprenticing in handicraft trades, the city council did not want to hinder whites from taking on black apprentices. Instead, the ordinance required that any white mechanic or tradesman who apprenticed four enslaved black workers to take on one additional white apprentice.

The final line in the ordinance, however, maintained the legal status quo regarding skilled enslaved workers and the tradition of slave hire. Though Charleston administrators gestured toward providing legal remedies to white Charlestonians who competed with enslaved workers for employment, the council ultimately reinscribed the legal supremacy of Charleston's slaveholding class. City administrators reassured slaveholders that they would not impede in the legally protected dominion of enslavers over the enslaved. "Nothing in this ordinance shall be construed," they noted, "to prevent any owner of a mechanic slave or slaves, from hiring him to any free man whom he shall please, or employing him or them in his own work as he pleases."[79] Despite the city council's feigned attempts to limit enslaved peoples' visible competition with white laborers in the Charleston marketplace of labor, the understanding between lawmakers and enslavers regarding slave employment superseded any complaints filed publicly by disgruntled white workers.

The General Assembly also intervened on the issue of slave labor competition and responded to outcries from white residents. In December 1796, state lawmakers revised statutes that they hoped would quell increasingly rowdy white workers, while attempting to better regulate economic interactions between enslaved people and the shopkeepers with whom they traded. Specifically, legislators believed it was necessary to adopt more effective measures to "prevent slaves without tickets from dealing with shop-keepers, traders and others." In this 1796 statute anyone—particularly shopkeepers or traders—found guilty of trading or bartering any goods with slaves without a valid ticket from his or her master, mistress, or temporary hirer would be fined no more than $200.[80] This statute was not unlike the previous 1787 version; however, lawmakers in 1796 specified the financial penalties levied against whites caught illicitly trading with enslaved blacks. The penalty rose from an unspecified sum to a defined amount of $200.

Though enslaved people in the Lowcountry garnered the majority of the legislative attention, as South Carolina's Upcountry began to expand, so too did the region's enslaved population. In 1760, less than 10 percent of enslaved people in South Carolina lived outside of the Lowcountry. By

1800, over 33 percent of bondspeople lived outside of the Lowcountry, in regions of the state that quickly began to adopt a different form of plantation agriculture from those that existed in the Lowcountry.[81] Enslaved people in the Upcountry did not shy away from developing their own networks of enterprise. In fact, bondspeoples' engagement in trade elicited white complaints similar to those from white Lowcountry residents. Enslaved people in the Edgefield District had been evading slave patrols and had been successfully carrying on their informal trading pursuits, specifically a trade in tobacco that they had grown for themselves. According to white Edgefield residents, slaves had been cultivating and locally trading their own tobacco. With a slightly paternalistic undertone, they stated that such activities were dangerous, not because of increased slave autonomy, but because slaves may have been trading with "unprincipled white men."[82] The Edgefield residents believed that framing their discussion in terms of protecting slaves as property would encourage lawmakers to offer a response in their favor. However, one could surmise that the white complainants did not want to contend with market competition from enslaved people, especially in an economically burgeoning region of the state.

In the summer of 1800, the Charleston City Council again ratified a set of ordinances "for the better ordering and governing of Negroes" in the city to ameliorate the difficult-to-regulate situation of slave hire in the city. To accomplish this goal, Charleston administrators sought to eliminate slave badge counterfeiting and reduce the number of yearly badges slaveholders could purchase for their hired-out slaves. To begin, the city council reiterated the ban on whites employing black slaves without a valid ticket. The ordinance revised the fee structure for slave badges, with badges costing $3 for enslaved people working in the handicraft trades, $2 for porters or draymen, and $1 for washer women or house servants. In a departure from the 1783 ordinance, this updated city law required "every huckster or vender (male or female)" to pay $6 for a yearly badge, the highest fee in the slave badge system.[83]

As in previous versions of the Charleston slave hire and badge ordinance, no slave owner was allowed to hire out a slave without a badge. However, in this revision, the city council limited the number of badges that a slave owner could purchase. City administrators argued that there were too many slaves in the city, more than "necessary for the servile business therein." To ameliorate what council members believed was a growing problem in the city, they mandated that no slaveholding inhabitant of Charleston would be allowed to purchase more than six badges (up from two as mandated in 1786) for slaves to hire themselves in Charleston. Yet if an enslaver wanted to purchase more than six badges for his or her slaves, each additional badge would cost three times the regular amount.[84] The ordinance included various new financial penalties for anyone in breach of the law. Anyone caught illegally hiring enslaved workers would forfeit $10 for each offense. Slaves found working without a badge or neglecting to wear a badge would be publicly whipped and confined in the stocks for no less than an hour. The enslaved person in violation of the Charleston decree could be saved from suffering in the stocks if the slaves' owner paid the requisite fine imposed by the court. Moreover, the statute made enslavers responsible for any expenses that arose from public punishment of their offending slaves.[85]

Enslaved people ignored the statute and even used the badge system as a way to live a life of semifreedom in the Lowcountry. In particular, enslaved women had become adept at taking advantage of the gaps between the regulations as written and how they were applied in practice. In 1801, an enslaved woman named Hagar fled her enslaver to James Island and sought refuge there with her children, who had presumably been sold away from her. She had a few items in her possession: a blue wrapper, a coat, and most importantly a badge, which confirmed that she had her enslavers' permission to find her own employment. It was this last item that garnered Hagar more attention than she probably desired. She stole a badge, perhaps in an effort to disguise herself as a hired-out bondsperson and to provide for herself as she evaded her enslaver's grasp. Her owner, Captain Gracia Rivers, urged all those tempted to bring her into their employ to contact him because he believed that she "most likely will say that she has permission to work out."[86] He wrote that she was "both artful and knowing enough to make her story good that she is not run away."[87] It is possible that Hagar understood the landscape of regulations enough to know the frequency with which city administrators enforced the slave hire and badge laws.

Enslaved women exposed the underlying challenges with Charleston's system of badges to regulate slave hiring. It was not uncommon for enslaved women in the early nineteenth century to use their knowledge of the badge system, slave hiring laws, and work opportunities to live as free women. They took advantage of inconsistencies in the system of slave hiring and badges to escape from their enslavers. In July 1804, Daphne ran away from her enslaver and fled to Charleston where her enslaver suspected that she was "working about town with a borrowed badge."[88] Betty made the decision to flee in April 1804, a month after she was sold to Sarah Harth, her fourth enslaver. She absconded with not only her young child, Nelly, but also with a badge to seek out work.[89] An enslaved woman, Dinah, worked as a washerwomen around Charleston to support herself after she escaped her enslaver in the spring of 1801. She was described as being "very artful" and was "in the possession of one of the city badges for working out as a washerwoman," which she used to help her find employment.[90] Though her job as a washerwoman provided her with a level of protection, she made sure to take a badge with her before she ran away, to validate her search for employment in the city. These women connected their ability to successfully abscond to their possession of badges. Enslaved women had to become adept at navigating the precarious legal landscape that characterized slave hiring in the early nineteenth century. They demonstrated that even though the badge system was enacted to regulate their efforts to earn money from their waged labor, bondswomen would continue to find white employers willing to ignore laws that did not benefit them.

Perhaps it was the increased attention that enslaved peoples' economic practices gained from white citizens in the post-Revolutionary period that spurred lawmakers to erect hurdles to enslaved people who successfully turned their hard work into freedom. Or maybe it was the small increase in the numbers of free people of color in South Carolina, from .72 percent to .92 percent of the state's population.[91] But in December 1800, state lawmakers revisited the issue of slave manumission. Before 1800, private manumission—when an enslaved person negotiated directly with their enslaver for their freedom—was the most common process by which an enslaved person could be emancipated. It was an ad hoc process and there were few legal obstacles to an enslaver manumitting an enslaved person, either because of dedicated service or because an enslaved person had saved enough money to negotiate the terms of freedom. After 1800, the barriers to manumission for enslaved people became even steeper. Lawmakers sought to standardize private manumission because they argued that the legal status quo had "been found insufficient for keeping [enslaved people] in due subordination."[92] They expressed concern that enslavers were emancipating enslaved people with "bad or depraved character, or, from age or infirmity" or slaves who were "incapable of gaining their livelihood by honest means."[93] In order to ensure that emancipated people of color were of good character and could provide financially for themselves, lawmakers mandated that enslavers prove that the enslaved person would not be a legal or economic burden on the state. To initiate the process, enslavers would tell a local magistrate of their intentions to emancipate a slave. The magistrate would then bring together five white male property holders who would then interview both the enslaver and the enslaved person. The enslaver would then have to make a public case for the enslaved person's good character and testify that the bondspeople could "gain a livelihood in an honest way."[94] If the magistrates and freeholders approved the manumission, then they would draft a certificate recognizing that the enslaved person was legally emancipated.

Despite the intervention by state lawmakers, and the additional burden that they put on enslaved people, the higher standards for slave manumission did not hinder or change enslaved peoples' economic behavior, nor the behavior of their white trading partners. In fact, a wide swath of white South Carolinians indirectly benefited from the manumission law. If enslaved people faced even tougher barriers to freedom, and their earnings and wages would not guarantee that they could buy their emancipation, then enslaved people were faced with a choice: save or spend their earnings. Even though enslaved people did not stop searching for opportunities to make money and buy goods, they continued to hire out their time to white employers and trade with and buy goods from whites. And enslaved enterprise and consumerism did not occur without white partners. Enslavers willingly rented out their slaves, gave enslaved men and women permission to hire out, and consented to enslaved people engaging in trade. White employers and merchants hired slaves and sold goods, even liquor, to enslaved customers. Despite white South Carolinians' complaints, enslaved peoples' economic practices remained a fundamental aspect of South Carolina's culture and economy of slavery in the early national era. White residents benefitted economically from enslaved peoples' investment in their own economic networks.

White citizens' appeals continued to rise during the first decades of the nineteenth century, as white workingmen turned to state lawmakers arguing that slave hiring threatened social and economic stability in early national South Carolina. At the same time, enslaved enterprises shifted in the midst of social and economic instabilities caused by the Revolution. The reconfiguration of the relationship between enslaved people and enslavers in the Revolutionary and post-Revolutionary eras influenced every aspect of South Carolina's slave society. While enslavers hoped to re-establish their prewar dominance over their slaves, enslaved people internalized the revolutionary spirit around them and used the small advantages that they gained during the war to ameliorate their lives after it.

The series of petitions and legislative interventions reveal the stark reality of slavery in Revolutionary and early national South Carolina: the economic activities of enslaved people often occurred outside enslavers' purview and control. In this period, enslaved people continued to engage in self-hire and participate in the burgeoning economic culture that defined America during the late eighteenth and early nineteenth centuries. They saved money and used their free time to cultivate goods for themselves. They bargained for waged labor and occupied marketplaces selling their merchandise at a profit. Enslaved people continued to pursue their economic goals in hopes of surviving the Revolutionary era's uncertainty. They acted as—and perhaps thought of themselves as—actors, consumers, and participants in their local economies. Yet the continued legislative and judicial tension around their commercial practices grew as the stakes rose amidst a dramatic economic change marked by one product: short-staple cotton.

In the early nineteenth century, enslaved people repeatedly encountered both barriers and openings to their engagement in local economies. Despite the social unrest wrought by the Revolution, networks of enslaved enterprise did not go underground, perhaps because of its visibility and acceptance in the South Carolina milieu. The traditions that enslaved people fought to maintain during the Revolutionary War became an enduring aspect of life for not only enslaved black people, but also for whites of every economic class. The conspicuousness of enslaved peoples' economic interests became so entangled in the fabric of life in South Carolina that those white citizens concerned with hindering slaves' economic pursuits faced an uphill battle. The upheaval that surrounded enslaved entrepreneurship would only continue in the nineteenth century.

3

"A DANGEROUS AND GROWING PRACTICE"

Enslaved Entrepreneurship and the Cotton Economy in the New Nation

The staple commodity of the State is rice, but cotton is now eagerly cultivated," observed traveler John Davis at the end of the eighteenth century. "It is to the crop of cotton," he noted, "that the Planter looks for the augmentation of his wealth."[1] The transition from a rice-dominated economy to one driven by short-staple cotton transformed South Carolina's economy of slavery. As one historian has argued, "cotton seemed like a gift from heaven, especially to those [farmers and planters] who had relied on indigo, tobacco, and wheat."[2] The slow and steady decline in the importance of rice production in the Lowcountry to the state's economy is well documented. The Lowcountry's rice industry made South Carolina's coastal districts, and the slave owners, planters, and merchants who inhabited the region, the wealthiest in colonial America during the eighteenth century.[3] At the beginning of the nineteenth century, however, South Carolina's export economy—and therefore the economy of slavery—shifted. Short-staple cotton quickly eclipsed rice as the dominant export that enslaved people in South Carolina produced. However, cotton, as a commodity, was not new to the South Carolina marketplace. Long-staple cotton had been an export product in South Carolina's Sea Islands beginning in 1754.[4] But the introduction of new tools to grow cotton cheaply and more efficiently unleashed the economic potential of the South Carolina Upcountry, with short-staple cotton molding the landscape as well as the economic culture of slavery.

Enslaved people were part of the Upcountry's agricultural and economic evolution. This generation of bondspeople would not have a strong familiarity with the culture of rice cultivation. Instead, their labor, their bodies, and their lives went to building the state's economy of cotton. The experiences of a formerly enslaved man, Charles Ball, are particularly enlightening.

On his forced journey from Maryland to Columbia, South Carolina in the early 1800s, Ball witnessed how the introduction of short-staple cotton to South Carolina transformed not only the physical landscape, but also the experiences of enslaved people in the state. Weighted down by the chains and iron collar that connected him to a coffle of fifty-one other enslaved men and women, Ball ambled for over a month from Maryland to be sold to enslavers in Columbia, South Carolina. On the journey, he overheard conversations between slave trading merchants about the potential profits they would make from the sale of enslaved people. He overheard the traders discussing the value of young enslaved girls and boys under twenty years of age. According to Ball, they speculated on how much young bondspeople could fetch in the Columbia marketplace because of their physical abilities to labor and bring wealth to aspiring cotton planters. The cotton economy had become so lucrative that enslavers would have paid almost any price to buy prime hands who they believed could easily learn how to pick cotton. Instead of taking the coffle of bondspeople to the Lowcountry to be sold to rice planters, the slave trader, according to Ball, earned much more of a profit by selling the slaves to cotton planters in the Upcountry. As he left southern North Carolina tobacco country and entered Upcountry South Carolina, Ball traversed newly created roadways that bound disparate regions of the increasingly interconnected Southern plantation states. The harrowing journey introduced him to the sheer sprawl of short-staple cotton, which began to dominate the Upcountry landscape.[5]

Cotton fields in bloom defined Ball's first impression of South Carolina. He related that "little attention was paid to the cultivation of anything but cotton," a judgment that belied the reality of agricultural life for bondspeople in South Carolina.[6] Short-staple cotton quickly overtook the state's agrarian landscape as cotton began to eclipse rice as king. "Now this plant," Ball noted, "was almost the sole possessor of the fields. It covered the plantations adjacent to the road, as far as I could see, both before and behind me, and looked not unlike buckwheat before it blossoms."[7] The ascendancy of cotton as the driver of South Carolina's economy of slavery made an indelible imprint on Ball.

Short-staple cotton transformed South Carolina's plantation economy in the early nineteenth century. A more nuanced perspective of enslaved peoples' networks of enterprise also emerges in this period, as the slaves' economy collided with the economic animation of South Carolina's Upcountry. This agricultural and economic invigoration thrust enslaved entrepreneurship more visibly into the public sphere and into public discourse. As South Carolina underwent dramatic economic, social, and environmental changes, the slaves' economy began to diversify as well. Enslaved people had access to wider diversity of goods and interacted economically with a wider group of people. Enslaved enterprises were not relegated to the more urban centers in and around Charleston and the Lowcountry. Bondspeople in newly developed regions of the South Carolina Upcountry entered into economic exchanges with other enslaved people and with white South Carolinians along the economic spectrum. It is clear that enslaved people responded to the changes that were beginning to take place within South Carolina's economy of slavery. In the regions outside of the wealthy Lowcountry, enslaved people adapted their profit-seeking motives to the growth of a commodity that came to define slavery in nineteenth-century South Carolina and America more broadly—short-staple cotton.

Enslavers' adoption of short-staple cotton as a major cash crop reshaped the lives of enslaved people such as Charles Ball in dramatic ways. As a result, enslaved entrepreneurship evolved as an extension of the state's burgeoning cotton economy. The culture of cotton cultivation that swept through South Carolina brought Upcountry planters into economic competition with their Lowcountry rice and indigo planting counterparts. For white South Carolinians, short-staple cotton began to democratize access to economic prosperity. For enslaved people, the emerging cotton economy brought more trading partners, with a more diverse array of goods, out of the woodwork. With the sweeping economic changes brought about by the short-staple cotton boom, enslaved enterprises departed from the previous century of enslaved peoples' independent marketing, trade, and exchange. But the explosion of the cotton economy did not make slaves' lives any easier. Though enslaved people developed more marketing skills and economic savvy and had access to more goods, the cotton economy did not alleviate the burdens of their enslavement.

Just as cotton planters invested in new technologies to cultivate short-staple cotton more profitably—which comprised the seeds of capitalist explosion in the early nineteenth century—enslaved people sought out opportunities to increase investment in their own economic pursuits. Bondspeople found themselves at the center of a commercial whirlwind, wherein enslavers capitalized on their labor and their bodies in new ways. At the same time, white South Carolinians of all economic classes became more eager participants in the growth of both economies—cotton from the top-down and enslaved entrepreneurship from the bottom-up.

The technological innovations made to the cotton gin drove South Carolina's cotton boom in the late eighteenth and early nineteenth centuries. The gin revolutionized the process of cleaning short-staple cotton, which proved to be labor intensive and time consuming. Mechanical improvements to the cultivation and harvesting processes in the late eighteenth century made short-staple cotton cultivation profitable, initiating an unprecedented explosion of economic enterprise in South Carolina, the expanding slave South, and the American economy writ large. South Carolinians who lived outside of the Lowcountry quickly took notice and took advantage of the invention. Cotton gin technology modernized cotton cultivation, allowing a wider swath of white yeoman and aspiring planters entrance into the economy of slavery and the profits that soon followed. Also, short-staple cotton required less initial capital investment than did rice as a profit-making venture.[8] In 1802, South Carolina governor John Drayton celebrated cotton cultivation, connecting it to American independence and the "peace of 1783."[9] He observed that the integration of cotton as an export product brought "extraordinary profits" to the state's planters, even declaring that cotton had surpassed rice and indigo as the most valuable crop grown in the state.[10]

The transition from a rice-based to cotton-based economy occurred relatively quickly. Cotton exports from South Carolina in 1793 amounted to 94,000 pounds, most of which was the long-staple variety grown on coastal Lowcountry plantations. By 1800, a mere seven years later, 6.5 million pounds of cotton was exported from South Carolina, the majority of which was the short-staple variety grown in the Upcountry. In 1810, enslaved people had cultivated 50 million pounds of short-staple cotton. The historian Lacy Ford has argued that the cotton boom at the beginning of the nineteenth century offered white yeoman economic alternatives to simply providing Lowcountry plantations with subsistence.[11]

Short-staple cotton production brought white South Carolinians who resided outside of the Lowcountry into the capitalist fold. Yeoman who had been relegated by their wealthier and more politically connected Lowcountry counterparts to the backwaters of South Carolina had the opportunity to invest in cotton's promise of economic prosperity. These white South Carolinians who lived outside the Lowcountry believed that in order to fully profit from their investments in cotton, they also had to invest in slaveholding. One could not occur without the other. The number of enslaved people outside the Lowcountry increased steadily between 1790 and 1810 to supplement future cotton planters' quest for profits. In 1790, there were approximately 21,000 enslaved people in the Upcountry. The number of bondspeople increased to over 70,000 by 1810, a jump of 233 percent. Moreover, by 1810, there were enslaved men and women in over a third of households in the Upcountry.[12]

The increasing numbers of bondspeople sold to enslavers in the Upcountry coincided with unmistakable levels of material deprivation among enslaved people on new cotton plantations. Charles Ball noticed immediately the poor conditions of the land, the livestock, and the enslaved people on the cotton plantations that he passed on his way to Columbia. "The horses and mules that I saw in the cotton-fields," Ball described, "were poor and badly harnessed, and the half-naked condition of the negroes, who drove them, or followed with the hoe, together with their wan complexions, proved to me that they had too much work, or not enough food."[13] The bondspeople were inadequately dressed and malnourished. He witnessed the physical toll that enslavement on a cotton plantation had on the enslaved. The asymmetry between the bounty of cotton and enslavers demands on their slaves' labor affected the lives of the enslaved, leaving them without enough food or proper clothing. This vision filled Ball with palpable fears of the suffering that his future as a bondsman on a South Carolina cotton plantation would portend.

During his seven years as an enslaved man in Columbia, Ball remarked on the array of strategies that enslaved people used to fulfill their material needs. But Ball also explains that enslaved enterprises were not only found among enslaved people in South Carolina. Indeed, he describes that in Calvert County, Maryland, his birthplace, slaves attempted to make their lives better through economic enterprise as well.

> The slaves were also permitted to work for themselves at night, and on Sunday. If they chose to fish, they had the privilege of selling whatever they caught. Some expert fishermen caught and sold as many fish and oysters, as enabled them to buy coffee, sugar, and other luxuries for their wives, besides keeping themselves and their families in Sunday clothes; for, the masters in Maryland only allowed the men one wool hat, one pair of shoes, two shirts, two pair of trousers—one pair of tow cloth, and one of woolen—and one woollen jacket in the year. The women were furnished in proportion. All other clothes they had to provide for themselves.[14]

Ball was accustomed to enslaved peoples' participation in local economies. It was the sheer scale and prevalence of enslaved enterprise in South Carolina that surprised him. While he was enslaved in South Carolina, he witnessed enslaved women and men completing extra work for neighboring planters in order to buy goods such as salt and sugar. One enslaved man divulged to Ball that his enslaver did not provide his bondspeople with enough food, and certainly did not offer his slaves salt, a product which enslaved people used to preserve meat and season otherwise bland meals. In order to obtain salt and other "articles of convenience," the enslaved man worked on Sundays for "neighboring planters" who paid him fifty cents per day for his labor.[15] To Ball, the tradition of enslaved people seeking out opportunities to earn money and buy goods was the norm, from Maryland to South Carolina. But his experience with enslaved enterprise in South Carolina during the cotton boom turned the slaves' trade into something more devastating. Instead of enslaved people buying luxuries or "Sunday clothes," enslaved people engaged in commercial activities to survive.

The sight of enslaved people working on Sundays for wages and toiling on individual garden patches was common, a ubiquity sanctioned by enslavers, accepted by white freeholders, and embraced by bondspeople. By the first decade of the nineteenth century, as Upcountry planters invested in land, slaves, and the technologies of short-staple cotton production, enslaved people entered into a delicate negotiation with their enslavers to work for wages. Ball observed that "when the slaves go out to work for wages on Sundays, their employers never flog them . . . The practice of working on Sunday is so universal amongst the slaves on the cotton plantations, that the immorality is never spoken of."[16] In the spring and early summer, times of the year when the rain prevented them from completing plantation work, enslaved people spent their down time making goods such as "baskets, brooms, and horse collars," items that they subsequently sold to local slaveholders.[17] Bondsmen and bondswomen transformed the goods that they had at their disposal—from hickory trees for baskets and horse collars made from corn husks—to earn money. "The money procured by these," he recalled, "and various other means . . . is laid out by the slaves in purchasing such little articles of necessity or luxury, as it enables them to procure."[18] Enslaved people purchased a range of goods, from sugar and molasses, to coffee and rum. In the winter, they received a set of woolen and linen clothing from their enslavers. But these items were of poor quality and did not last the entire year. For this reason, the enslaved people that Ball encountered had to use their earnings to buy clothing, which suggests that cotton planters and slaveholders were finding ways to make their investments in cotton cultivation in the early nineteenth century pay off. Ultimately, slaves continued to lack basic necessities, such as adequate clothing and food. They had to spend their free time completing extra work to earn money to purchase the most basic of necessities. According to Ball, one enslaved man had been spending his free time working to provide clothing for his children and his wife. He went without shoes for many years, instead creating moccasins for himself out of tree bark. The moccasins did shield his feet from the frost, but they did a poor job of protecting him from the wet and humid weather.[19]

Ball's revelations about enslaved peoples' lives in the cotton-cultivating Upcountry contextualizes why they were so dedicated to participating in economic enterprise. Bondspeoples' investment of their time and meager resources into market activities was not simply a matter of improving their material conditions; it was also a matter of survival. They overworked and saved as much as they could. They organized themselves into family units and pooled their shared resources to ensure that they could feed themselves and their kin. Ball recalled an act of kindness by Dinah, an enslaved woman who "was at the head of our family." She shared her family's molasses with him, a small act of generosity that encouraged Ball to forge even stronger ties with Dinah and her kin. Remembering Dinah's kind gesture, Ball promised her and her husband that he would "bring all my earnings into the family stock, provided that I be treated as one of its members, and be allowed the proceeds of their patch or garden."[20] Ball understood the material and emotional benefits of aligning himself with a family and community. He recognized that his survival—and his own economic goals—depended on it.

The introduction of short-staple cotton also altered the ways in which slaves' accessed trading partners. Cotton, combined with the opening up of South Carolina's Upcountry to cotton's profitability, cleared the way for enslaved people to establish new and fertile commercial relationships with whites. The experience of an unidentified enslaved person in 1805 serves as an example. On July 14, 1805, an enslaved person sold a variety of goods—including one pound of meat, two bushels of corn, and one bushel of corn meal, all valued at $5—to John and Lucy Miller, two white Union District residents. The Millers were subsequently brought before a Union District magistrate and charged with stealing corn and "indecent dealing with a Negro."[21] Though the records do not reveal the enslaved person's name, the magistrate called the slave's owner, Richard Farr, to account for the validity of the claims against his slave. Perhaps the bondsperson had an individual plot of land, allocated by Farr, on which to grow his or her crop of corn. It is possible that the enslaved person used the corn to supplement the meager provision of food provided by Farr. Or the slave used his or her independent cultivation to earn money by selling the yield of their crops. It is possible that the enslaved person had been growing crops that he or she knew that white members of their communities wanted to obtain. John and Lucy Miller were so eager to obtain the goods from the enslaved person that they ignored the laws that made their trade illegal. Nevertheless, the transactions between the Millers and the enslaved person were not uncommon.

Against the backdrop of the state's economic growth, enslaved people innovated ways to participate more directly in local networks of exchange. But for enslaved people, the transition from rice to short-staple cotton as the primary driver of the state's economy proved to be a double-edged sword. On the one hand, enslaved enterprise had grown into a more recognizable and accepted facet of South Carolina's culture of slavery. On the other, the development of South Carolina's cotton economy meant that bondspeoples' lives and livelihoods would be even more tethered to enslavers profit-making motives. The tactics that enslaved people used to connect with trading partners evolved in tandem with the changing nature of slavery in the South Carolina economy in the early nineteenth century. Between bondspeople, free blacks, and white South Carolinians of all classes, enslaved entrepreneurship morphed as bondspeople more frequently traversed country roads and inhabited marketplaces entering into a wide variety of exchanges with whites.[22]

Indeed, biracial networks of trade spread throughout the Upcountry in the early nineteenth century as enslaved people and whites sought out opportunities to trade with one another. On September 4, 1808, an enslaved woman named Suckey brought a number of items with her to an exchange with a white woman, Nancy Edwards. Suckey, perhaps well-acquainted with the Union District roads and country paths to get to the meeting, brought with her one peck of wheat flour, two pounds of dried beef, and one gallon of corn meal. She arrived without a ticket from her slaveholder to legalize the exchange, as required by South Carolina law. Nancy Edwards did not ask for one. There is no information that reveals if Suckey received anything from Edwards for her goods. However, a trade did take place, with both Suckey and Edwards leaving the transaction with tangible markers of their interaction, Edwards with goods and Suckey with perhaps another commodity. It is possible that Suckey requested that Edwards compensate her in money. Or maybe she required another item, perhaps whiskey, in exchange for the items that she traded with Edwards; an illicit substance to finalize what would become an illicit transaction.[23]

The illegal nature of the trade between Suckey and Edwards was put on public display the following month. In October 1808, a Union District judge summoned Edwards to appear before him and a jury of local freeholding white men, charging her with violating laws that restricted whites from trading with slaves without a ticket from the slave's master or hirer. Edwards was charged with illegally "trading with a Negro" because Suckey did not present her with a ticket before the exchange took place. Moreover, during the trial a local white freeholder, Thornton Stringfellow, argued that Suckey stole from him the items that she sold or traded to Edwards. While it is possible that Suckey told Edwards where and how she procured the goods that Edwards ultimately purchased, it is also probable that Suckey did not offer this information and Edwards did not ask for it. On October 7, 1808, Edwards was tried before a magistrate and thirteen jurors. They found her guilty of illegally trafficking with a slave. In an interesting twist, no information exists as to whether Suckey was even brought before the Union District magistrates court on similar charges.[24]

The economic rendezvous between Suckey and Nancy Edwards—this brief, albeit illicit exchange—exemplifies how the transformations that began to occur in South Carolina's economy of slavery during the early years of the nineteenth century influenced the lives of all South Carolinians, white and black, enslaved and free, enslaver and yeoman. The exchange between the two women represented the extent to which people at every rung of South Carolina society depended, in some way, on enslaved peoples' entrepreneurial pursuits. This was especially true for whites on the economic and social fringes of society. Though there is no extant census information about Nancy Edwards, the court records refer to her as a "single woman," which suggests that she was an unmarried white woman.[25] Enslaved peoples' extralegal networks of trade necessarily involved unpropertied and poor whites because, as historian Jeff Forret has argued for the antebellum South, they comprised an economically dependent population who lacked the financial security afforded to landowners and slaveholders. This dependence made them, as Forret contends, "attractive potential economic allies for enterprising slaves in the region."[26]

For poor and single white women, that dependence may have been even more acute. Edwards may have been facing a pressing material need, where she was willing to run afoul of the law to obtain necessities. It is not surprising then that Nancy Edwards and Suckey would establish even a fleeting economic bond, with Suckey willing to exchange wheat, beef, and cornmeal with Edwards and Edwards keen to complete the trade. Ultimately, Edwards was found guilty of circumventing the legal channels to trade with Suckey. It is possible, though, that her precarious economic situation led her to take the calculated gamble of seeking out Suckey, knowing that Suckey could provide goods that would be difficult to get elsewhere.

This exchange reveals just how universal enslaved peoples' engagement in trade had become in the early nineteenth century. Nancy Edwards stood before the Union District Circuit Court charged with publicly breaching the legal codes that made the types of exchanges between a slave and a white person illegal. However, just because Edwards's participation in the trade may have been illegal, the legality of Suckey's role was not as clear. Though Suckey, for example, did not bring a note from her enslaver, Bird Bluford, to the trade, we cannot immediately assume that Bluford did not know about or support Suckey's enterprising activities. Bluford was a planter, owning nineteen enslaved people in 1800 and it is possible that he did not discourage Suckey from seeking out legal and extralegal entrepreneurial opportunities.[27] Perhaps he benefited economically from Suckey's investment in trade and saw her economic pursuits as a way to make his own investments in slave labor pay off. All of this might explain why the court indicted and charged Edwards, while Suckey was shielded from prosecution.[28]

The burgeoning short-staple cotton economy may have brought Suckey and Edwards together. They lived in a region of the state that many South Carolinians in previous generations believed could not compete with the agricultural promise of enslavers in the Lowcountry. The state's Upcountry districts began to coalesce in the late eighteenth and early nineteenth centuries, allowing enslaved people such as Suckey to harness their economic interests to create more avenues through which to develop their networks of exchange.[29] Furthermore, Suckey and Nancy Edwards resided in the Union District, founded in 1785 at the end of the Revolutionary War and located in the northwestern part of the state, just south of the North Carolina border. The Union District represented one of the Upcountry districts that experienced the most dramatic of the economic transformations brought on by cotton planters' investments in the technologies of short-staple cotton cultivation at the beginning of the nineteenth century.[30] Therefore, the interaction between Suckey and Edwards perhaps occurred within close proximity of a cotton plantation and it is likely that their trade was made possible *because of* the expansion of the cotton economy.[31]

Short-staple cotton restructured the Upcountry in the early nineteenth century, bringing economic opportunity to those invested in cotton, land, and slaves. White farmers transitioned from subsistence cultivation to investing in cotton for export.[32] As a single woman, Edwards may have found herself in an untenable position—perhaps without land, without slaves, and certainly without capital. The experience of living in an environment without the necessary tools of economic survival may have pushed Edwards to take the calculated risk of trading with Suckey.

Enslaved peoples' networks of exchange represented the economic atmosphere that characterized the burgeoning cotton South in the early national period. It also exemplified the ways in which enslaved peoples' commercial practices were a component of the capitalist energy that propelled regions of the lower South to economic prominence. Both enslaved people and the whites with whom they traded invested in illicit economic relationships because each party had something to gain. For enslaved people it was access to goods, money, or perhaps the psychological benefits of engaging in trade. For some white trading partners, it was sometimes swindling enslaved people out of their cash and goods because of the asymmetrical power dynamic that existed between them. Charles Ball illuminated how white shopkeepers exploited enslaved peoples' interest in trade. Slaves frequented local shops and stores near rich cotton plantations, often after the overseer went to bed and sometimes without slave owners' consent. The white storekeepers were enthusiastic trading partners, "always ready to accommodate the slaves."[33] Enslaved people, according to Ball, often purchased goods with cash, not credit like white patrons, and a storekeeper could "demand any price he pleases for his goods."[34] In welcoming enslaved consumers into their stores, even under the cloak of darkness, white storekeepers maintained their economic interests, bolstered their profit-making capabilities, all while increasing their cash-based—not credit-based—businesses. The historian David Patterson argues that for white merchants, bondspeople occupied two spaces during their transactions: that of property and that of a customer.[35] White shopkeepers eagerly sold goods to local bondspeople because they reaped the financial rewards from welcoming enslaved people as customers, despite the legal risks that they were taking. Apparently, the benefits were worth it.

As biracial networks of exchange continued to expand, lawmakers continued to receive complaints about the slaves' trade in the first two decades of the nineteenth century. Petitioners expressed their frustrations about the frequency of "illicit trafficking" between whites and black slaves, and the failure of enslavers to control the slaves' economy. These white petitioners reveal a lot about the atmosphere of economic exchange. Bondspeople introduced a variety of goods into their local marketplaces in the early nineteenth century, including corn and cotton. And there was a ready market of white South Carolinians—from slaveholders to yeoman and shopkeepers—who desired enslaved peoples' goods. This trade had become so widespread that groups of Upcountry white residents, in particular, complained to state lawmakers, accusing certain white South Carolinians of willingly engaging in illegal economic activities such as "trading with Negroes" and "retailing spiritous liquors" to slaves. They argued that when slaves "hire[d] their own time" and took apprentices, as white working men did, these activities threatened the stability of entire slaveholding communities, including the whites who lived in close proximity.

Petitioners from around the state were highlighting the prevalence of biracial economic exchange and the investments that white South Carolinians put into maintaining their trade with and their employment of enslaved people. While some white citizens expressed frustrations with whites "trading with Negroes," the reality was that there were two parties to each of the trades, one enslaved and black, the other often white. And both parties were eager to complete the transactions.[36]

The residents who publicly lamented the continued presence of the slaves' economy were concerned with one issue above all else: how the slaves' trade undermined racial solidarity among whites. They maintained that whites who profited from their investments in the slaves' economy put their personal economic interests over protecting their fellow white citizens. That is to say, it was not uncommon for enslavers, merchants, and even poor whites to put their economic goals and material needs above those of other whites in the society. White grog shop owners, for example, willingly accepted money from enslaved customers, even daring to traffick in illegal goods with slaves, to keep them as patrons. Again, the words of Charles Ball are particularly poignant. Ball described the eagerness of white shopkeepers to attract enslaved people as customers. He argued that enslaved people were "better customers than any white people" because instead of acquiring goods on credit, enslaved women and men paid cash or "make their payments by barter."[37] Ball indirectly gets to the heart of how the rise of capitalism in the early nineteenth century undermined racial solidarity among white South Carolinians, while still keeping enslaved people in bondage.

Ball also perceived underlying tensions between the whites with whom he engaged economically. From shopkeepers to his enslavers, Ball witnessed how white South Carolinians sometimes lacked a shared commitment to the privileges of whiteness in a society characterized by both capitalism and racial slavery. This failure of whites to cohere around the advantages of whiteness had real economic consequences for white South Carolinians. Enslavers, merchants, shopkeepers, and even employers who wanted to hire enslaved workers put their own financial security over protecting the economic interests of other whites. In this way, capitalism in early national South Carolina undermined white racial solidarity. If whites willingly put their economic engagement with slaves and the profits to be made from such arrangements above any sense of camaraderie that they felt with other white people, then the slaves' economy would continue to grow. White South Carolinians who relied on the labor of and commerce with enslaved people did not want anything to get in the way of their economic relations with slaves. As long as enslaved people continued to patronize their shops, sell them goods at a reasonable price, and work for lower wages than white laborers, then whites would continue to encourage the expansion of slaves' economic networks.[38]

One strategy used by whites to curtail the slaves' trade and better regulate trafficking was slave patrols. In the Lowcountry, enslaved people in Georgetown and St. George's Dorchester had been engaging in self-hire, selling rice to white shopkeepers, and using cash that they had at their disposal to buy liquor. Bondspeople in the Lowcountry's eight districts had remained so vigilant in maintaining their own networks of trade that white Georgetown residents made an official appeal to state lawmakers. In November 1810, one hundred and four white residents of the Georgetown District petitioned the state legislature for financial assistance to help support a town guard. The guard had been having a hard time eradicating whites' "illicit traffic with Negroes," and they believed that enslaved people had been procuring and selling sizable portions of rice to "petty shopkeepers" without tickets from their masters.[39] Ultimately, the proliferation of the slaves' trade caused these white residents to believe that the same people who supported "the prospect of accumulating property by fraudulent means" would attempt to set Georgetown ablaze and plunder the community's law-abiding citizens.[40] They urged lawmakers for financial support for a slave patrol, arguing that slaves' illicit traffic threatened the peace and tranquility of their communities. Consequently, lawmakers responded in December 1810 to Georgetown residents' complaints, writing that they would support the request for patrol funds.[41] Enslaved people had been developing their networks of trade in the Lowcountry for over a century by this point, so it was not surprising that white residents continued to face an uphill battle in their attempts to restrict the slaves' trade. In particular, the petitioners did not ask lawmakers to increase fines or otherwise reprimand shopkeepers, merchants, or even slaveholders who did not intervene to stop the illicit traffick. They hoped that slave patrols—and the legal apparatus created to regulate enslaved people—would solve this problem.

In general, the perceived fragility of South Carolina's laws of slavery, as they related to enslaved people with access to cash and goods, were on full display in white South Carolinians' complaints about the slaves' trade in the early nineteenth century. It is notable, however, that neither the white residents nor the state officials who responded to residents' petitions suggested re-evaluating or revising the laws. In the Lowcountry complaints, residents did not suggest making slaves' economic activities illegal. Instead, the white citizens requested that lawmakers offer financial assistance for slave patrols instead of intervening more directly in the local business of slaveholding residents.[42] These interchanges, between white residents and state lawmakers, presented a conundrum. Perhaps most whites did not actually object to trading with, selling to, or employing enslaved people. It is possible that their reluctance to stop their economic engagements with slaves belied a broader recognition that enslaved enterprise filled important economic roles within their communities. While they may not have fully supported enslaved peoples' customary economic privileges, they did want to eradicate the trade either. But why was that the case? Why did whites' recommendations fall short of demanding harsher sentences for those involved in enslaved entrepreneurship? Maybe their calls to augment the region's slave patrols was the most effective way to regulate—not eliminate—slaves' involvement in market activities. White investment in enslaved peoples' networks of enterprise fueled its growth, despite the sometimes illicit nature of the exchanges.

Enslaved peoples' sometimes illegal economic practices spurred slaves to incorporate stolen goods into their trade networks. Enslaved people had always, to some extent, stolen goods that they then wanted to sell as their own—or stolen merchandise that they wanted to keep for themselves. Yet the public mechanisms, namely the magistrates' courts, attempted to do a better job of holding enslaved people accountable for such behavior in the early nineteenth century. In January 1805 an enslaved man, Bob, stood before magistrates and local white freeholders in the Kershaw District, charged with petit larceny for stealing a pair of boots. Bob's trial included the testimony of one witness, that of merchant James Pearl. Pearl testified that he noticed a pair of boots missing from his shop and upon visiting the stable of Kershaw slaveholder John Kilpatrick, believed that he saw the same pair of boots. He had "every reason to believe . . . that Bob a Negro fellow the property of said John Kirkpatrick did take and carry away the said Boots."[43] After considering Pearl's testimony, the freeholders found Bob guilty of petit larceny and sentenced him to receive forty-five lashes on the bare back. However, the details of the case and Pearl's testimony suggest that the magistrates and freeholders may have made a hasty decision about Bob's guilt. The entire case rested on Pearl's accusation of Bob. First, Pearl did not say, with absolute certainty, that Bob stole boots from his store. He stated that he had "reason to believe" that Bob had stolen the boots. Moreover, Pearl did not give the reason for why Bob would want to steal Pearl's boots. Had Bob and Pearl traded goods informally on previous occasions? Was this case retribution by Pearl on either Bob or Kilpatrick for an economic relationship gone sour? In addition, it is not clear that Pearl knew to check the stable of John Kilpatrick for his purloined boots; it was a very specific place in which to look for stolen goods. In the end, Bob was found guilty. Though he received a brutal physical punishment, Bob did not serve as an example for other enslaved people, as members of the court had perhaps hoped. That is to say, theft remained an integral and conspicuous facet of enslaved peoples' economic networks.

And bondspeople stole a variety of goods. They pilfered bacon from local smokehouses, cattle from neighboring plantations, and ran off with horses.[44] Enslaved people such as Bob did not distinguish between stealing goods from their enslaver—for their own consumption or use—and theft with the intention of redistributing stolen goods within their local networks of trade.[45] For many bondspeople, theft and trade were intricately linked. Charles Ball offers perhaps one of the most direct explanations for why enslaved people resorted to stealing as a means of acquiring desired goods in the early national period. He argued that enslaved people rationalized stealing and its place within the economy of the enslaved, declaring, "The slave sees his master residing in a spacious mansion, riding in a fine carriage, and dressed in costly clothes, and attributes the possession of all these enjoyments to his own labour."[46] He expressed no qualms about stealing from his master to procure bacon, a good that he considered to be a luxury item. Ball traded fish that he and his fellow enslaved men caught for their master for bacon that he procured from a local white trader. Even though he realized that the exchange between himself and the white trader ran afoul of the law, "a very high offence in Carolina," such a realization did not stop him from using the tools at his disposal to obtain an item that he desired.[47] He recognized that he was selling goods that did not legally belong to him. But Ball still believed that he had the right to take his owner's goods, sell them, and make a profit for himself. In fact, he argued, "I felt in my conscience that I had a better right than any other person."[48] Ball was unequivocal in his thinking about the relationship between stealing and slaves' profit-oriented activities. Enslaved people such as Charles Ball and Bob expressed little shame about stealing goods for themselves—if not for their own use, then to sell or trade for other goods with people within their communities.

The pivotal concern at the heart of Bob's case and Ball's rationalizations, and instances of bondspeoples' engagement in theft more broadly, was enslaved peoples' motivation. When Charles Ball compared his experience surrounded by family in Maryland to his experience in South Carolina, one that was "cheerless" and "hopeless," he highlighted "the pains of hunger and the sting of the lash."[49] As historian Alex Lichtenstein has argued, physical punishment "could hardly overcome the hunger that drove many slaves to steal."[50] Ball not only discussed the trauma of forced separation from his family, but he revealed the physical hunger pangs, the ever-present feeling of physical deprivation, and the subsequent emotional and psychic toll that enslavement in the cotton South had on him. The hopelessness and the hunger, the violence and the punishments, that characterized his life and the lives of other enslaved people illuminates why Ball and other enslaved people resorted to theft to fulfill their immediate material needs.

Though the relationship between theft and slave resistance has been well-established by historians, when viewed through the lens of enslaved peoples' networks of exchange, theft takes on a different meaning. When bondspeople resorted to theft, these incidences were not acts of rebellion.[51] Instead, when enslaved people engaged in theft, survival was their upmost concern, not resisting enslavers' domination and violence. Enslavers in the early nineteenth century began to construct a culture of cotton cultivation that under-provisioned enslaved people. They deprived slaves of proper food in adequate quantities. This strategy worked to enslavers' economic advantage because they ultimately spent less on food for their slaves. Moreover, this new generation of enslavers invested not in rice and indigo but in short-staple cotton, and adapted slave management techniques that mirrored their Lowcountry counterparts. They embraced enslaved peoples' marketing activities, a vestige of Lowcountry rice culture. Cotton planters diverged in other important ways. They began to adopt a more profit-oriented approach to slaveholding. For this reason, enslaved people invested in their economic enterprises by more fully incorporating theft—to survive the increasing material deprivations that began to categorize slavery in South Carolina.

Bondspeople trafficking in stolen goods fit into the architecture of the early national economy and when enslaved people incorporated enslavers' goods into their networks of exchange, they created black markets in the process. From the birth of state-sponsored banks to the rise of counterfeit paper notes, enslaved people cultivated underground networks that were emblematic of the wide-open landscape of early republican economic activity. The slaves' economy and the ways in which theft fit into it reflected the capitalist evolution that took place in the American economy. Though bondspeople traded in stolen items, even in legitimate bank notes, they defended how theft fit neatly into their economic lives.[52]

It is no surprise, therefore, that one of the more valuable items that circulated within enslaved peoples' networks of trade was paper money. In the summer 1812, Sukey,[53] an enslaved woman from Camden, stood accused of stealing from a local merchant named Ignas Folmer. On a Saturday evening in July 1812, Sukey, owned by free man of color Bond Conway, stole several items from Folmer's store. Harriet, Conway's daughter, stated that she saw Sukey on the following Sunday morning with a variety of colored cloth, "the size of a man's hat."[54] According to Peter, an enslaved man owned by a neighboring slaveholder, Sukey approached him on the following morning and told him that she had paper money that she wanted to change. On August 10, 1812, another witness, a white Camden resident named Martin Genley, maintained that he gave Folmer a five-dollar bill for safe keeping prior to Sukey invading Folmer's store. Genley testified that the bill was the same one presented to the court as evidence of Sukey's guilt. After hearing the witnesses' testimonies, members of the court found Sukey guilty of stealing and they ordered that she be punished with fifty lashes on her nude back to be administered in front of the Kershaw District's common jail.[55] The details of this case provide an impression of Sukey's understanding of the relationship between theft and the slaves' economy. Even if Sukey did enter Folmer's store and did steal the cloth and the bank note, her intention was to find ways to use both items. The fact that she wanted to change the note for something that could possibly be of more immediate value to her suggests that she may have tapped into a network of people with knowledge of how to transform stolen goods into tradable commodities. Or perhaps Sukey was indicted, found guilty, and subsequently punished with fifty lashes because she was owned not by a white slaveholder but by Bond Conway, a free man of color. It is also possible that the magistrates wanted to use Sukey as an example, to convince other enslaved people in the Kershaw District that they had no business keeping or trying to obtain paper money.

The circulation of paper notes within enslaved peoples' networks of trade cannot be overstated. Bondspeople were just as eager to procure bank notes as they were to purchase or trade for other goods. They understood the value of a cash-based economy and the power of utilizing money to obtain items that they desired or needed. Enslaved people were embroiled in relatively high-stakes networks of exchange, where trust dictated whether or not the transaction would be completed.[56] They willingly straddled the boundary between legal and illegal commercial pursuits to bring cash into their extralegal economic networks. In some cases, for bondspeople, getting caught with stolen or counterfeit bank notes meant the difference between life and death. In early January 1816, three enslaved men from the Kershaw District were charged with burglary for entering the store of Hugh M. Call, a Camden merchant, and stealing money from him. According to Call, on the night of January 10, 1816, the three enslaved men broke into and robbed his store. Call singled out Frank, Dick, and Milton on the following day, January 11, and made a formal complaint to the district's two magistrates who presided over the Court of Magistrates and Freeholders, the court that handled cases involving enslaved people. After the magistrates gathered three local white male freeholders—Phineas Thornton, Lewis Ballard, and John Naudin—the trial began on January 15. After the first of twelve witnesses, Abraham Dickinson, testified that he saw only one man, Dick, with an ax on the evening of the crime, members of the court dismissed the charges against Frank and Milton, focusing the trial on Dick as the sole perpetrator. When the magistrates asked Dick if he was going to plead "guilty" or "not guilty," he chose the "not guilty" plea, perhaps believing, as Charles Ball did, that there was no crime in appropriating goods for himself.[57]

The case proceeded against Dick on January 15, 1816, when members of the court heard additional witness testimony. Abraham Dickinson continued his testimony and expounded on his observations of Dick on the night in question. However, in recounting Dick's supposed criminal activities, Dickinson revealed that he was "uncertain whether he [Dick] had the ax or not."[58] He did claim to have seen Dick at a local drinking establishment owed by proprietor W. Nixon. Other witnesses corroborated this important clue about Dick's whereabouts and his inebriation, including the person who hired Dick on the day of the alleged crime. On the day of the crime, Dick hired himself out to Peter Adamson. Adamson, during the day of hire, asked Dick to fetch his tools. He also admitted that he saw Dick during the evening and he "appeared to be in liquor."[59] Perhaps with the money he earned from his work for Adamson, Dick spent the evening drinking at W. Nixon's grog shop. Another witness, Stuart Andrews, worked at McCall's store until 11:00 p.m. on the evening of the crime. He testified that he did not hear any noises nor did he see anyone on the street at the time that he tended to the store. Five white witnesses in total—Peter Naudin and Jim Naudin, relatives of one of the trial's freeholders, John Naudin; John Cunningham, an apprentice to Peter Adamson, who hired Dick for the day; and Anthony Adamson, perhaps a relative of Peter Adamson—observed Dick drinking earlier in the evening at W. Nixon's establishment. Each witness who testified to having seen Dick intoxicated during the evening supported Dick's claim that he carried neither an axe nor any other weapon on the evening of the crime.[60]

Three enslaved people even testified on Dick's behalf. Dinah—an enslaved woman owned by slaveholder Elisha Bell, who also owned Dick—was on her way home after the evening bell tolled on January 10 and saw Dick enter his living quarters, presumably after he had been drinking. She admitted that he did leave the quarters during the evening, but his absence only lasted a few minutes. Somersett, another enslaved man, maintained that he had witnessed Dick on the evening of the alleged burglary and that Dick was inebriated. A third enslaved person—Jim, owned by Elisha Bell—informed the court that Dick returned home from his hire at around 10 or 11:00 p.m. But he also revealed that Dick told him that "if anyone inquired to tell them that they came home together."[61]

The trial records do not reveal the extent of the deliberations, but after hearing all witness testimony, members of the court found Dick not guilty of burglary. The trial's outcome presents an opportunity to consider how South Carolina's early nineteenth-century district courts handled cases that involved enslaved people and theft. It brings the concept of localism in Southern legal culture to the fore.[62] The freeholders had a vested interest in the enslaved men not being charged with any crime. The complicated relationship between kinship, ownership, and perhaps visibility that existed between the white freeholders, the witnesses, and the enslaved defendants may have influenced the outcome of Dick's case. First, one of the enslaved men, Frank, was owned by one of the court's freeholders, Lewis Ballard. Even though the magistrates dropped the case against Frank, perhaps at Ballard's behest, Ballard may have persuaded the other members of the court to use extreme prejudice when considering Dick's fate. Second, two of the witnesses that testified in defense of Dick—Peter and Jim Naudin—were related to another freeholder on the court, John Naudin. Third, Dick's owner, Elisha Bell, was a rising Upcountry slaveholder whose slaveholding increased in the first two decades of the nineteenth century. In 1810, Bell was a middling slaveholder who owned six enslaved people.[63] In 1820, he augmented the number of slaves on his plantation to twenty-eight, placing him in the category of not a middling slaveholder, but a planter.[64] It is possible that Bell's influence in Camden grew in tandem with the number of slaves he owned. And in addition to witness testimony, Bell's influence within his community may have shaped the outcome of Dick's trial, thereby protecting his investment in his human property.[65] It is probable, though, that perhaps as Bell's influence grew, Dick also became an important economic actor within his community. Perhaps his ability to obtain goods, such as cash, influenced the outcome of the case.

Enslaved people clearly had access to paper money and a veritable marketplace of goods. Access to money provided bondspeople with the purchasing power to acquire a variety of items. Just as Sukey and Dick attempted to exchange a paper bill for other goods, Charles Ball used his skills as a carpenter, making and selling wooden bowls with matching ladles to a local merchant. In these exchanges Ball received compensation in cash, accumulating about $30 in a year. He used the money, earned during his free time, to buy blankets for his family, molasses, and "some other luxuries."[66]

Just as enslaved peoples' economic pursuits were placed under a microscope within the public sphere of the courtroom, the slaves' trade placed bondspeople in the crosshairs of white fears about slave rebellion. During the summer of 1816, a group of fifteen enslaved people were suspected of waging the first nineteenth-century slave uprising in South

Carolina. According to newspaper reports and court records, bondspeople in Camden allegedly planned to carry out a revolt on July 4, 1816, during an annual celebration of the United States military defeat of England in both the American Revolution and the War of 1812. On July 2, the *Camden Gazette* reported that a group of fifteen to twenty slaves had been arrested on suspicion of planning to carry out an insurrection. The group of the enslaved rebels—allegedly lead by enslaved men March, Ned, Jack, Cato, Abram, Renty—intended to engulf the town of Camden in flames, armed with guns and ammunition. As a writer for the *Camden Gazette* stated, "the reader can imagine the course that would have been pursued" had the enslaved people carried out their violent plan.[67] In the end, six enslaved people were executed for their participation in the planned insurrection.[68] The entire sequence of events—from whites' suspicions of enslaved peoples' plans to raze Camden to the subsequent trials of the alleged conspirators—suggests that it was white panic more than actual facts of conspiracy that caused white Camden residents to believe that they successfully thwarted a planned slave rebellion. There is no evidence, other than the court records and petitions, that could offer a more complete picture of whether enslaved people in Camden actually planned to burn down the town and kill as white residents in it. Therefore, it is entirely possible that enslaved people did *not* plan an insurrection in 1816 and that white fears of slave rebelliousness—and the specter of slave vengeance on whites—resulted in the hasty conviction and execution of six innocent enslaved people.

However, while white fears of bloodthirsty slaves were ever-present, it was white suspicions of enslaved peoples' commercial savvy that fueled their rush to judgment and cost six enslaved people their lives. Whites in the Kershaw District used various justifications to gain the attention of state lawmakers. Hoping that lawmakers would recognize that the existing statutes failed to keep their community safe from rebellious slaves, they made two competing arguments about why enslaved people planned the revolt. First, the residents made a direct connection between insurrection and enslaved peoples' independent trade with white vendors, specifically the illicit traffic in liquor. Second, they argued that enslaved people enjoyed the latitude to steal goods and use those goods to procure liquor, a substance they contended "encourage[d] the commission of crime" without repercussion.[69] If the concerns expressed by white Camden residents were representative of the issues that preoccupied Kershaw District's white citizens more generally in the fall of 1816, then it is clear that they attempted to convince lawmakers that there was an association between enslaved peoples' attempts to rebel with their independent and conspicuous engagement in Camden's economic life. In the end, they used these arguments to petition legislators to enact stronger laws to prevent "persons dealing and trafficking with slaves, and more especially in selling them ardent spirits."[70]

The Camden residents did not fully comprehend how ingrained enslaved peoples' entrepreneurship had become in the social and economic fabric of slave society. Enslaved peoples' investments in trade would continue because the extralegal networks for slave goods persisted and the economy of cotton cultivation produced increasing profits to enslavers and merchants. Moreover, as long as enterprising bondspeople maintained their trading partnerships and encountered white people who had no qualms with engaging in trade with enslaved men and women, slaves' networks of economic enterprise would exist and grow. For example, enslaved people in the Amelia Township had been exploiting their customary privileges to sell the yields of their independent cotton cultivation and engage in the local market economies by selling or trading goods that they cultivated for themselves. The enslaved population of Amelia adopted the same market-based economic knowledge that had swept other regions of the United States during the early nineteenth century.[71] They embraced, in their own way, the emerging economic principles of capitalism.

Enslaved peoples' conspicuous participation in trade—particularly trade in cotton—angered some white residents, especially if the cotton was stolen.[72] In December 1816, whites from the Amelia District asked lawmakers to consider passing a new law that would have prohibited slaveholders from allowing their slaves to raise their own cotton or livestock. They claimed, "Every nuisance that may lessen the dependence of a slave on his master would . . . be lending to dangerous consequences. The more privileges a slave obtains the less depending he is on his master and the greater nuisance he is likely to be to the public."[73] They argued that enslaved people had been engaging in the types of economic activities that threatened white peoples' safety because of slaves' public displays of autonomy. This included taking advantage of free time every other Saturday to venture into town, maintain and ride horses, keep pigs, and "cultivate for themselves everything for home consumption and for market, that their masters do."[74] In the list of nefarious activities in which enslaved people involved themselves, the most pernicious was the illicit sale of cotton. They asserted, "Cotton is Subject to the depredation of the night walking thief and when left, it would be the height of folly to attempt finding it among negroes who all have cotton of their own."[75] The petitioners, though, did not interrogate—or highlight in their petition—the people with whom slaves traded. If enslaved people in Amelia were trading in cotton, one can assume that they were trading with local factors or merchants who were interested in procuring cotton at a low price. For this reason, they did not indict the failures of local policing forces or administrators in curtailing the illicit cotton trade between slaves and cotton factors. Instead, they shifted the blame onto enslaved people in hopes that lawmakers would put in place stronger laws that would better regulate slaves' engagement in trade.

The white petitioners requested legislative intervention because they believed that when slaveholders allowed their slaves to plant, harvest, and subsequently traffic their own cotton, bondspeople disrupted the natural order of race relations within South Carolina slaveholding society. To be clear, the Amelia petitioners did not object to slaveholders who "encouraged the industry" of their slaves.[76] Some enslavers embraced instances when enslaved people cultivated their own cotton and then sold the cotton to their masters for better food, clothing, or shelter. This cadre of whites began to support enslaved peoples' demonstration of economic innovation, but only when bondspeople were trading with their masters or mistresses. They did, however, challenge slaveholders who did not prevent their slaves from acting independently as vendors of goods that they cultivated. They asked state lawmakers to enact a law that would officially make slaves selling cotton on their own illegal. The Committee on the Judiciary responded to the Amelia residents' petition in the same year, but the outcome did not fulfill the petitioners' requests; the committee replied that they had considered the request but believed that lawmakers should not intervene in the issue. The General Assembly's stance of nonintervention shifted responsibilities for slave regulation to local authorities: slaveholders, slave patrols, and justices of the peace. If these local authorities did not believe that the slaves' trade posed a serious threat, then they did nothing. In this response, state lawmakers opted to protect not only bondspeoples' customary rights, but more importantly, the right of slaveholders to allow slaves to market and trade.[77]

Enslaved people encountered a legislative intervention on another issue. In December 1817, the General Assembly worked to strengthen the state's statutes in an effort to better regulate slaves trading, and specifically, slaves purchasing liquor from white vendors. Perhaps the appeals of whites from Kershaw and Amelia influenced lawmakers to revisit state statutes on slaves' trading. Ratified in December 1817, the act made instances in which white vendors sold or traded for liquor with bondspeople illegal and imposed a fine of $1,000 and prison time for white offenders—a very steep financial penalty. Though the General Assembly had already rendered enslaved people trading on their own without a ticket illegal as of 1784, the 1817 statute singled out enslaved peoples' attempts to obtain liquor as the legislative focus.[78]

Lawmakers wrote that despite receiving appeals from whites, they had done enough to revise the laws in a way that local administrators could curtail the trade on their own. Regardless of increasing fines for whites found guilty of illegally trading in liquor with enslaved people, state lawmakers continued fielding complaints about the ineffectiveness of the new laws. White residents' concern about the dangers of slave hiring and slaves' trading seemed to have presaged the social unrest in South Carolina that was on the horizon in 1822, as they bombarded lawmakers with complaints about unruly slaves, greedy merchants, and seemingly oblivious slaveholders. These expressions of unease about the 1817 act almost universally concerned the laws' failure to regulate slave hiring and local challenges with preventing slaves from purchasing goods such as liquor. Yet as enslaved people continued creating avenues through which to buy their own goods, trade in cotton, and practice self-hire, they also angered white South Carolinians who opposed such activities. Between 1818 and 1820, debates about the act's failure continued to infiltrate the legislative sphere. After redefining their stance on enslaved enterprise in 1817, the General Assembly maintained a position of nonintervention in local affairs, especially when the issue revolved around slave hire or the visibility of slaves' trading.

Ultimately, the Act of 1817 did not obstruct enslaved peoples' quest for money and goods through hiring out. In particular, the tradition and prevalence of slaves' self-hire caught the attention of white mechanics. A group of eighty-seven white mechanics from Columbia petitioned the General Assembly in 1818, asking lawmakers to "prohibit masters from permitting their mechanic slaves to hire their own time."[79] Enslaved people, according to the mechanics, had been granted the freedom not only to engage in the mechanical pursuits, but enslaved mechanics had been taking on apprentices as well. The white mechanics made the argument that enslaved mechanics challenged the labor prospects of equally skilled—and even less-skilled—white laborers. They beseeched lawmakers to impose even higher penalties on slaveholders who allowed and encouraged slaves to hire their own time, imploring them to enforce strict guidelines on the arrangements of slave hire made between slaveholders and those who contracted slaves' labor. Ultimately, the white mechanics sought a set of newer and more effective laws that endowed white citizens to punish enslaved people for hiring out their own time and for taking on other slaves as apprentices.[80] Bondspeoples' money-making activities through self-hire, the mechanics believed, undermined the racial and economic hierarchies that were supposed to have structured South Carolina's slave society—a structure that the white mechanics assumed they had the racial privilege from which to benefit.

The General Assembly's Judiciary Committee responded to the Columbia mechanics' complaint. However, they did not side with the mechanics. The committee did not believe that they needed to intervene and wrote, "it is inexpedient for the Legislature to interfere in the internal regulations of the town of Columbia."[81] In this rejoinder, lawmakers conveyed to the mechanics that the laws were sufficient as written and that they would not place more regulations on enslaved peoples' economic activities or further intercede on slaveholders' approval of such pursuits.

Enslaved peoples' networks of exchange expanded, and this expansion is exposed in the number of complaints that white citizens made to state lawmakers. White residents made thirteen complaints to the General Assembly between 1818 and 1820. These complaints were a clarion call to lawmakers that enslaved people had not ceased their economic pursuits, and that the Act of 1817 had failed to curb white encouragement of slaves trading and self-hire.[82] Not only did enslaved people not stop seeking out opportunities to make money and buy themselves goods, but they found willing white economic partners. Grievances from white residents in Lowcountry districts such as Georgetown and St. George's Dorchester and Upcountry districts such as Kershaw and Sumter flooded lawmakers with protestations about the rebelliousness of enslaved people in their unabashed pursuit of money and merchandise. In addition to engaging in self-hire, enslaved people had been selling their own cotton to local merchants using local river systems as informal marketplaces and competing with white workers for employment in skilled positions. Indeed, in cities such as Columbia and Charleston, enslaved people skilled in mechanical trades had been "taking apprentices in the mechanical arts," traditionally a practice in which only white artisans engaged. Not only were enslaved people depriving white workers of "jobs and imployment [*sic*] in their respective trades"; white skilled workers argued that bondspeople were doing so with "the liberty granted" by their enslavers.[83]

Despite white complaints, lawmakers responded that it was "inexpedient" to intervene, and they would not enact further legislation on skilled slaves' self-hire and enslaved peoples' engagement in trade for two reasons. First, the law allowed enslavers to use their slaves' labor in any way they wanted. This included the practice of slave hire. Enslaved people, therefore, were sometimes forced by their owners to seek external employment. Second, enslaved people took advantage, when possible, of the customary right to seek hire with slaveholder permission.[84]

After members of the General Assembly made repeated efforts to enact laws that to regulate bondspeoples' participation as agents in local economic life more effectively, one must begin to question the efficiency of the statutes. Why would the General Assembly create another statute to make whites' trade in liquor with enslaved people illegal? Knowing that slaves did not heed the restraints outlined in the law, why did white South Carolinians also fail to abide by the law? It is clear that some white South Carolinians disregarded the law, perhaps because there were no swift consequences for their actions and they benefited economically from having enslaved people as customers. It is revealing that white merchants in the Kershaw District objected publicly to such strong prohibition on their trade with slaves, despite the failed rebellion just two years earlier. The Kershaw merchants did not ask lawmakers to strengthen the laws. Instead, they petitioned for the opposite. In 1818, forty-nine merchants and storekeepers from Camden complained about the 1817 law, arguing that the increased penalties unduly punished merchants who regularly traded *legally* with enslaved people. They argued that the law penalized merchants who carried on legal trades with slaves, with slaveholder permission and with slaves who held valid tickets. For these merchants, their concerns with profitmaking outweighed their concerns with the rebellious activities of a few enslaved people. To the merchants, money—made legally—was their primary concern. They did not want lawmakers to interfere with their legal trade with enslaved people.[85] And lawmakers proved that they prioritized the rights of enslavers and merchants over the economic prospects of white skilled workers.

Perhaps the Camden merchants were referring to unlawful merchants among them, such as one Francis Anone. In an intervention from the South Carolina Court of Appeals, Anone stood before the Court of Appeals in May 1819, charged with violating the Act of 1817, specifically the decree that made instances in which whites traded with slaves for liquor illegal. According to court records, a slaveholder sought to entrap Anone for trading with a slave without a ticket. The unnamed slaveholder directed his slave to exchange a bag of corn for goods sold in Anone's store. The enslaved person travelled to the store, sans ticket, and exchanged the bag of corn with Polydore—Anone's slave and also the store's clerk—as the slaveholder's overseer witnessed the illegal transaction. According to witness testimony (the witnesses included Anone's former white store clerks), Anone had regularly relied on Polydore's assistance in managing the store during his absence. According to a former clerk, in 1817 and 1818, after the General Assembly passed the Act of 1817, Anone directed Polydore to purchase as much corn from local slaves as possible, even slaves who did not possess valid tickets from their enslavers. The judges subsequently rejected Anone's motion for a new trial, which upheld the lower court's guilty verdict.[86]

The verdict in *State v. Anone* established that the struggle over enslaved peoples' participation in local markets and their competition with white workers did not always place slaveholders in support of such slave pursuits against white workers and residents who rejected enslaved enterprise. In fact, slaveholders situated themselves on both sides of the debate about slaves' independent trade with local merchants.[87] The slaveholder's entrapment of Anone, however, does not shroud the fact that Polydore served as the intermediary between Anone and enslaved people who were willing to trade not only with Polydore, but also with Anone. It is worth noting that the slaveholder in this case gave Polydore permission to take bags of corn to Anone for exchange.

The South Carolina Supreme Court's decision on *State v. Anone* encouraged the justices to consider another similar case in the following year. In January 1820, the Court of Appeals decided on the fate of Charleston merchant Jacob Sonnerkalb and the future effectiveness of the Act of 1817 as well. The lower court found Sonnerkalb guilty of two crimes: selling liquor to an enslaved man without a liquor license, in violation of the Act of 1784, and trafficking with a slave without a ticket, violating the Act of 1817. Sonnerkalb, however, did not believe that he violated two separate statutes. The judges were determining whether Sonnerkalb could be guilty of violating two statutes that forbade his engagement in trade, particularly with a slave. According to court testimony, a bondsman owned by slaveholder Samuel Dubose entered Sonnerkalb's store with a bag of corn and an empty bottle. While Dubose did not witness an exchange between the enslaved man and Sonnerkalb, he did testify that he heard corn poured out and "liquor pour[ed] into some vessel."[88] When the enslaved man and Sonnerkalb finished the transaction of the corn for the vessel of liquid, which turned out to be whiskey, the enslaved man left the store. Once this occurred, Dubose entered the store with the enslaved man in tow and confronted Sonnerkalb on the illicit transaction that he had just completed. Indeed, the bondsman did not possess a requisite ticket that would have made the transaction legal. According to Dubose, Sonnerkalb confessed to having committed two illegal acts at that moment: first, he traded the enslaved man's corn for whiskey without a valid ticket from Dubose, and second, he sold the enslaved man a handkerchief for $0.25, also without a ticket. Upon further examination, Sonnerkalb revealed that even though he did not have a license to sell liquor, Dubose's presence at the exchange validated the corn-for-whiskey trade with the enslaved man. This argument did not satisfy the judges and they dismissed the case, upholding the lower court's conviction of Sonnerkalb.[89]

While the General Assembly and the state Supreme Court attempted to mitigate the outcry from white residents about the ineffectiveness of the Act of 1817, surprisingly few enslaved people and few whites were being tried in local courts for economic crimes in this period. Between the summer of 1816 and the summer of 1822, in the Kershaw District only three enslaved people were tried for economic crimes, and in the Laurens District only two enslaved people were brought before the magistrates' court for crimes of economy such as larceny.[90] In the Union District, during the same six-year period, the district court tried only two cases where white Union residents were charged with illicitly trading with enslaved blacks.[91] It is possible that the Act of 1817 caused enslaved people to be more careful with putting their independent engagement in local commercial networks on public display. Or perhaps whites who would have usually traded with enslaved people exercised extra caution in their illicit engagement in trade with them.

On March 24, 1820, a series of illicit economic interactions between an enslaved man named Jack and a white freeholder names James Graham gained the attention of white Union District residents. Jack, owned by attorney and slaveholder Amos Davis, sold James Graham corn and corn fodder on more than one occasion. Because Jack did not possess a valid ticket from Davis to sell the corn products to Graham, Davis subsequently reported Graham to a local judge, charging him with illegally trafficking with a slave. After a brief judicial examination, Graham was found guilty and fined $500 for his role in the illegal exchange. The major question that this incident introduces is this: Why did Amos Davis report James Graham? Perhaps Davis brought Graham to court because he wanted to manipulate Jack's access to trading partners, and therefore Jack's income. It is possible that Jack had been growing corn on an individual plot of land allotted to him by Davis and Davis saw an opportunity to not only exert more influence over Jack's independent economic pursuits, but to control the profits that Jack earned because of his investment in trade.[92]

By the antebellum period, enslaved entrepreneurship became more than just a way for enslaved people to survive the institution of slavery.

Just as Amos Davis attempted to control Jack's access to James Graham as a trading partner, so too did a new generation of enslavers. It became standard practice for slave owners to place more constraints on enslaved people as their investments in cotton and slavery influenced their perspectives on slaveholding and therefore, the slaves' trade. These constraints did not merely take the form of whippings and other violent forms of coercion. Beginning in the 1820s, enslavers devoted more time and energy toward discovering new ways to extract as much labor from enslaved people as possible. They began to fully embrace seemingly simple aspects of finance and the technologies of capitalist investment. Though Charles Ball may not have been privy to the newest tools of financial innovation that began to infiltrate South Carolina's slaveholding and merchant classes, he was surely exposed to transformations that these economic practices produced.

As enslavers clung to the profit-making potential of cotton production, they also discovered that they could capitalize on enslaved peoples' unshakable interest in improving their material conditions through embarking on their own moneymaking activities. A symmetry emerged between slaves' immediate economic goals and enslavers' monetary motives. It culminated in a transformation of the way that enslaved people interacted economically with their enslavers, as well as the ways in which slaves' networks of enterprise fit into slaveholders' quest to reap the financial gains from their investments in slave labor.

4

"THE FACILITY OF OBTAINING MONEY"

Violence, Fear, and Accumulation in the Vesey Era

In some ways, the man who came to be known as Denmark Vesey led an exceptional life. Many believe that he was born enslaved on the island of St. Thomas in the late 1760s with the name Telemaque.[1] In 1781 he was purchased by a slave trader named Captain Joseph Vesey, and along with 390 other enslaved people that Captain Vesey bought in St. Thomas, he was taken to St. Domingue to be sold. It is possible that his purchaser expected Telemaque to spend his prime years laboring on a sugar plantation on the island colony, the crown jewel of the French colonial empire in the eighteenth century.[2] On a subsequent trip to St. Domingue, Joseph Vesey learned that Telemaque would be returned to him, as the enslaver who purchased him "represented him unsound, and subject to epileptick fits."[3] Young Telemaque allegedly captured the captain's attention with his "beauty, alertness and intelligence."[4] The captain decided to purchase the then fourteen-year-old in 1771. Telemaque was enslaved in the captain's service for the next nineteen years. During this period, they relocated to Charleston.[5]

For a short time, Telemaque's life as an enslaved man in Charleston mirrored those of other bondsmen in the city. He developed marketable skills as a carpenter. He also gained membership into a large network of both enslaved and free artisans who worked (and networked) in Charleston. Telemaque's experiences reflected those of another enslaved skilled man named Peter. Peter was a "first rate ship carpenter" who "enjoyed all the substantial comforts of a free man" and also had the autonomy to manage his own time.[6] He also kept "a large proportion of the profits of his labour at his own disposal" and "even kept his master's *arms* and sometimes his money."[7] Perhaps Telemaque, like Peter, enjoyed a higher level of control over his daily life than other enslaved people in the Lowcountry. Surely within this dynamic urban community, black men such as Telemaque and Peter took advantage of opportunities to work on their own, saving their earnings to make their lives a little more comfortable. Maybe Telemaque saved the wages he received as a carpenter. It is possible that he benefitted from the relative autonomy that he enjoyed as an enslaved skilled worker. One could speculate that his carpentry skills, combined with Charleston's urban employment landscape, provided him with the means to carve out a life of relative semi-independence for himself. And Telemaque's skilled work in Charleston would prove to be his ticket out of slavery.

In November 1799, his life took a dramatic turn. That fall Telemaque purchased a $6 lottery ticket, perhaps using his earnings to do so. With the purchase of the ticket, No. 1884, he participated in Charleston's East Bay Street lottery, a lottery sponsored by city administrators to raise capital to fund internal improvement projects.[8] The results were published in the *City Gazette* on November 9, 1799. The person who possessed the winning ticket won the lottery's biggest prize, $1,500. The person who possessed ticket No. 1884 was Telemaque. Though no extant records reveal his reaction to the news, Telemaque surely exhibited an equal amount of surprise and jubilation that he was the ticketholder—$1,500 was a staggering sum of money by any estimation, but in particular for an enslaved person.[9] However, just because he had a winning lottery ticket did not mean that he could immediately use the prize money. Telemaque must have appealed to his legal owner, Mary Clodner, Joseph Vesey's common-law wife, to negotiate the terms and price of his emancipation. They came to an agreement because less than a month later, on December 7, 1799, Telemaque, Mary Clodner, and Joseph Vesey stood before St. John Berkeley district magistrate Daniel James Ravenel, attesting to the terms of Telemaque's manumission.[10] According to the manumission deed, Telemaque paid $600 for his freedom, an amount that some believed was "much less than his real value."[11] It is not known why Joseph Vesey and Mary Clodner agreed to manumit Telemaque. Perhaps

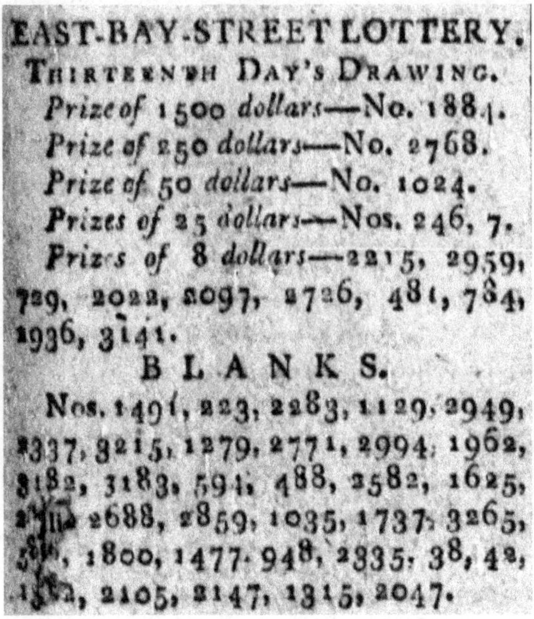

EAST-BAY-STREET LOTTERY.

THIRTEENTH DAY'S DRAWING.

Prize of 1500 *dollars*—No. 1884.
Prize of 250 *dollars*—No. 2768.
Prize of 50 *dollars*—No. 1024.
Prizes of 25 *dollars*—Nos. 246, 7.
Prizes of 8 *dollars*—2215, 2959, 729, 2022, 2097, 2726, 481, 784, 1936, 3141.

B L A N K S.

Nos. 1491, 223, 2283, 1129, 2949, 3337, 3215, 1279, 2771, 2994, 1962, 3182, 3183, 594, 488, 2582, 1625, [illegible] 2688, 2859, 1035, 1737, 3265, [illegible], 1800, 1477, 948, 2335, 38, 42, [illegible], 2105, 2147, 1315, 2047.

FIGURE 4.1 Denmark Vesey's winning ticket, No. 1884 (1799)

they had an immediate need for the money that he was willing to pay. Or maybe they did in fact believe that he had been "a most faithful slave" and rewarded his steadfastness with the opportunity to purchase his freedom.[12] His emancipation was made legal on December 31, 1799, and he entered the nineteenth century as a free person.

After he invested his winnings in his own liberation, Telemaque emerged as Denmark Vesey. He arose as a new member of Charleston's free black community. From there, he became an early congregant of the city's African Methodist Episcopal church and continued to work in Charleston as a carpenter, a vocation that provided him with the means to survive as a free man of color in a city characterized by slavery.[13]

However, twenty-one years later, Vesey would become a martyr, celebrated by African Americans and villainized by whites. As quickly as the lottery and his purchase of freedom transformed Vesey's life, so too did the conviction for his supposed involvement in arguably one of the most infamous slave rebellion conspiracies in American history. The legal account of Vesey's life and actions place him at the center of a thwarted insurrection plot, set to have taken place on July 14, 1822. But his plans were spoiled in June 1822 when two enslaved people disclosed the plot to their masters, who then relayed the information to local authorities.[14] According to trial records, the testimonies of white Charlestonians, and the confessions of supposed black participants, Vesey attempted to arm as many as six hundred free black and enslaved people, to lead them in an attack on Charleston's white citizens. Charleston administrators charged and executed thirty-five conspirators for "attempting to raise an insurrection among the Blacks against the Whites."[15] White Charlestonians were convinced that enslaved people and free people of color had planned to demolish South Carolina's most valuable city. They believed that this conflagration was led by skilled bondsman turned freedom-fighter Denmark Vesey.[16]

The conspiracy exemplified more than black Charleston's ever-present push for liberty; it also exposed white anxieties about enslaved people who took advantage of their labors' economic potential. These anxieties were realized by white Charlestonians who feared enslaved people with access to money and markets. The Vesey plot transformed the significance of the slaves' economy not only among Charleston residents, but within South Carolina slaveholding society writ large. In the fall of 1822 lawmakers made a desperate effort to further regulate enslaved peoples' economic practices, but they realized that the slaves' economy was far too important to South Carolina's culture and economy of slavery to curtail it. In the aftermath of the Vesey conspiracy, fear of violence from whites did not stop enslaved people from seeking out opportunities to maintain their networks of exchange and enterprise. Furthermore, white South Carolinians did not let the specter of black violence keep them from engaging economically with enslaved people. In fact, in the post-Vesey years, the slaves' economy became a more recognized aspect of the economy of slavery despite white fears of enslaved people and free people of color waging a violent uprising to take their freedom by force. Ultimately, enslaved peoples' economic networks proved too valuable to the economy of slavery. The Denmark Vesey conspiracy revealed that white South Carolinians, enslavers in particular, were willing to risk safety and psychological security to maintain their investments in not only slavery, but in the economies of the enslaved.

By most measures, the Vesey conspiracy had the potential to completely upend South Carolina's slaveholding milieu. The plot involved armed slaves ready to kill white citizens and a free black community with the money and mobility to fund an insurrection. At the center was a former bondsman who did what few enslaved people had the economic ability to do: he freed himself. Though Denmark Vesey's fate was stamped as soon as his supposed coconspirators uttered his name, the effects of the failed slave revolt that bore his name lingered far beyond his death.

On the surface, it may appear as though white Charlestonians were concerned primarily with the prospect of black violence. After all, according to the official Account of the "negro plot," the conspirators held "malignant hatred of the whites, and inordinate lust of power and booty."[17] The reality, though, was much more complex. The Vesey plot invites us to explore the real influence of enslaved and free black people with access to money and markets. If, as white Charlestonians believed, black residents of Charleston planned to carry out an insurrection because of their "hatred of the whites" and "lust for power and booty," what happened to enslaved peoples' networks of commodity exchange after the thirty-five supposed coconspirators were executed?[18]

White Charlestonians believed that the Vesey conspiracy represented not only an anti-slavery revolution, but an anti-capitalist one as well. They framed the planned insurrection as a plot engineered by Vesey and his fellow organizers to destroy the city, kill white residents, and violently dismantle slavery as an institution. Because the conspirators sought to take their freedom, attempting to demolish the foundations of slavery in Charleston in the process, white Charlestonians believed that the participants' ultimate goal was to not only upend the institution of slavery, but also obliterate the economy of slavery. After all, South Carolina's economy of slavery had become increasingly profit-oriented in the 1820s. With the rise of cotton cultivation and global cotton exportation, slaveholding capitalists sought to reap the ever-increasing financial benefits of enslaved peoples' labor. The real and perceived threat of slave rebellion had the potential to interfere with the burgeoning slave-labor based cotton economy—and the profits that enslavers and investors had in the economy of enslaved peoples' labor.[19]

Yet for enslaved people, the Vesey conspiracy was proof that their networks of economic enterprise would survive. Moreover, bondspeople would continue to find trading partners in white South Carolinians. The Vesey plot made clear that though whites of every social class feared rebellious slaves, they would not unilaterally stop engaging economically with enslaved people. The economic desires of white South Carolinians—and in some instances their survival needs in terms of foodstuff and products they purchased from slaves—superseded their concerns about enslaved violence.[20] It was in this way that enslaved enterprise evolved in the years after the plot. The Vesey conspiracy put the slaves' economy front and center in conversations about the economic future of slavery in South Carolina. Ultimately, the Vesey plot proved that bondspeoples' networks of trade and commerce could withstand the social instability wrought by the specter of enslaved violence.

Over the past several decades, historians of African American life in antebellum America have looked to the Denmark Vesey conspiracy as proof of enslaved peoples' willingness to organize, fight, and die for their freedom. But there has been a recent push by scholars to reimagine the Vesey conspiracy. The historian Michael Johnson in particular has argued that "instead of an insurrectionist, perhaps Vesey was a fall guy for both the court and the witnesses who repeatedly testified against him."[21] The quickness with which the trials of suspected insurrectionists occurred, the haphazard record-keeping by court officials, and the real or imagined terror felt by white Charlestonians—all of which infiltrated the court proceedings—should complicate our understanding of Denmark Vesey and the thirty-five people executed for their participation in Vesey's supposed plan.

Though the scholarly contestations about the veracity of the historical record are important, they reveal little about how the conspiracy influenced the economic culture of slavery in Charleston and in South Carolina more generally. What can white fears about rebellious African Americans in Charleston during the summer of 1822 tell us about the threats of black economic power in the early antebellum era? Moreover, how were the economic activities of enslaved people affected by the Vesey plot? The official documentary records created by the city's administrators show the level of anxiety among white Charlestonians about the increased autonomy of enslaved people and free people in the city. As historian Douglas Egerton has contended, the Vesey plot reveals the ways in which members of South Carolina slaveholding society had come to believe that the bonds of the interactions between enslavers and the enslaved had become "dangerously loosened."[22] Economically minded enslaved people continued to challenge the structures of control that enslavers erected to protect their investments in wealth and status. This is where the slaves' economy emerges as a major hinge around which the Vesey conspiracy revolved.[23]

The Vesey plot epitomized white ambivalence about the capitalist turn in South Carolina's economy of slavery. The events that led to Vesey's capture and eventual execution were perhaps visualized by enslaved and free blacks, but actualized in the minds of white Charlestonians who were afraid of the subversive reality of slaves with access to money and the purchasing power of their labor. This fear was not relegated to Charleston. One group of white citizens from Columbia declared, "We have long viewed with great interest and concern the serious and alarming consequences arising from owners permitting their slaves to hire their own time, upon the payment of certain wages."[24] These residents connected enslaved people earning wages for their labor to "the recent and serious occurrences in the city of Charleston, in which the principal plot and scheme originated and was matured by the machinations of this very class of our black population."[25] This group of white citizens from Columbia echoed a widespread belief about both the culture of slavery and the culture of capitalism that had been emerging in the state. They feared that well-equipped and well-funded enslaved people, cognizant of the state's reliance on their labor, could upend the economy of slavery in South Carolina. Enslaved peoples' roles not only as laborers in cotton fields, rice plantations, and in enslavers' households, but also as sellers of goods and purveyors of services within their local communities, became an increasingly prominent feature of white South Carolinians' reliance on the technologies of capitalist innovation. The continued visibility of bondspeoples' investments in their own economic goals threatened whites' perceived sense of security. For this reason, the Vesey conspiracy was as much about real and imagined black violence against the institution of slavery as it was about what whites believed capitalism meant in the lives of bondspeople in South Carolina. Thus, enslaved enterprise emerged as the central issue in the Vesey conspiracy and its aftermath.

The alleged masterminds behind the insurrection plot were the first to face a judicial inquiry. On June 19, 1822, Peter, Ned, Rolla, and Batteau, the first group of four alleged rebels, were tried in private, after members of the city's policing authorities arrested them. Each entered "not guilty" pleas, attempting to prove that they were not involved in the plot to terrorize the city's white residents.[26] Denmark Vesey was subsequently captured on June 22 and brought to trial on June 27. After his arrest, according to witness testimony, Vesey made no confession. His reticence led Charleston administrators and legal authorities to conclude that "any opinion formed as to the numbers actually engaged in the plot must be altogether conjectural."[27] While each of the accused insurgents entered a "not guilty" plea, by the end of the summer, thirty-five black Charlestonians, along with Vesey, were tried in the local magistrates' court, found guilty, and executed for their supposed role in the conspiracy. Charleston magistrates decided that another forty would be transferred out of state, shipped to a workhouse, or banished from the United States altogether. But the trials and subsequent punishment of the conspirators did not quell white fears. White paranoia remained high as the investigators struggled to gather information about the scope of the conspiracy.

The swift judicial decision-making did not obscure the ways in which the slaves' economy emerged within the inquiry. According to the *Official Report*, a majority of the 135 African Americans tried by Charleston magistrates for their participation in the Vesey conspiracy worked as hired-out laborers in Charleston. "The enlistments appear to have been principally confined to Negroes hired or working out," the *Official Report* revealed, and "in short those who had certain allotted hours at their own disposal, and to the neighbouring [*sic*] country negroes."[28] The investigators believed that there was a direct connection between the enslaved people involved in the insurrection plot, slaves hiring out in Charleston, and bondspeoples' use of self-hire to earn their own money.

In the months after the slave executions, white South Carolinians from all economic classes used the Vesey conspiracy to vent their growing frustrations with the obstinance of the enslaved and free people of color. In fact, after the first trials, white Charlestonians struggled to understand why enslaved people not only decided to follow Denmark Vesey, but why they had a "malignant hatred of the whites, and an inordinate lust of power and booty."[29] They believed that enslaved Charlestonians "had no individual hardship to complain of, and were among the most humanely treated negroes in our city."[30] At the same time, Charleston's magistrates and white freeholders believed that they had dispensed justice, using the perpetrators as examples to dissuade the free and enslaved black population of Charleston from following in the conspirators' footsteps.

In the fall and winter of 1822, the fear of slave insurrection infiltrated conversations among white slaveholders and nonslaveholders alike. They struggled to contend with the social disruption caused by even the whiff of violence waged by enslaved and free black people. White South Carolinians did not believe that the legal constraints designed by lawmakers to curtail enslaved peoples' behavior succeeded in containing the state's slave and free black communities. White citizens called attention to enslaved peoples' potential for violence, arguing that even small acts of insubordination, such as slaves "strolling about" by themselves in the country and engaging in "theft and trading" outside their "master's premises," threatened the safety of South Carolina slave society.[31] They connected the specter of slave rebelliousness and disorder to enslaved peoples' market ambitions. Throughout the 1820s, groups of white citizens professed continued frustrations with lawmakers and slaveholders who failed to place the necessary constraints on slaveholders' investments in slavery and on enslaved people and the whites—both slaveholding and nonslaveholding—who enabled slaves' felonious economic pursuits.

Whites levied the harshest condemnations against slave hiring. The critiques revolved around the tradition of slaves hiring their own time, employers hiring enslaved people as workers over white laborers, and enslavers who allowed bondspeople to seek their own employment. Petitioners called on lawmakers to provide more funding for slave patrols, to stop the "illegal trade with Negroes," and to better regulate "the practice of negroes navigating the rivers and creeks in floats and boats, for cutting wood and other purposes and in this way carry on a traffic with Negroes in the neighboring plantations."[32] Above all, white South Carolinians called attention to the slaves' economy in the aftermath of the Vesey conspiracy, with enslaved peoples' economic autonomy coming under heavy scrutiny.

The petitioners also offered a variety of solutions. They connected the Vesey plot to the continued visibility of bondspeoples' moneymaking activities. Some white South Carolinians pleaded with lawmakers to endow their local social and agricultural organizations with the authority to police free black and enslaved members of their communities. Others implored politicians to provide financial support for increased militia forces to protect whites from rebellious and enterprising slaves.[33] Petitioners connected Vesey's conspiracy to the unrelenting conspicuousness of the slaves' economy. From such suggestions, they believed that the thwarted rebellion could have toppled completely white South Carolinians' capitalist aspirations.

Though most requests came from Lowcountry residents, white South Carolinians from other regions expressed their distress as well. They vented myriad concerns. One of the most prominent of white criticisms was how they believed that enslaved peoples' opportunities to work on their own and keep their earnings fomented the rebellious plan of attack. "In a prominent degree is this evil exhibited among that class of slaves," white citizens from Columbia argued, "who have been trained and instructed in the various mechanical professions."[34] They connected the pervasiveness of bondspeoples' engagement in exchange to enslaved and free black peoples' perceived attempts to strike a violent blow to slavery. For example, in the fall of 1822, 289 Richland District residents signed a petition responding to the Vesey plot; approximately 12 percent of the free white men in the Richland District signed onto the petition.[35] The Richland petitioners, comprised of both slaveholding and nonslaveholding white men, used the Vesey conspiracy to advocate for "such laws or legislative provisions, as will immediately and effectually suppress" the "dangerous and growing practice" of slave hire.[36] The petitioners challenged state lawmakers to consider the events in Charleston and the potential destruction that the city's enslaved people and free people of color could have caused had they carried out their plans. The petitioners' main concern was the threat that slave hire posed to the stability of Charleston, as well as other less well-regulated regions of the state.

One of the 289 petitioners was Henry W. DeSaussure. A prominent South Carolina judge and politician, DeSaussure penned a series of essays in the months after the Vesey plot. He made a series of observations about the nature of slavery in the United States, primarily in response to northern spectators who blamed slaveholders for enslaved peoples' rebellious inclinations. Black people, both enslaved and free, he contended, should have been prohibited from working as mechanics and artisans. Enslaved peoples' labor, he argued, should have been confined to agricultural work. DeSaussure believed that black skilled laborers—draymen, artists, and wharfingers, for example—who worked in coastal cities such as Charleston succumbed to "false notions and delusive hopes . . . which render[ed] them dissatisfied with their condition, and prepare[d] them for plots and other mischief." Enslaved peoples' dissatisfaction threatened the master–slave relationship, he argued. He believed that skilled slaves set poor examples for other slaves because of their independence and the ways in which they put their economic prospects on public display. In a paternalistic tone, he concluded that enslaved mechanics "acquired vicious habits, injurious to themselves" and their owners.[37]

What DeSaussure did not convey was a full understanding of the complexities and the realities of enslaved hired labor. The habits that enslaved people adopted included working and living autonomously, saving hard-earned money, and challenging equally skilled white workers for employment. But enslaved people did not engage in such work without white complicity. Not only did skilled slaves find employment from white hirers, but bondspeople were being encouraged (and sometimes forced) to do so by their enslavers. They were hired by white employers who were all too eager to exploit the glut of cheap enslaved labor. And enslavers profited from slave hiring, especially during the cyclical nature of agricultural life in the antebellum South.

As DeSaussure offered his perspective as a member of Columbia's political elite, DeSaussure's friend and Charlestonian Thomas Pinckney put his thoughts into words as well and published his reflections in November 1822 under the pseudonym "Achates." In his *Reflections*, Pinckney outlined five threats to successful slave regulation that needed immediate attention in the aftermath of the thwarted slave insurrection. The first threat was the specter of St. Domingue and the rebelliousness of slaves in the French colony. He argued that the violence waged by African slaves in St. Domingue influenced enslaved people in South Carolina and spurred them to take up arms against whites.[38] Pinckney's second complaint highlighted the rising abolitionist sentiments espoused by Northern anti-slavery activists. He believed that Northern agitators were provoking black slaves in Southern slaveholding states such as South Carolina, and with prescience, he argued that if any issue could divide the Union, it would be slaveholding states defending the institution of slavery. The third threat that Pinckney outlined in *Reflections* was the indulgences that whites allowed enslaved people to enjoy, especially domestic workers. In particular, he maintained that enslaved people had been wielding "dangerous instruments of learning" or learning how to read and write in greater numbers. Literacy among enslaved people, he feared, would only increase, despite efforts to curtail it. And Pinckney's fourth concern regarded the slaves' economy. He contended, "The facility of obtaining money afforded by the nature of their occupations to those employed as mechanics, draymen, fishermen, hucksters, butchers, porters . . . increase their ability to do mischief."[39] The enslaved people who were employed in these jobs, he claimed, almost always spent the money they acquired purchasing liquor. He ultimately acquiesced on this issue, admitting that the only way to remedy the overpopulation of skilled slaves in Charleston would be to manage the black majority in the city. This argument led to Pinckney's fifth concern: the disparity between the white and black population in Charleston, with blacks outnumbering whites.

Pinckney admitted that no effective strategies existed to ameliorate the first four problems, including enslaved people employed in positions outside of their enslaver's purview and making money from such pursuits. Echoing DeSaussure, Pinckney recognized that Charleston's economy relied on employers hiring enslaved laborers, in particular enslaved draymen and mechanics. Employers would have found it difficult to recruit white laborers to complete the same work that enslaved people did for a fraction of the costs. He believed, therefore, that slave hiring was the oil that lubricated South Carolina's bustling economy. Ultimately all members of South Carolina's slaveholding society—black and white, enslaved and free, slaveholder and nonslaveholder—would be inconvenienced in some way by the very nature of slavery.[40]

Pinckney and DeSaussure questioned the utility of slave hire, but surprisingly, both avoided the topic of the slaves' trade. They argued that slave hire was a problem that required immediate attention. What was it about slave hire, but not slaves' trading or the slaves' economy writ large, that concerned these two writers? Could it have been that they wanted to do away with the scourge of slave hiring, but they realized the material benefits of encouraging the enslaved economies? Pinckney and DeSaussure also recognized that when enslaved people worked for wages, they earned money that they then spent in dangerous and idle pursuits. But they did not address instances in which enslaved people earned money and did not purchase liquor, but instead bought clothing, shoes, or other consumable goods such as sugar and coffee. It was enslaved peoples' engagement in local market economies that supported white merchants and sellers. Perhaps they understood the important niche that enslaved people filled when they spent their free time cultivating, selling, and trading their own goods, because Pinckney and DeSaussure did not malign this customary practice in the public sphere. Instead, their silence on slaves' trading—and their direct criticisms of slave hiring—suggests that enslaved peoples' economic engagements bolstered South Carolina slaveholding society.

White residents such as Henry DeSaussure from the Upcountry regions of the state expressed their fears about skilled slaves working in cities such as Charleston and Columbia. This was because even the hint of slave insurrection sparked doubts about the slaves' trade and the supposed freedoms that such pursuits provided. The Vesey conspiracy stoked white fears about slaves not succumbing to white control. Citizens from Columbia used the specter of the Vesey revolt to emphasize the social and economic disturbances generated by slave hire. Specifically, they voiced concerns that slave hire threatened the job prospects of equally skilled white workers. While white residents and members of white workingmen's organizations had been appealing to lawmakers since the eighteenth century, the tenor of these appeals changed in the aftermath of the Vesey conspiracy.

Ultimately, the Vesey plot stoked white fears of slaves' defiance. The image of enslaved people earning an independent living terrified some white South Carolinians. Many believed that this image was almost as alarming as black people wielding weapons to upend not only slavery as an institution, but white supremacy at its foundation. In an attempt to placate or perhaps empower whites, local legislators made changes to the law. The white residents of Charleston Neck, for example, expanded the duties of the local slave patrol "to controul [*sic*] and keep in order the numerous black population" of the neighborhood.[41] The revised statute empowered members of the patrol to enter into any "disorderly house, vessel or boat" if they were suspicious of "unlawfully trafficking or dealing with slaves."[42] Legislators did not discriminate based on race or status, meaning that the statute included whites who were continuing to support the proliferation of illicit trading with slaves.

As some white citizens made public pronouncements and others appealed to the General Assembly to assuage their fears of rebellious bondspeople, members of local courts responded swiftly to the fear engendered by the Vesey plot. In one instance, the court's response was abrupt and violent. One such case involved an enslaved man, Jim, from the town of Camden. On the night of October 21, 1822, Jim broke into merchant John B. Merges's store and pilfered goods and money. Jim stole a two-dollar bank note that a store employee, Samuel Saul, left on a store counter when he closed the store for the night. On October 24, the two magistrates, George Gillian and William Nixon, and three freeholders, Alexander Young, Henry Abbott, and Thomas Warren, heard the testimony of two witnesses, Mary Cunningham and Samuel Saul. Cunningham testified that she received a two-dollar bank note from Jim in exchange for allowing him to spend the night at her home. After examining the money, she believed that Jim had "fraudulently come by" it.[43] Cunningham used the bank note to pay a local butcher and the butcher then used it to purchase goods from Merges. When Merges saw the note, he inquired from where it came. Saul offered details of the two-dollar bill allegedly stolen from Merges's store. Saul affirmed that Merges's missing bill was a bank note from the Bank of Cape Fear, marked with the number 355, the same bill that Merges argued was stolen from his store.[44]

During the seven-day trial, Jim was imprisoned in the Camden jail, awaiting the court's decision. He received it on October 28. Despite his "not guilty" plea to the felony burglary charge, the court found Jim to be guilty. However, Jim did not receive the customary punishment for enslaved people found guilty of burglary. Indeed, his sentence did not include the customary number of lashes. The court ordered a sentence for Jim that was in excess of any sentence that the magistrates' court had ordered for a similar crime: death by hanging. The members deemed Jim's supposed infraction to be so egregious that it warranted him to be sentenced to death. Jim was hanged on November 13, 1822.[45] The members of the court sent enslaved people a strong message through Jim's sentence: subversive behavior, real or perceived, would not be tolerated. The Vesey conspiracy, and the violence that white Charlestonians meted out on enslaved people and free people of color, surely influenced the court's decision to kill Jim for his supposed crimes.

It is not clear if Jim burglarized the Camden store or if the case against him represented a carefully orchestrated maneuver by the magistrates, freeholders, and witnesses to quell Camden's white residents' fears of potentially rebellious slaves. In fact, the trial records did not include testimonies from two key interlopers: John B. Merges and the butcher. The court did not summon Merges or the butcher to offer their sworn testimonies about the night in question, the stolen bank note, or how the note circulated between the night of the burglary and the fortuitous moment when Merges noticed the butcher paying for goods with his stolen bank bill. Yet despite this seemingly decisive omission, the court found Jim to be guilty and sentenced him to die for his alleged crimes. It is possible that Jim's trial served as an example to enslaved people in Camden that pushing the legal boundaries of their subordinate status would have dire consequences. It is even probable that white residents gained a temporary sense of relief, knowing that local judicial authorities were taking black rebelliousness seriously. Even though the General Assembly had not intervened to offer white citizens the palliative measures they had solicited, members of the Kershaw District's Court of Magistrates and Freeholders demonstrated their vigilance in attempting to regulate enslaved peoples' economic behavior in the aftermath of the Vesey conspiracy.

While Kershaw District residents resorted to punishment as an example for enslaved people, white citizens from Columbia used the Vesey plot to emphasize the social and economic disturbances generated by enslaved peoples' quest for economic independence through self-hire. They voiced two sets of concerns. The first was that when enslaved people hired themselves out to white (or even free black) employers that they consciously threatened the job prospects of white workers. They did not merely single out enslaved people who were earning money for themselves. Instead, they connected bondspeoples' economic enterprising to the violence that they believed Vesey and his coconspirators attempted to wage on Charleston's white residents. In the months after the Vesey trials ended, Charleston's City Council pleaded with state lawmakers to restrict the numbers of enslaved men brought into the state, especially skilled enslaved tradesmen. Members of the City Council did not want enslaved men to practice—and profit from—self-hire.[46]

Though some whites denigrated the presence of skilled enslaved tradesmen, the petitioners did not fully object to bondspeople finding their own employment and earning compensation. After all, whites frequently leased enslaved people for short periods of time, particularly in the nineteenth century. As historian Jonathan Martin has explored, white Southerners writ large benefited economically from hiring enslaved people to perform discrete agricultural tasks.[47] Slave hiring as a labor practice shepherded more whites from nonslaveholder to slaveholder status, especially during the explosion of the cotton economy. White Southerners understood that with the rise in socio-economic status came the potential for increased financial profits from their investments in slaveholding. But for enslaved people, slave hiring could be used as a tool to keep a portion of their earnings. Enslaved people hired in cities such as Charleston and Columbia experienced a wider range of opportunities to keep some of their wages instead of paying all of their earnings to their enslavers. This practice had become so rampant that 111 white workingmen in Charleston urged lawmakers, white hirers, and enslavers to prevent enslaved workingmen from negotiating the terms of their hire to prevent them from saving even a small portion of their earnings. They contended that Charleston "had become so unprosperous" because enslaved tradesmen were stealing the jobs of white men, specifically white tradesmen employed in carpentry, bricklaying, painting, shoemaking, and plastering.[48] White citizens believed that when enslaved people worked as laborers, without reaping the economic benefits of slave hiring, the practice posed no social problem. It was only when enslaved people negotiated for the price of their wages in an effort to profit from their labor, or when equally skilled white men were losing their economic prospects to skilled bondspeople, that some white South Carolinians became frightened and concerned.

The second set of white concerns revolved around ideas of slaves increased economic and legal freedom. They argued that if the state's enslaved population believed that they could achieve even a modicum of freedom through making their own money and capitalizing off of their work, then whites needed to thwart the slaves' trade. This perspective obscured the true nature of enslaved peoples' economic behavior. Not only did bondspeople trade with one another; some of their primary trading partners continued to be white residents. In October 1822, only four months after the Vesey conspiracy was disrupted, an enslaved man named Jerry purchased a variety of goods from Randolph Alexander, a white Union District resident. No charges were brought against Jerry, perhaps because his owner David N. Saunders punished his actions. Alexander, on the other hand, was subsequently charged with "clandestinely trading" with an enslaved man and charged a $100 fine for his participation in an illicit trade.[49] The transaction between Jerry and Alexander suggests that neither party allowed rampant white anxieties of enslaved people with money to intervene in the economic and material demands that each brought to the trade.

After a tumultuous summer and fall, the General Assembly attempted to assuage anxious white citizens. The historian Walter Johnson has asserted that slaveholders attempted to suppress enslaved enterprises after almost every staged or realized slave revolt in American history.[50] The aftermath of the Vesey plot was no exception. State lawmakers met in December 1822 and passed a revised version of "An Act for the Better Regulation and Government of Free Negroes and Persons of Color; And For Other Purposes" as a legislative panacea to social unrest in the post–Vesey period. In this revised set of statutes, lawmakers sought to rid the state of the most pernicious threat to slaveholding society: free people of color. The 1822 statute declared that "no free negro or person of color, who shall leave this State, shall be suffered to return."[51] Therefore, if any free black person elected to leave the state, they would not be able to legally return. The statute maintained that free people of color would be charged a $50 annual tax to remain in the state and that any free person of color who arrived to any port or harbor via foreign vessel or ship would be imprisoned until the vessel departed.[52] The 1822 act placed more restrictions on enslaved people in their attempt to earn money through self-hire. The act stipulated that it would be unlawful for any white person to hire "any male slave or slaves, his or their time," which meant that enslaved people would find it more difficult to negotiate the terms of their hire with potential white employers.[53] Though past statutes allowed slaves to hire their own time with enslaver permission, the General Assembly made slaves who engaged in hire "liable to seizure and forfeiture," even with slaveholder consent.[54]

The language that lawmakers used in the 1822 Act singled out enslaved men. By attempting to restrict only the independent economic activities of bondsmen, the legislature revealed their perspective on enslaved women's labor in three ways. First, the new statute highlighted the economic prospects available to enslaved men while not contending with enslaved women's economic activities. Because enslaved men's skilled employment and hire in the mechanical trades directly threatened equally skilled white men, their economic pursuits came under more scrutiny than the independent economies in which enslaved women participated. Second, because the supposed conspiracy only involved black men—and only men were tried and executed for their alleged participation in the insurrection—the General Assembly instituted restrictions *only* against enslaved men hiring their own time. Third, by omitting enslaved women from the 1822 statute, lawmakers established that enslaved women's work was too valuable to impose additional regulations on it. Legislators may have not perceived enslaved women as a threat to social stability on par with enslaved men. Yet legislators were reflecting enslavers' interests and they deemed enslaved women's work as necessary, valuable, and not deserving of extra regulations.[55]

During this period, neither white residents' nor state lawmakers emphasized enslaved women as targets of their contempt. However, though enslaved women do not appear in the archival records in the same numbers as enslaved men, their absence does not suggest that enslaved women were not deeply engaged in their own forms of resistance and subversion.[56] In fact, despite enslaved women's continued visibility in local marketplaces as vendors, white freeholders did not single out enslaved women who worked as hucksters, laundresses, or maids. It is possible that lawmakers did not believe that enslaved women posed as much of a threat to social stability as enslaved men did. The lack of slave women charged with economic crimes, however, does not suggest that they were not integral participants in local market economies. In fact, as historians Stephanie Camp and Amrita Chakrabarti Myers have shown, enslaved women pursued a wide range of independent employment opportunities because of the nature of women's external work.[57] Enslaved women's labor and the subversive ways in which they exercised their economic autonomy meant that they did not appear in the public record for their economic pursuits in numbers similar to enslaved men.

Though legislators approved the revised set of statutes in 1822, surely as a way to protects slaveholders' interest, a question remains unanswered: How dedicated were enslavers to cracking down on the slaves' trade after the summer of 1822? Though in public, slaveholders such as Thomas Pinckney criticized both lawmakers and enslavers for their support of slave hiring, the ways in which slaveholders behaved in private would have revealed something different. Slaveholders' concerns about their slaves' economic lives were superseded by their economic aspirations. Despite the Act of 1822, whites were terrified of armed, violent, and well-funded slaves. But white fear did not dramatically alter the economic behavior of enslaved people. Nor did white South Carolinians, especially those who benefited from the slaves' trade, halt commodity exchange with them. Enslavers continued to support the slaves' economy in both public and private ways. In general, despite the initial violent blowback against black South Carolinians, whites continued to seek out opportunities to engage economically with slaves, despite the new set of regulations. Enslaved people, facing the increased specter of violence, simply forged ahead, not allowing white anxieties to hinder their market ambitions.[58]

In fact, in the years after the Vesey melee, the slaves' economy did not abate. Perhaps enslaved people realized that barriers erected by South Carolina's planter politicians to regulate slaves' trading were meant to deter whites, not enslaved people themselves. After all, if white concerns about the Vesey conspiracy superseded black Charlestonians' economic autonomy, then lawmakers would have created a more stringent set of laws to regulate the behavior of both blacks and whites more effectively. The experience of Isaac, an enslaved man from the Anderson District, serves as an example. On September 20, 1830, Isaac stood trial for illicitly selling liquor. The magistrates summoned two witnesses, enslaved men named Washington and London, to testify. The trial lasted less than a day, and after deliberating on Washington and London's testimony, the magistrates and freeholders found Isaac guilty. However, Isaac did not receive the customary twenty to forty lashes that the magistrates typically mandated. Instead, Isaac received a single lash.[59]

It is clear that enslaved people had become more adept at maintaining strong economic ties with black and white members of their communities after the Vesey plot. The threat of increased violence from local policing and judicial authorities did not deter those who were not dissuaded by the violence that ensued in Charleston in 1822. Similarly, white South Carolinians attempted to maintain their economic ties to enslaved marketers, even if it meant subjecting themselves to judicial penalties and judgments.[60] In April 1826, an enslaved man named Solomon sold a bag of potatoes and corn to Thomas Spurrier, a white freeholder. This trade would have been a legal one if Solomon had brought a ticket from his master, legalizing the transaction. In an attempt to backtrack on his participation in this illicit exchange, Spurrier argued that Solomon had indeed provided him with a valid ticket.[61] In the Union District in 1822, enslaved people were brought to court to account for their participation in trade on no less than five occasions. This means that most of the transactions between enslaved people and whites occurred in private. Therefore, these were only incidences when the slaves' trade came to light, often in judicial proceedings, and when enslaved peoples' perceived transgressions prompted a white person to file a complaint.[62]

Even so, the threat of violence in the aftermath of the Vesey plot did not discourage bondspeople from continuing to invest their labor and their time in productive economic agendas. An escaped bondsman retold the story of an enslaved man named Peter who would steal wood near the Ashley River, about twelve miles outside of Charleston. Peter intended to build his own stack of wood, load it onto one of his master's boats along with his master's wood, and sell the wood that he stole in Charleston for a small profit. He had only accumulated five or six sticks of wood, a relatively meager number, but Peter believed the small risk was worth a small reward. However, his enslaver, Davy Cohen, discovered Peter's scheme. The punishment was a violent one. According to the escaped bondsman, "They carried Peter to his hut, and tied him up so that his feet could not touch the ground, then tied his feet together and put a great log between them, to keep him stretched tight. Then they whipped him till he fainted twice in the rope. They did not leave off whipping him till midnight."[63] Though Peter took the risk, putting his enterprising to good use, his master did not want to allow Peter to exercise even a degree of economic autonomy. For that, he suffered great physical trauma. Perhaps Peter's gamble reflected the calculated risk that enslaved people took in an attempt to ensure their survival. Peter could have netted a small sum of money had he been able to hawk the few pieces of wood, but he made a strategic choice that in the end subjected him to his enslaver's violent whims.

Peter's experience, one that aligned a bondsperson's efforts to earn a bit of money with a slave owner's brutality, reflects the perspective of the slaves' economy that some white South Carolinians did not fully understand. Some did not—and could not—reconcile that enslaved peoples' efforts to earn the buying power to obtain goods was borne out of survival and that they would risk physical safety and emotional duress to make their lives better. An enslaved woman named Amey was brought to court during the summer of 1825, tried for stealing three hogs from a white neighbor, killing them, and "converted said hogs to her own use and to the use of the other negroes."[64] She was subsequently found guilty and sentenced to receive a punishment of thirty-nine lashes. Amey's enterprising move suggests that enslaved peoples' participation in networks of exchange were a result of necessary economic innovations and, most importantly, a strong sense of self-preservation.

The legislative and judicial measures in the aftermath if the Vesey plot were only a temporary salve. In order for the revised laws to be effective, all South Carolina residents, enslaved and free, black and white, alike needed to heed the directives. This did not happen. As swiftly as the General Assembly revised the existing laws in the 1820s, especially regarding enslaved people trading illegally with whites, the trade between blacks and whites continued. But in the antebellum era the trade revolved around a few goods: whiskey, corn, and most importantly, cotton. Enslaved people quickly discovered that the key to more material comfort was in the cotton trade. Perhaps this realization is why in

January 1824, Bartlett, Trim, and Alexander, enslaved men from Pendleton, South Carolina, were suspected of "stealing a certain quantity of cotton, between three and four hundred weight."[65] In addition to the cotton, they also sought out a cotton gin. Perhaps the three bondsmen realized that they could find a buyer for their stolen cotton more quickly if they could sell ginned instead of unginned cotton.[66]

Enslavers could not ignore the dire conditions in which bondspeople worked and the degradation that enslaved people experienced, especially on cotton plantations. After all, slaveholders were directly responsible for providing their slaves with the raiment necessary for their survival. However, enslavers were all too eager to profit from their slaves' struggle to survive. Slaveholders' profitmaking aspirations superseded their fears of armed and well-funded slaves. At the same time, enslavers worried about how the practice of enslaved people stealing food and livestock affected their profit margins. Slaveholders were considering how to increase the profitability of their plantation enterprises, and by extension how the slaves' economy could then fit into their overall investment in slave labor as a profit-making venture.

The Vesey conspiracy exposed deep-seated contradictions within South Carolina's culture of slavery. The conspiracy represented white South Carolinians worst fears—armed, organized, and well-funded enslaved people and free people of color who were ready to die for their freedom, killing anyone who stood in their way. Denmark Vesey embodied all of their anxieties about enslaved people with access to money and markets. He was a skilled enslaved man who, with a combination ingenuity and luck, purchased his own freedom. The conspiracy also exposed fundamental inconsistencies in South Carolina's slaveholding ethos. Whites believed that the black community sought to upend the culture of capitalism that had begun to characterize the economy of slavery in the state. Despite the specter of slave violence and in the face of white anxieties about enslaved people with money, the slaves' economy had become an even more important aspect of slaveholding life in South Carolina during the antebellum period. On the one hand, enslaved people clung to their own economic pursuits before, during, and after the Vesey conspiracy occurred. On the other hand, white South Carolinians made public proclamations about the need for more regulations to guard against slaves and free people of color accumulating goods and making money. In private, however, whites continued to secure their economic relationships with bondspeople.

The Vesey conspiracy was a flashpoint that put the specter of enslaved violence on display, and also thrust the slaves' trade into South Carolina's public discourse. White South Carolinians vocalized their rejection of enslaved peoples' and free blacks' participation in the public sphere. However, there were prominent groups of whites who inadvertently safeguarded the economic networks of enslaved and free black people—those who benefitted economically from their trade with slaves. Black South Carolinians, both enslaved and free, did not let white fear keep them from continuing to invest in their own economic pursuits. In the years after the Vesey conspiracy, enslaved peoples' investment in economic enterprise grew to an even more prominent position in the economics of slaveholding life in nineteenth-century South Carolina.

5

"THE NEGROES' ACCOUNTS"

Capitalist Influences in the Slaves' Economy

John Andrew Jackson was born in Sumter, South Carolina in 1825, the son of an enslaved woman named Betty and an enslaved man, a healer, known as Dr. Claven. As a young bondsman, Jackson's life was filled with the horror and trauma characteristic of plantation slavery until he made a daring escape to Massachusetts in 1846. His earliest memory was not of his family, but of his abusive mistress. "My earliest recollection was of my mistress," he chronicled, "whom I feared above all persons, as she used every means in her power to spite me."[1] Jackson's enslavers, especially the aforementioned mistress, utilized a veritable toolbox of violent and coercive techniques against him and other enslaved people. The memories of his enslaver's brutality shaped his childhood. At the tender age of ten, a childhood competition with his enslaver's son lay bare how the specter of white violence against enslaved people could shape even a childhood rivalry. Jackson and the enslaver's son were amusing themselves by digging for hickory root. Upon seeing that Jackson more quickly acquired a piece of the root, the enslaver's son kicked him in the nose. Jackson wiped the blood that streamed from his nose onto the young boy. "He ran and informed his mother," Jackson recounted," who whipped me on my naked back, to console her son, till the blood ran down."[2] The twin engines of fear and physical punishment instilled in Jackson a vivid awareness of enslavers' destructive potential over his life.

It was not uncommon for enslaved people to find ways to cope with their enslavers' brutal practices, be it their use of a cat o' nine tails to whip them into compliance or the promise of liquor with which enslaved people drowned their physical and psychic ills. By the time Jackson reached adolescence in the 1830s, enslavers in South Carolina had developed an index of coercive practices designed to compel slave compliance and above all else, productivity. Jackson's life as a bondsperson was shaped by a transformation that had begun to occur in Southern states, with enslavers working to perfect slave management techniques, which included violence to extract as much labor from enslaved people as possible.

Jackson divulged how his enslavers deployed economic incentives to control enslaved peoples' lives, and then began to profit from their use of coercion. His first master established a store on his plantation, out of which he sold liquor to whites during the day and at night traded with slaves to supplement his own income. However, Jackson's enslaver did not want to trade with enslaved people for just any commodity. He encouraged local bondspeople from surrounding plantations to bring him stolen cotton. In return, they received whiskey. Whether the cotton had been cultivated by the bondspeople themselves on their own individual plots of land or whether it was pilfered from their enslavers' own stock is not clear. No matter the cotton's origins, the economics show that Jackson's enslaver not only enticed enslaved people with the promise of spirituous liquor, but he also swindled them in the exchange. According to Jackson, the enslaver could sell 100 pounds of cotton for $14 in the local marketplace. A gallon of whiskey was worth $1. Therefore, the slaveholder made $13 for every 100 pounds of cotton that local slaves brought to him. This enslaver's trade with enslaved people helped him gain the financial footing to expand his investments in both land and slaves. "This method of getting rich," related Jackson, "is very common among the slaveholders of South Carolina."[3]

John Andrew Jackson depicts a system of commodity exchange, one filled with participants at opposite ends of the Southern economic spectrum: enslavers at one end and the enslaved at the other. But the transactions that Jackson described do not merely uncover how one aspect of the slaves' economy functioned. Jackson's words also reveal how such exchanges helped enslavers profit even more from enslaved peoples' labor. And his testimony was not singular. Though some enslavers believed that the trade with bondspeople would undermine not only the power that they possessed over their slaves but also their own financial well-being, others disagreed wholeheartedly. These enslavers, including the man who owned Jackson, embraced the belief that allowing—or forcing—enslaved people to work independently for compensation benefited both themselves and their slaves. They encouraged enslaved people to act as capitalists. That is to say, they not only believed, but openly touted, the advantages of encouraging bondspeoples' economic pursuits. Both Jackson and his enslaver understood the power dynamics at play. While Jackson and other enslaved people acquired goods and earned money for themselves, enslavers had begun to develop a more violent regime of slaveholding that fully commodified the enslaved: their bodies, their labor, and their economic aspirations.

The aftermath of the Vesey conspiracy marked a dramatic shift in the ways in which enslaved people engineered their own small-scale capitalist ventures, as well as how enslavers approached bondspeoples' interest in the market. For enslavers and members of the South Carolina elite writ large, a new economic rationality took hold. Though enslavers had been witnessing and supporting the slaves' economy since the colonial period, the rise of the cotton economy convinced enslavers that not only could they exert even more control over enslaved peoples' market activities, but they could profit from them in real and valuable ways. Moreover, if the Vesey conspiracy proved anything to slaveholding capitalists, it was that enslaved peoples' investment of time and energy in their own economic arrangements could coexist with the more formal avenues of economic enterprise and profit-making. Slaveholders realized that enslaved enterprise and entrepreneurship did not destroy the foundation of slavery. Instead, enslavers emerged as the ultimate beneficiaries of enslaved peoples' investments in commodity exchange.

Enslaved people experienced firsthand how slave owners' innovations in capitalist enterprises led to more violence and exploitation. During a period in which enslavers were aware of the increased profits to be made from slave-produced cotton, enslaved people lived with a new level of slaveholder control. John Andrew Jackson's experience demonstrates this turn. The new methods that slaveholders used to enrich themselves beginning in the 1820s were widespread. Though slaveholders pushed enslaved people toward higher levels of productivity, often with the threat of violence and familial separation, slave industriousness came with another cost: free time. While it may seem as though bondspeople were given opportunities by their enslavers to work for themselves, the opportunity quickly turned into a mandate. Enslavers steadily tempered enslaved peoples' autonomy to trade with whom they selected, a move that suggests enslavers were approaching their slaveholding investments as businesspeople, not merely as paternalist masters and mistresses. Bondspeople may have enjoyed more access to consumer goods and other commodities, but acquiring material goods had its limits. For enslaved people, economic exchange alone could not secure for them what they ultimately wanted: freedom from bondage. Enslavers recognized this fact clearly in the 1820s and 1830s, as they responded to instabilities in the American economy catalyzed by events such as the Panic of 1819. It was in this period when the slaves' economy went from being a source of autonomy for bondspeople to the source of their increased exploitation by enslavers. This evolution epitomized the ways in which enslavers championed new technologies to increase their profits and secure their economically risky investments in slavery. These efforts began in earnest in the 1820s, in the aftermath of the first financial panic in American history.[4]

An important facet of this shift was accounting. As enslaved people weathered the economic storm that characterized the antebellum South Carolina economy through clinging to their networks of exchange, enslavers were integrating accounting as a tool in their economic arsenal. They attempted to approach their plantation enterprises and modulate their ideas about slaveholding mastery not as paternalists, but as businesspeople. Slaveholders implemented a new framework of coercion, as they innovated strategies to make their capital investments in slavery as profitable as possible. These innovations incorporated enslaved enterprises. Though John Andrew Jackson, for example, does not explore whether his enslaver formally accounted for his trade with local bondspeople, it is possible that Jackson's enslaver had begun to track his trade with slaves in written form. Indeed, if Jackson's enslaver traded with enslaved people to enrich himself, then he may have accounted for his trade with enslaved people, even if it was illicit. Enslavers and other businesspeople with whom enslaved people marketed their goods began to write down their engagement in the slaves' economy, giving a level of validity and formality to enslaved peoples' experiences as actors within an increasingly capitalist economy.

In a December 1828 letter to the *Southern Agriculturist*, plantation overseer R. King Jr. revealed, "Every means is used to encourage them, and impress on their minds the advantage of holding property, and the disgrace attached to idleness."[5] King argued that slaveholders, above all, sought an industrious enslaved labor force. They strove to create an environment where instances of slaves' absconding were a rarity. In the antebellum era, enslavers developed new, perhaps less blatantly violent methods to compel enslaved people to remain on plantations as productive and dutiful workers. After all, if a bondsperson escaped successfully, the enslaver lost a capital investment. King assured readers that slaveholders made decisions about plantation management and slave labor through the filter of profitability and cost-effectiveness. This overseer noticed that if enslaved people were "industrious for themselves," then they would be so for their enslavers as well. No enslaved person "with a well stocked poultry house, a small crop advancing, a canoe partly finished, or a few tubs unsold, all of which he calculates soon to enjoy," he contended, "will ever run away."[6] Again, the cost that enslavers incurred by pursuing a runaway slave was higher than the cost of forcing enslaved people to earn money to feed and clothe themselves. As the profits to be made from cotton and slavery rose, enslavers coerced enslaved people toward higher levels of productivity. In addition to using violence and fear, enslavers mandated that bondspeople to put their economic skills to good use.

Enslavers possessed a warped sense of charity when it came to encouraging enslaved people to invest their time, energy, and resources into their own small-scale enterprises. King argued that when enslavers allowed enslaved people to hold property and work for themselves, these activities minimized the time and money that slaveholders spent retrieving runaway slaves. Bondspeople allowed to earn money were less likely to run away, he asserted, because they had the opportunity to control this small aspect of their lives. In King's estimation, enslaved peoples' desire for freedom were quelled by the opportunity to hold property and earn money. He concluded that such dedication to their own semi-independent work engendered in enslaved people a sense of industry, which ultimately produced a sense of devotion to their masters. King noted, "Many may think that they lose time when Negroes can work for themselves; it is the reverse on all plantations under good regulations—time is absolutely gained to the master."[7] Enslavers believed, according to King, that their investment in the slaves' economy made financial sense. This overseer acknowledged the advantages gained by enslavers when they validated enslaved peoples' tradition of holding of property and working for themselves. He framed his assertions in terms of productivity and industriousness.

Yet King overlooked what enslaved people gained by participating in their own networks of trade. Enslavers' primary incentive for sanctioning—or encouraging—slaves' investments in their economic activities was a fiscal one. Enslavers implemented management systems that prioritized slave productivity and sought, above all, to protect investments in slaves as capital. If permitting enslaved people to accumulate goods and work for themselves reduced absconding and augmented profit margins, some slave owners allowed such activities to continue, within reason, and always under their supervision.

King reflected enslavers' evolving understanding of the economics of slaveholding during an era of unprecedented economic promise. But enslavers did not begin to reconceptualize of the slaves' economy in a vacuum. Indeed, the global market for slave-produced goods from the American South, short-staple cotton in particular, proved to be rapacious yet unpredictable during the 1820s through the 1840s. The demand for Southern cotton that came from northern manufacturers and industrialists across the Atlantic enticed cotton slaveholding capitalists with the promise of wealth. However, as is typical with economic booms, there was a bust.[8] Economic depressions in 1819 and 1837—which were national crises—hit the South Carolina economy particularly hard, destabilizing the Southern cotton economy. Meanwhile, enslavers invested in South Carolina's cotton industry failed to gain sure footing in the competitive market for American cotton, as production thrived in fertile soils of newly opened territories in Alabama and Mississippi.[9]

Furthermore, the price of the state's major exports—cotton, rice, and corn—fluctuated greatly in this period. The cotton economy in particular remained unstable. For example, cotton prices in Charleston fluctuated from as high as $0.35 per pound in January 1818 to as low as $0.075 per pound in January 1830.[10] The subsequent expansion of cotton-growing plantations in newly incorporated lands west of South Carolina increased the supply of American cotton, which lowered the price of short-staple cotton prices in regions of the southeast. Furthermore, Charleston, the location of the state's most important port, lost its place as one of America's premier port cities. Between 1821 and 1839 Charleston lagged behind New York, Boston, and New Orleans in the value and size of exports.[11] All of this meant that enslavers and investors in South Carolina's cotton-based economy of slavery faced a potentially lucrative, but ultimately unstable, economic environment.

Enslaved people were also shaken by the unpredictability of enslavers' investments in the marketplace for slave-produced commodities. Just as they dealt with the real fear of family separation due to enslavers' overleveraging themselves in their investments in slavery, bondspeople also had to use all the tools at their disposal to shield themselves from starvation.[12] Charles Ball described the tradition of enslaved people maintaining individual "patches," or gardens, on which they grew pumpkins, melons, potatoes, and corn for themselves not as a luxury, but as a necessity. These patches were located usually in "unprofitable" parts of plantation estates, meaning that if the land on which enslaved people grew their own produce could have been used to plant cotton, slaveholders would not have allocated it for enslaved peoples' independent agricultural pursuits. But even Ball recognized the cotton economy's volatility. "The land is constantly becoming poorer," he claimed, "and the means of getting food, more and more difficult."[13] As long as enslaved people could grow corn and sweet potatoes for themselves, he argued, they rarely went hungry. Yet as large-scale cotton cultivation took priority, foodstuff became scarce. Ball observed that when a slaveholder had to purchase corn, "the [enslaved] people must expect to make acquaintance with hunger."[14] The cotton economy's instability, combined with enslavers' financial insecurity, shaped enslaved peoples' lives. But as Ball detailed, if enslaved people grew food for themselves, then they could withstand the vagaries of slave owners' investments in the cotton economy.

To adapt to the cotton market's unpredictability, enslavers adopted new techniques to control enslaved peoples' economic activities—often for their own financial benefit. Enslavers began to consider enslaved peoples' full income-generating potential in broader ways. Bondspeoples' labor would always generate a profit for enslavers, such as through slave hiring. However, slave labor to produce export commodities such as cotton alone would not ensure a return on investments in the cotton economy. Enslavers' investments in cotton had become less secure in the antebellum era.[15] The downturn in Atlantic demand for American cotton combined with a series of financial crises brought economic terror to South Carolina capitalists invested in the market for slave-produced cotton exports. The precipitous drop in the price and demand for American cotton had a devastating effect on the South Carolina economy that forced slaveholders to re-evaluate their investments in their plantation enterprises.[16] The historian Theodore Rosengarten points out that in response to the economic crises of the 1810s and 1830s, enslavers began experimenting with more innovative cotton cultivation techniques in hopes of rebounding economically and salvaging their risky investments in cotton and enslaved labor.[17] Taken one step further, it stands to reason that enslavers also innovated more creative slave management techniques to ensure, as much as possible, a return on their investments. Forced by fears of financial insolvency, enslavers reconceptualized the utility of enslaved peoples' eagerness to participate in their own economies.

To compete in the competitive marketplace for slave-produced commodities, enslavers began adopting more exploitative approaches to their slaveholding enterprises. Slaveholders recognized that they could fully commoditize and further control enslaved peoples' dedication to their own networks of enterprise and entrepreneurship. Enslaved people were on the receiving end of slaveholders' efforts to extract as much labor from them as possible, in order to make plantation enterprises more self-sufficient and more lucrative. Enslavers' intrusion on the slaves' economy belied their ever-growing avarice for profit and their concerns about South Carolina's waning economic power during the antebellum period. Bondspeople experienced enslavers' efforts to reap the financial benefits of their ever-increasing capital investments in slavery.

One slaveholder's words exemplify this shift. In June 1837, South Carolina slaveholder Charles C. Pinckney (nephew of namesake and South Carolina Constitutional Convention delegate Charles Cotesworth Pinckney) penned a letter to the *Southern Agriculturist* in which he called attention to a subject that legislation had "in vain endeavored to control." The subject was "the trade of bond with free." Pinckney maintained that in South Carolina, laws designed to regulate trade between enslaved and free people were a "dead letter." He wrote that neither lawmakers nor the laws that they created could curtail such exchanges when the parties involved—black slaves and the whites with whom they traded—had a vested interest in disregarding the law.[18]

Pinckney clarified his perspective on why enslaved people sought out opportunities to "clandestinely" sell their products to external buyers. It was customary, he acknowledged, for slaveholders to allot slaves a portion of land on which to cultivate their own goods—such as rice, corn, or even cotton—during their free time. With the surplus of their individually cultivated product, bondspeople traded for clothes, bacon, sugar, molasses, and tobacco—items that Pinckney ungenerously designated the "luxuries of life." Though he recognized enslaved peoples' enduring interest in selling their goods to willing customers, he also expressed the belief that slaves' fascination with trading left them in an untenable situation. Indeed, he conveyed a paternalistic concern for enslaved peoples' welfare. He believed that white buyers took advantage of bondspeoples' ignorance when transactions between them occurred. When a bondsperson sold his or her goods in local marketplaces, he claimed, they were at the mercy of unscrupulous shopkeepers and roguish merchants. "The prices of his sale and purchase," he wrote, "depended on the will of the tradesman." If enslaved people were in fact "defrauded," they had no legal redress against the perpetrators because of their subordinate status before the law. Unless enslavers introduced legal claims against white merchants, black slaves had few avenues through which to address fraudulent economic transactions with whites.[19]

Pinckney offered a solution, however. To remedy the dangers posed by trade between white and enslaved people, he proposed that enslavers put themselves in the buyers' place. He believed that slaveholders should purchase enslaved peoples' goods at full market price to "drive the illicit trader from the neighborhood." Pinckney also advised fellow slaveholders to keep an accounting of the goods that they transacted with enslaved people. Though bondspeople and enslavers in South Carolina had been trading with one another since the late seventeenth century, in the antebellum period slaveholders such as Pinckney and Jackson's enslaver decided to integrate networks of enslaved enterprises more fully into their plantation's profit-making efforts. Pinckney contended, "Much facility in this business arises from keeping a regular book of entries," and he suggested that "this can be done by every planter who understands his factor's accounts." He went on to note that "by carefully entering dates and amounts . . . the time thus employed does not much affect the interests or comfort of the planter, whilst it materially promotes those of the slave." He urged slaveholders to follow his example and more closely track their trade with slaves to protect their slaves' economic interests, and to ensure the profit-making potential of their investments in slavery and slave labor.[20] Pinckney advocated a new and novel concept: enslavers accounting for their trade with slaves.

On the surface, Pinckney's proposition appears to be an altruistic one. Certainly, offering to purchase his bondspeoples' products at full market price suggests that he was acting with benevolent concern toward his slaves' independent economic ventures. However, this act was not an unselfish one. Pinckney, like enslavers of his ilk, sought to control every aspect of enslaved peoples' commercial endeavors, which entailed eliminating external patrons and situating himself as the only person with whom his slaves traded. He wanted to fully capitalize on his slaves' interest in independent commodity production and exchange, realizing that he could co-opt an aspect of enslaved peoples' lives over which they had maintained the largest amount of autonomy. In doing this, the enslaved people owned by Pinckney lost the privilege to select with whom they traded. By 1837, if not before, enslaved people owned by Charles Pinckney lost their autonomy to trade within their community. Pinckney did not disclose that in fact he had adopted a new method of controlling his slaves' economic pursuits. He fully co-opted and manipulated what was once under enslaved peoples' control—and he used accounting to do it.[21]

Enslavers such as Pinckney intervened in what had become steady and reliable business for local white merchants from enslaved people and free people of color. In 1827, forty-two Charleston grocers complained about an 1815 city ordinance that forbade any black person from buying liquor from them after 8 p.m. during the fall and winter and 9 p.m. during the spring and summer. They argued that since the city's black population enjoyed the latitude to "dispose of their commodities," the grocers should also enjoy the right the sell liquor to these same people.[22] The grocers were not concerned with the race of their patrons, but rather the "depressed state of business" without the patronage of black customers.[23] As enslavers attempted to control where and with whom enslaved people interacted economically, white businesspeople expressed concerns about the potentially depressed profit margins from a lack of enslaved patrons.

Enslavers made the slaves' economy an important component of their overall investment and profit-making strategies. Indeed, this move proved to be a dramatic shift from enslavers of previous generations. This new breed of slaveholder rode the economic waves of profit and insolvency between the 1820s and 1840s. They utilized every facet of enslaved peoples' lives to protect their investments in slave labor, from outright violence to economic coercion.[24] For example, Pinckney disseminated his counsel during a period of increasing economic unpredictability. His words epitomized the ways in which enslavers were consciously resituating enslaved peoples' autonomous buying, selling, bartering, and trading activities, making slaves' networks of trade a prominent facet of slaveholders' own profit-minded goals. Slowly, enslaved peoples' economic activities were no longer defined by informality or relegated to the underground. In its place arose a more formal, even more visible, economy of the enslaved. The slaves' economy became an aspect of the capitalist economy of slavery. In a pernicious way, however, enslaved peoples' long tradition of controlling this aspect of their economic lives—their abilities to trade, market, and make money for themselves—was being intercepted by increasingly profit-hungry enslavers who strove to keep their plantation and slaveholding enterprises afloat.

Bondspeople were on the receiving end of enslavers' efforts to not only profit from but to modernize their investments in slavery. Beginning in the 1820s, pressured by domestic and international challenges to the state's cotton and rice plantation economies, slaveholders enacted more exploitative plantation management techniques over the enslaved people that they owned. Despite the perspective that Charles C. Pinckney articulated about protecting the enslaved people that he owned from unscrupulous traders, slaveholders often substituted one dishonest trader with another: themselves. Pinckney did not track enslaved peoples' trade for their benefit. Instead, his new tool of choice was an economic one—accounting—to manipulate bondspeoples' interest in trade to scaffold his quest for profits from his investments in slavery.

Enslaved people, however, were not mere units of capital, unwilling to pursue their own avenues of economic advancement. They too were economic actors, despite having far fewer tools at their disposal. They had to protect themselves from not only the vagaries of the global marketplace for commodities that they produced, but they also had to contend with enslavers' profit-seeking motivations. Enslaved people responded to what Governor George McDuffie observed in 1840, that "cotton is the only crop that will command money, and as money is the most pressing want of a man in debt, everything is directed to that object."[25] Ultimately, bondspeople pushed back against slaveholder control by selling cotton—the one item that they desired above all else—to others who desired it.

Enslaved people sold cotton to anyone willing to purchase it. Joe, an enslaved man from the Union District, decided in 1842 to find a buyer for the over thirty pounds of seeded cotton that he had in his possession. On December 9, 1842, under the cover of night, Joe entered into merchant Matthew Hartford's store with his cotton in tow. We do not know if Joe's cotton was stolen or if he grew it on his own, but he handed his cotton over to Hartford, who then weighed it for accuracy and offered Joe $2.00 for the entire amount. Hartford even offered to "give a credit on the said Joe's account" for future use in his store, a move suggesting that Joe was not only a regular customer and had an established economic relationship with Hartford, but that Hartford and Joe trusted one another.[26] It is unclear whether Joe was cognizant of the going price for short-staple cotton, but the range of prices for December 1842 in Charleston was between $0.575 and $0.775 per pound.[27] This meant that the total value of Joe's cotton was between $18.40 and $24.80. At this point, Joe decided to negotiate. He initially rejected Hartford's extremely low offer of only

$2.00, instead telling Hartford that "he wanted a bottle of whiskey, and some tobacco and that he . . . would place the tobacco to his credit."[28] Joe and Hartford agreed to the terms, with Joe walking away with three and a half pints of whiskey, tobacco, and credit on his account in Hartford's store. Hartford had seeded cotton that he could sell for a much higher price than he exchanged in goods with Joe.[29] Bondspeople such as Joe fueled enslavers' concerns about their inability to control the slaves' trade, and therefore their own investments in slavery. It was the behavior of enslaved people such as Joe and whites such as Hartford that Pinckney and other enslavers believed undermined not only their financial stability, but also their status as enslavers.

The evolution of slaveholding practices in the antebellum era reflected enslavers' ideas about the economic interactions between enslavers and the enslaved. However, in practice, coercion and control as business practices lay at the heart of enslavers' ideas about enslaved enterprise. One slaveholder described the coercive techniques that he used to compel bondspeople to dedicate their free time to subsistence gardening. In 1830, he argued that every plantation should have a garden that was "sufficiently large to grow such quantities of the more common vegetables on, as may supply the wants of each slave on the place."[30] Enslaved people would not suffer from hunger, he contended, with readily available produce cultivated by younger and older bondspeople on the plantation. If enslaved people were healthy, he assumed that they would be more willing to labor on tasks that benefited him economically. Yet this slaveholder quickly exposed his belief that coercion was necessary to compel enslaved peoples' participation. He wrote, "The indolent nature of negroes, so well known to us, and the experience of our whole lives, forbid us to expect that they will ever be induced to undertake the least work which does not result in their immediate benefit, without coercion, for, of all beings, the negro appears to be the most indolent and the most improvident."[31] He described what appeared to be a communal garden for which his plantation's enslaved people were made responsible. He then shifted a responsibility that had, in past decades, resided with enslavers onto enslaved people themselves. His seemingly paternalist rhetoric was overshadowed by his ultimate goal: to induce enslaved people to be more productive and therefore more profitable. Though this enslaver communicated an overarching concern about hunger among his slave population, his real concern focused on slave indolence, a problem that he believed affected his bottom line.

The idea of reciprocity—one that many enslavers believed dictated the power dynamic between themselves and their slaves—crumbled when they exploited paternalist rhetoric to shift more work onto enslaved people. In explaining the coercion that he believed was required to compel bondspeople to tend a communal garden, the aforementioned slave owner instead revealed the extent to which he believed that coercion was required to force enslaved people to comply with his wishes. He was willing to overwork and overburden enslaved people—to the point of starvation—in order to extract as much labor as possible from his human property. Though he utilized a paternalist's rhetoric of care for enslaved peoples' well-being as the guise under which he communicated his real economic plans, his words belie another goal. This enslaver approached enslaved people not only as a slaveholder but as a businessperson, concerned with productivity and profitability. He induced the bondspeople that he owned to increase their labor output.[32]

It is clear that by the 1830s, enslaved peoples' economic gains reinforced enslavers' own profit-making interests more directly than in previous generations. As bondspeople dedicated themselves to independent cultivation and trade, they also became entrenched in an economic system that thrived even more off of *every* aspect of their labor. Ultimately, enslaved peoples' dedication to their own market ambitions directly buttressed enslavers' investments in their own plantation enterprises. The enslaved people on the Pooshee plantation in St. Berkeley's Parish serve as an example. As early as 1827, enslaved people on Pooshee had been patronizing a plantation store, maintained by the overseer. The overseer purchased products that slaves produced, including chickens and eggs, and he paid market price for these goods. A handful of enslaved people purchased goods from the store in 1827. One enslaved man, Daniel, purchased blue homespun for $1 and one enslaved woman, Jenny, borrowed $0.45 to buy cloth. The following year, Jenny repaid the money. Seventeen enslaved people took advantage of the opportunity to obtain goods on credit from their enslaver, Henry Ravenel. The bondspeople on Pooshee most frequently purchased homespun, handkerchiefs, molasses, and kitchen goods—items that perhaps would have made their daily tasks easier to complete and, in prior generations, would have been provided by their enslaver.[33]

Increasingly, enslaved people shouldered the burden of slave owners not outsourcing the manufacture of items such as clothing and blankets. The bondspeople on Pooshee produced clothing and blankets for themselves and other members of the slave community. They were also forced to absorb the additional burden of processing the wool and cotton that they produced. While they had been in the habit of wearing clothes that their enslavers had purchased from various vendors, in the late 1820s, Ravenel and other enslavers stopped using external vendors for goods such as slave cloth and blankets.[34]

In the 1830s, as enslaved people in South Carolina experienced slaveholders' increasing efforts to control their economic activities, they witnessed their relationship with local entrepreneurs evolve as well. Bondspeople in one Lowcountry community traded with Society Hill cotton factor Leach Carrigan. Between 1836 and 1838, enslaved people from sixteen different Lowcountry plantations sold over 10,000 pounds of independently cultivated seeded and unseeded cotton to Carrigan. Enslaved people were on the receiving end of a financial arrangement that Carrigan made with numerous slaveholding cotton planters to purchase enslaved peoples' independently grown cotton. During this three-year period, fifty-three enslaved people earned a total of $627.91 from Carrigan.[35] His trade with local slaves, in fact, represented a noticeable component of his yearly income. Between 1837 and 1839, these transactions comprised 9.3 percent of Carrigan's total purchases. While that was not a large share of Carrigan's business, enslaved peoples' trade with Carrigan represented a recognizable component of this cotton factor's financial investments.[36]

While it is significant that fifty-three bondspeople earned money from Carrigan for the cotton they cultivated independently, Carrigan's official documentation of such trades reveals a different perspective. The trades between the slaves and Carrigan were not illicit backdoor financial interactions. Instead, Carrigan legitimated the trades between himself and the enslaved people by writing them down alongside his other transactions. The practice of enslavers and merchants tracking, in written form, not only their trade in commodities with bondspeople but also the amount that they offered slaves in compensation for their labor or products they cultivated, suggests that they figured out how to capitalize on enslaved peoples' interest in trade and enslaved peoples' quest to earn wages. Merchants and enslavers made decidedly rational choices about incorporating enslaved peoples' trading activities into their official record-keeping practices. Ultimately, merchants such as Carrigan implemented new strategies to exploit slaves' interest in gaining even a modicum of purchasing power. Accounting was one strategy.

Accounting factored prominently as one of the new economic approaches embraced by enslavers and merchants in their trade with enslaved people. Indeed, beginning in the 1820s, accounting was a harbinger of change; enslavers became increasingly interested in understanding their plantation enterprises as capital investments. As proposed by enslavers such as Charles C. Pinckney and put into practice by merchants such as Leach Carrigan, the introduction of accounting to track the slaves' trade brought the slaves' economy from the realm of the informal to the formal realm of economic productivity. White investors in the economies of slavery understood that they could use simple, yet sophisticated accounting techniques to formally monitor their investments in the labor of enslaved people as well as their trade with them. They openly embraced accounting as a buffer against the capriciousness of the market, especially in response to the financial downturn in 1819. Accounting historians, in particular those who examine the relationship between accounting practices and the genesis of capitalism, contend that when businesspeople track their expenditures and profits, they are making "rational" choices to legitimize the economic pursuits in which they are engaged.[37]

The mere act of account-keepers writing down their transactions legitimized the economic exchanges, the values of the goods exchanged or labor compensated, and also the economic actors who were privy to the transactions. Accounting scholar Peter Miller suggests that accounting is not merely a technical practice, meaning that an accounting ledger does not simply depict the debits and credits or appreciation and depreciation of assets or other goods. Instead, financial record-keeping reproduces in written form an account-keeper's conscious commercial and social decision-making processes.[38] For investors who sought to profit from the labor of enslaved people, accounting represented the act of *rationally* reckoning with one's expenditures and earnings. The practice of maintaining financial records validates the record-keepers' economic interactions and recognizes the people with whom the record-keeper engages. Businesspeople who invested in slavery began to deploy accounting techniques to track—and ultimately profit from—their trade with enslaved people in a more detailed way. In doing so, they were acknowledging enslaved people as independent economic actors, thus legitimizing enslaved peoples' customary right to accumulate property and earn money. But this recognition did not diminish the efforts of slaveholders and merchants to exploit bondspeoples' market ambitions. In fact, it was *because of* enslaved peoples' participation in economic enterprise that white capitalists relied on, increasingly accounted for, and ultimately affirmed their trade with enslaved people.

The connection between slavery and accounting became a marker of Southern slaveholding entrepreneurs' embrace of modern capitalist principles. Historians such as Robin Blackburn and Caitlin Rosenthal have explored the ways in which slavery became a more modern economic institution as enslavers adopted new strategies to make their investments in land, materials, mechanisms, and enslaved people produce visible economic benefits. Enslavers began accounting for the complexities in enslaved peoples' value, including depreciation and productivity.[39] Though some planters were more strategic in how they accounted for their trade with slaves, many enslavers kept haphazard record, often tracking the slaves' trade in "Negro accounts" or "Negro books." In the end, however, the move that slave owners made by adopting accounting methods did not benefit enslaved people. Instead, it harmed the same enslaved people who were attempting to ease the burden of being enslaved.

Plantation accounting in general, and shopkeepers' tracking of their trade with enslaved people in particular, were components of a movement spearheaded by enslavers to adopt more strategic approaches to the economics of slaveholding. Exemplified in the accounting strategies outlined by King and Pinckney, enslavers and overseers shared their plantation management strategies in the pages of Southern magazines. Slaveholders used the periodicals as an outlet to express their ideas about mastery, plantation management, and regulating enslaved people. Topics including slave control and plantation management grew in popularity among Southern planters in the antebellum period, as readership of these magazines increased and new publications emerged. As South Carolina's rice and cotton-producing slaveholders endeavored to find tools and strategies to make their slaveholding enterprises more profitable, they turned to agricultural journals to gain and disseminate such information. The topic of enslaved peoples' independent cultivation framed myriad arguments about how to successfully manage a profit-generating plantation in the antebellum period. Armed with advice about how to control the daily lives of enslaved people most effectively, enslavers and overseers invested not only in the process of spreading the gospel of slaveholding mastery, but also the gospel of plantation profitability, above all else. In the pages of Southern agricultural magazines, enslavers learned about how to approach their plantations as business enterprises, treating enslaved people as both property *and* employees in the process.[40]

The more controversial matters, slave productivity and management—which included discussions of slaves' independent crop cultivation, bondspeople hiring out their own time, and slaves' possession of property—produced conflicting opinions, as enslavers expressed inconsistent ideas about how to coerce their slaves into working more productively. Yet there were moments when planters used these forums to communicate their perspective on slave management using discourse imbued with the language of paternalistic mastery and concern over their slaves' well-being. Governor Whitemarsh Seabrook eagerly advertised his strategies for maintaining an income-accruing plantation in May 1829 to the *Southern Agriculturist*. Seabrook argued that he recognized the important role that slaves' customary rights played in how a profitable plantation functioned. In writing about the management strategies that he employed in running his family's Lowcountry cotton plantation, Seabrook believed that all planters sought "economy in the labor of our field negroes."[41] He recognized, though, that most planters did not understand, as he did, the importance of allowing enslaved people time to dedicate toward their "customary privileges."[42] He urged fellow planters to think critically about overburdening slaves with too much extraneous work, specifically work that did not relate in some way to preparing cotton to be sold in the marketplace.

Above all, though Seabrook expressed a paternalistic concern for the rights to which he believed enslaved people were entitled, he realized that respecting bondspeoples' customary rights positively influenced his plantation's productivity. That being said, Seabrook's commentary on his respect for enslaved peoples' economic privileges did not overshadow his more pressing concern about the financial viability of his Lowcountry cotton plantation. Ultimately, he only expressed his respect for slaves' free time and their customary privileges because he realized that it did not hinder his underlying concern for profit. According to Seabrook and many other slave owners, enslaved entrepreneurship and plantation profitability were not mutually exclusive. Instead, they could coexist to help slaveholders fulfill their economic goals. The benevolence with which Seabrook laced his ideas, however, could not shield his immediate focus on implementing strategies to ensure that his investments in both land and slaves would yield visible monetary returns. He reveals that enslaved peoples' investment of time and energy into participating in their local market economies would not hinder his ability to both control and profit from enslaved peoples' labor.

Other enslavers adopted management strategies that their colonial predecessors implemented in the late seventeenth and eighteenth centuries. Lowcountry planter B. McBride believed that *allowing* slaves to tend their own gardens and cultivate their own food thwarted enslaved peoples' engagement in other potentially nefarious pursuits. In 1830, McBride revealed that on his Hickory Hill plantation, "All my slaves are to be supplied with sufficient land on which [the overseer will] encourage, and even compel, them to plant and *cultivate* a crop, all of which I will, as I have hitherto done, purchase at a fair price from them."[43] Enslavers who supported trade with slaves described the economic exchange between themselves and enslaved traders as a mutually beneficial arrangement. McBride rationalized that interplantation commerce benefited both masters and slaves, albeit in different ways. On Hickory Hill, he compelled his slaves to cultivate their own crops, believing that slaves would be less likely to engage in criminal activities during their free time if they had the opportunity to earn money. McBride asserted that they would have no time to become embroiled in suspicious activities that might have resulted in "severe punishment" from himself or perhaps a slave patrol.[44] Therefore, to encourage both productivity and compliance, McBride argued that he paid his slaves "a fair price" for their goods.

McBride noted that he always purchased slaves' crops and considering that he controlled how much compensation his slaves received, he may have paid his slaves below market value for their goods. Such a move would have allowed him to spend less on provisions. By forcing his slaves to grow their own crops, he freed himself from having to provide essential provisions for his slaves.[45] One could also suggest that he sought to capitalize on his slaves' interest in profiting from their trade. Instead of allowing his slaves to venture outside Hickory Hill's boundaries to trade, he wanted to be his slaves' sole customer, thus controlling his slaves' economic autonomy. He strove to manipulate the extent to which his slaves engaged in their own economic activities and used slaves' independent cultivation as a plantation management technique to do so.

Enslaved peoples' access to economic opportunities were stymied by enslavers who sought to position themselves as the only person with whom their slaves traded. An "eminently distinguished" planter writing in 1833 shared this perspective in yet another article in the popular *Southern Agriculturist* magazine. The unnamed slaveholder asserted that he never allowed bondspeople to sell anything *without* his expressed permission. Though he never restricted enslaved people in "any acts of industry," he wanted to control the extent to which his slaves engaged in local market economies.[46] This planter believed that bondspeople created a dangerous black market when they traded without their master's direct involvement. To encourage enslaved peoples' cheerful submission, he wrote that he rewarded them "punctually for their exertions by taking from them at a fair price whatever they justly have to offer."[47]

However, this planter did not expand on what he considered a fair price. Was a fair price what the planter was willing to pay his slave for a product, or what consumers in local marketplaces would pay? Did enslavers who engaged in trade with their slaves operate under the same market practices that they did when trading with other whites? The larger question is, to enslavers, what constituted fair when it came to commercial exchange with their slaves? The notion of slave owners' fair and just compensation for enslaved peoples' independent cultivation was an important one because it brought economic rules that dictated their interactions with merchants into the power dynamic between themselves and enslaved people. Perhaps the "eminently distinguished" slave owner included the term "fair" to convey that he approached the exchange between himself and bondspeople as he did with other non-slave agents with whom he interacted economically. However, for enslavers, obtaining the highest price for goods was at the heart of the economic relationships that they forged with local rice merchants or cotton factors. If planters, as actors in the global economy for slave-produced commodities, wanted to maintain their economic and social positions as members of South Carolina's slaveholding class, then their financial successes hinged on their economic acuity. So it stands to reason that they would not hesitate to undervalue their slaves' goods.

Just as enslavers haggled with merchants and factors over cotton prices and the value of their cash crops in local, domestic, and the Atlantic marketplaces, they also applied these business practices to their dealings with enslaved people. While the "eminently distinguished" slaveholder did not restrict bondspeoples' assertion of industry, enslavers almost certainly did not want enslaved peoples' "act[s] of industry" to supersede their own economic imperatives. For this reason, as historian John Campbell has shown in Upcountry South Carolina, this enslaver sought to exercise ultimate control over how bondspeople realized their independent economic interests.[48] During the antebellum period, when planters traded with bondspeople they were the ones who determined the fair price—not enslaved people or larger market principles.[49]

Ultimately, enslavers wanted enslaved people to opt into trade as a way to not only increase their profit margins, but to also cut down on theft. It was not uncommon for enslaved people to appropriate enslavers' commodities for themselves, out of a sense of survival and a desire to possess their own goods. One runaway slave argued that because of the meager food allowance that he and his fellow bondspeople received from their enslaver, they resorted to stealing. He divulged, "I did not think it was wrong to steal enough to eat. I thought I worked hard to raise it, and I had a right to it."[50] According to historian Alex Lichtenstein, when enslaved people stole their owners' goods, they were challenging the dynamic of domination and servitude that characterized how enslaved people and enslavers interacted. While this dynamic may have been true in some circumstances, another perspective is that enslaved people were not trying to undermine slaveholder authority. Instead, they were attempting to not only secure the material tools necessary to survive, but they were also attempting to redistribute enslavers' wealth.[51]

Enslavers' fears of slaves stealing their cotton and selling it without their permission influenced some enslavers' decisions to restrict enslaved peoples' cultivation of their own products. Prominent South Carolina slaveholder and politician James Henry Hammond attempted to suppress slaves' assertion of economic independence in any form. In 1831, after marrying Catherine Fitzsimmons, daughter of wealthy Charleston slave trader and merchant Christopher Fitzsimmons, Hammond took charge of the Fitzsimmons' fledging Silver Bluff plantation in Aiken County, South Carolina. Silver Bluff was a sprawling 10,800-acre estate valued at $36,100 and was home to 147 slaves.[52] Upon taking control of Silver Bluff, Hammond ascertained quickly the importance of slave management as the key to turning his failing plantation into a profitable one. Hammond's first move as a newly minted enslaver was to eliminate any activity that would make the enslaved people that he owned less dependent on him. Hammond believed that when bondspeople had too much time to themselves, they inevitably became involved in dangerous activities. More importantly, Hammond feared that slaves' assertion of independence by engaging in their own economic pursuits reduced their dependence on him. For this reason, he designed a set of directives that he believed would transform Silver Bluff into a well-functioning and economically successful venture. Hammond implemented a system of regulations, rewards, and punishments in an effort to rehabilitate Silver Bluff. First, he set out to preside over his slaves with a sense of "justness and moderation in all things."[53] Hammond articulated his belief in moderation, which included tempering the use of physical punishments. He wrote that he did not want to rely on beatings to encourage slave productivity and obedience. Second, in directing his overseers, he argued for corporeal punishment only in instances of self-defense or in extenuating circumstances. Instead, he wrote, "Persuasion should substitute for severe punishment in getting work done as much as possible."[54]

Yet Hammond did not use moderation when he addressed one aspect of enslaved peoples' lives on Silver Bluff. He outlawed slaves travel to local merchant and grog shops, and prohibited slaves from selling the produce from their gardens to neighbors. Although he permitted his slaves to maintain "negro patches," which were located in close proximity to enslaved peoples' dwellings, he prohibited slaves from growing "crops of corn or cotton for themselves, nor to have any cattle or stock of any kind of their own."[55] Hammond did not want his slaves to cultivate commodities for their own benefit when they spent their time cultivating goods for him. Hammond opposed enslaved peoples' assertion of autonomy, as had been the norm at Silver Bluff before his tenure. Hammond's opposition to slaves' economic independence influenced his resistance to allowing his slaves to engage in trade.

Hammond's perspective on the slaves' trade was not unique. In fact, to combat the spread of enslaved peoples' commodity exchange with whites, one group made a stunning request. In the fall of 1831, white Spartanburg residents convened to find a viable solution to the enduring problem of the trade between whites and enslaved people. Specifically, they wanted to find a more effective punishment for "persons convicted of trading with slaves."[56] The law, as it stood, demanded that whites found guilty of illegally trading with slaves be made to pay a hefty fine and serve designated time in a local jail. But the Spartanburg District residents wanted more. They did not believe that the existing punishments—not for enslaved people, but for whites—went far enough to discourage them from fueling the slaves' trade; they wanted to find a "corrective to the evil." So they offered a solution. The answer was to add another layer of punishment to white offenders: whippings. They insisted that state lawmakers include physical punishment of whites to deter them from illegal commodity exchange with local slaves—punishments that African Americans typically received for acting unlawfully. The Spartanburg petitioners, however, faced a steep challenge from lawmakers, who responded with a resounding "no." In fact, state lawmakers countered that additional "legislation on the subject [was] unnecessary."[57] The response suggests that even though there were vocal detractors of the trade between enslaved blacks and whites, there was enough support from state lawmakers to ensure that the slaves' economy would continue to grow, with enslavers and other capitalists taking advantage of enslaved peoples' economic interests.

The eagerness with which enslavers and merchants scrambled to profit from enslaved peoples' entrepreneurship only increased after the Panic of 1837. General unease increased among enslavers amidst the backdrop of economic uncertainty, in particular the cotton market's unpredictability in the late 1830s. Economic forces compelled South Carolina planters to consider different ways in which to maintain their investments in monoculture as the international demand for Southern cotton waned. This volatility—or perhaps insecurity—affected cotton prices. Between 1837 and 1849, the price of short-staple cotton fluctuated between $0.05 and $0.10 per pound, the lowest prices since the beginning of the nineteenth century. Concurrently, global demand for Southern cotton weakened in the midst of financial turmoil. The cotton market's instability challenged South Carolina planters' enthusiasm not about cotton as an industry, but on cotton monoculture.[58]

Enslaved people endured more suffering when enslavers became dedicated to the cultivation of and profit from one product. When enslavers stopped providing food and raiment to them, bondspeople were coerced to spend their already meager free time cultivating not only food for themselves, but also other essential items for the entire plantation community. Though enslaved people were being compensated by enslavers and merchants for their independent cultivation, these same enslavers and merchants increasingly took advantage of these forced economic relationships to bilk slaves out of the fair market value of their goods.

Moreover, enslaved people absorbed slaveholders' increasing dependence on them to both harvest record amounts of cotton and dedicate more of their free time toward income-generating work. Enslaved woman Margaret Bryant witnessed her mother, a skilled weaver, work day and night to "make up that cloth to please the obersheer [*sic*]." She also invested her free time weaving extra yarn to sell to other enslaved people and poor whites.[59] She revealed that poor white men would "come there and buy cloth from Ma. Buy three or four yard."[60] In her cloth trade, when Bryant's mother sold cloth to other enslaved people, she often did not receive money as compensation. Instead Bryant's mother would receive hogs or other commodities as payment for her cloth.

In theory, enslaved peoples' extra work as producers of goods for the market allowed enslavers to maintain a singular focus on monoculture. Ultimately, enslavers' dedication to monoculture—first rice, then cotton—threatened plantation self-sufficiency. For example, a planter who neglected subsistence farming and forced enslaved people to focus singularly on cotton cultivation risked dependence on external growers to provide food for not only themselves, but their slaves and livestock as well. When slaveholders relied on and purchased necessary foodstuff from upper South states such as Virginia for the nutritional needs of their slaves, they risked undermining the financial stability of their plantation enterprises. This concern, however, did not deter enslavers from investing in cotton monoculture. The profits to be made from cotton were so seductive that slave owners, before the 1840s, ignored the clear benefits of subsistence farming.[61]

For enslaved people, however, neither the financial panic nor its causes thwarted their participation in trade with their enslavers or with local merchants. In fact, slaveholders began to depend even more on bondspeople to harvest record amounts of cotton and also dedicate their free time toward independent cultivation. In the late 1830s and 1840s, enslaved peoples' independent cultivation revolved around two products: cotton to sell and corn to consume. And slaveholders kept track of how much of each product slaves could cultivate in order to better calculate plantation profitability. Perhaps enslaved people were more forward-thinking on the issue of subsistence than their enslavers; slaveholders did not face the same daily struggles with food as did the enslaved. As enslavers exploited enslaved peoples' long-held investment in trade and barter to help plantations maintain their profitability, bondspeople necessarily dedicated more of their independent time toward economic activities that ultimately buttressed slaveholders' interests in profits above all else.[62]

The challenges that enslavers' singular dedication to cotton posed to both the environment and economy forced them to develop more strategic methods to ensure self-sufficiency. The data suggests that some slaveholders took the issue of self-provisioning seriously. In 1837, corn imports to Charleston totaled 393,400 pounds. The following year, that number surged to 456,718, an increase of 16 percent. In 1839, however, corn imports dropped significantly to 342,098 pounds and even further in 1840 to 322,080. Yet the most dramatic change in corn importation to Charleston came in 1843. In that year, only 169,777 pounds of corn were imported into the city. "The grain crops were unusually abundant this year," according to an 1850 trade magazine, "and a large portion of the receipts of corn in Charleston were the product of South Carolina."[63] The decline in corn imports into the state coincided with larger conversations among enslavers about self-sufficiency and the role of enslaved people in filling the subsistence lacuna created by slaveholders' dedication to cotton monoculture.

The agricultural crisis of the 1830s and 1840s plunged Southern enslavers and bondspeople into a complex system of exchange that hinged on the relationship between cotton and corn. As the cost of imported foodstuff increased in the late 1830s and early 1840s, enslavers depended on enslaved people to cultivate food that would not only feed themselves, but also feed entire communities. As slave owners became more systematic in how they tracked plantation expenditures and profits, incorporating their trade with slaves, the topic of self-sufficiency arose in the discourse about productivity, economic independence, and monoculture.[64]

In response, enslaved people were compelled to fill the gap between enslavers' dedication to monoculture and the lack of subsistence caused by their overreliance on a single crop for the marketplace. Bondspeople on Samuel Porcher Gaillard's Orangeburg plantation in Sumter planted, harvested, and sold Galliard their independently produced corn. On January 24, 1841, twelve bondspeople sold their corn to Gaillard.[65] Almost a fifth of the enslaved people on Orange Grove sold their corn to Gaillard, with a total corn amount of over 33 bushels. An enslaved woman, Widow Nancy, sold the most corn to Gaillard, with 7.5 bushels and 13.5 quarts, the equivalent of over 420 pounds of corn. Though Gaillard did not disclose the specific period of time over which the slaves had to cultivate the amount they sold to him, the record does offer another perspective on how this slaveholder defrauded the twelve bondspeople for their independent market cultivation.[66] In total, the corn cultivation for Orange Grove as of January 24, 1841, including the slaves' individual harvests, amounted to 675 bushels, worth $54.00. Gaillard valued corn cultivated by the slaves at Orange Grove at $0.08 per bushel. This means that the enslaved people, including Widow Nancy, were paid this price for their independent cultivation efforts. A closer look at the value of corn bushels in January 1841 on the open market, however, shows a different story than the one that Gaillard presented in his accounting.[67]

On January 23, 1841, the day before Gaillard recorded the transactions between himself and his slaves, a shipment of approximately 20,000 bushels of corn arrived in Charleston from North Carolina and Virginia. The corn was sold locally for between $0.52 and $0.59 per pound.[68] This information suggests that Gaillard failed to compensate the twelve slaves for the market value of their corn. With a difference of at least $0.44 and at most $0.55 per bushel, Gaillard undervalued the slaves' corn and the bondspeople failed to get the full market value that their independent cultivation efforts could have fetched. Widow Nancy received $0.62 for the over 420 pounds of corn that she grew. Had she been able to sell her independently grown corn in a Charleston market, she would have earned at least $3.90. What could she have purchased with the extra money? The compensation from Gaillard could have provided Nancy with the money to purchase fabric or shoes. As of January 25 of that year, linens, woolens, and other fabrics were selling in Charleston for about $0.35 per yard. Sometimes enslaved people splurged on items made out of silk and other fine fabrics, and it is possible that Nancy may have used her earnings to purchase more luxurious items that the ones provided to her by Gaillard. Had Nancy been able to both earn the market value of her corn and purchase these goods from a local merchant, she could have purchased a little more material comfort with better quality clothing. Indeed, she could have gained the psychic boost of earning a fair amount in compensation for her labor.[69] Instead, her extra labor filled Gaillard's coffers.

One might wonder why Gaillard, or any other enslaver or white entrepreneur, would agree to pay enslaved people at all. Absent information from Gaillard himself, one might conclude that Gaillard believed that the benefits of trading with his slaves far outweighed the disadvantages. He could coerce enslaved people like Nancy to work harder and for longer hours. He could get more corn for less money. And he could attempt to ensure that his slaves would not run away. Perhaps for Gaillard, the rewards were worth the financial risks.[70]

Enslavers profited from enslaved peoples' dedication to completing extra labor. Their exploitative practices, which co-opted the slaves' market participation, supported the growth of their own profit-making regimes. This move represented a dramatic shift in slaveholders' perspective on their investments in the labor of enslaved people. Indeed, in the 1820s through the 1840s, slaveholders cloaked their profit-seeking motives in the language of the economic activities of the enslaved. As Thomas Pinckney revealed in his 1837 letter, he allowed enslaved people he owned to trade for goods with him, but his seeming altruism shrouded his more immediate concerns about profits. Ultimately, enslavers traded with bondswomen and bondsmen in an attempt to extract more labor from them. As enslaved people participated as producers and consumers in their local market economies, during an era of economic uncertainty, exploitation was an indelible aspect of the slaves' economy.

Even in the tumultuous antebellum period, enslavers and merchants did not allow their fears of rebellious and armed enslaved people, who were also economically minded, to hinder their interests in profit-making incentives. Bondspeople continued to trade with whites. Perhaps enslavers did not fully realize that enslaved peoples' independent cultivation and their efforts to earn money or the buying power to obtain goods for themselves was borne out of survival. It is also possible that enslavers did not care about enslaved peoples' efforts to survive. The slaves' trade shielded them to an extent from the unpredictable economic instabilities inherent in the antebellum-era economy of slavery.

Enslaved people traded and bartered with their enslavers for commodities such as livestock and foodstuff. In exchange, enslavers entered into financial agreements with bondspeople based on monetary compensation or permitting slaves to purchase merchandise that they wanted or needed. Ultimately, however, the trade that occurred between enslaved people and slaveholders benefited slaveholders more than it did bondspeople, who spent their free time cultivating goods for their own consumption. And the exchanges revolved around slaveholders' exploitation of their slaves—and more directly, their slaves' micro-economies.

Enslavers adopted plantation and slave management strategies that began to influence the culture of slaveholding in the antebellum era. They reconsidered how to increase profits and encourage slave productivity in the midst of the changing economic and political landscape of slavery. Enslavers began to enact more strategic approaches to slaveholding, in hopes of making their investments even more profitable, with co-opting the slaves' economy as one of their primary tools. Some enslavers forced enslaved people to carve out time to work for themselves, as long as the practice proved profitable to slaveholders themselves, thereby transforming the slaves' economy into a technology of their own capitalist desires.

6

"A MONSTROUS NUISANCE"

Enslaved Enterprises, Class Anxieties, and the Coming of the Civil War

Charleston's suffocating heat and humidity blanketed the city's center marketplace during the summer of 1835. Under the night's sky, the swelter penetrated the myriad stalls inhabited by the city's enslaved marketers. It was a typical summer Saturday evening in Charleston. The weather proved no match for the swarms of enslaved people who flooded the marketplace, ready to sell their merchandise to eager customers. Earlier in the day, after they completed their tasks, bondspeople heaved their wares from plantations surrounding the city to the market, eager to begin the tradition of haggling with customers who came ready to participate in verbal banter with them for their goods. Perhaps some of the enslaved marketers used the various riverways to transport their wares to the market. Others may have traversed the county roads, all of which connected the Lowcountry's biggest and most bustling city.[1]

The enslaved vendors situated themselves in rows on the ground, their merchandise illuminated by lamplight. The marketers were selling an abundance of food such as bananas, apples, oranges, meat, and fish. This commercial hub was one of the most vital distributive networks for fresh produce and other commodities to Charleston's residents and visitors. Some enslaved people worked exclusively on behalf of their enslavers, while others negotiated with their owners for the privilege of maintaining a stall on their own behalf. Most slave owners levied a fee of $6 per week to each enslaved marketer. This sum may have been a large amount, but in comparison to the opportunity that the enslaved vendors had to keep whatever they made in excess, it was worth it.

The enslaved marketers brought a variety of goods to the marketplace. In Charleston's Centre Market, not only did bondspeople sell their enslavers' goods, but they also put their own products on display. Their merchandise represented an admixture of ownership and possession that historians Laura Edwards and Dylan Penningroth claim characterized the complex legal relationship between enslaved people and their claims to property.[2] Slaveholders held legal claims to all of the goods that slaves brought to the market. Enslaved people, however, *possessed* certain products, claiming informal legal rights over items that they cultivated and produced for themselves, with their enslavers recognizing enslaved peoples' claim over those goods. Their sales included boxes and baskets that they wove by hand, with their incredible skill and dexterity.[3] Enslaved women in particular controlled the pace at which they sold their products to interested buyers, their distinctive voices reverberating through the marketplace.

On Saturday evenings, the marketplace's vendors were black and enslaved and some, if not many, of the patrons were white. Perhaps white

FIGURE 6.1 Enslaved women selling sweet potatoes, Charleston (1861)

buyers entered the market wanting to purchase food or other commodities that they desired from the enslaved marketers at lower prices than they would receive from white vendors. The buyers knew that they would not wield absolute control over the outcome of the transactions; the patrons understood both the formal and informal rules of buying goods in public from enslaved vendors in the Centre Market. On the other hand, because enslaved people had been given tacit permission by their enslavers to sell goods in the marketplace, the enslaved people were, in some ways, proxies for their owners. White patrons had to remember that haggling with the enslaved marketers, especially the enslaved women, was part and parcel of doing business in the Centre Market on Saturday evenings. The enslaved people dictated the pace of sale and the price at which their goods would sell. This was perhaps the one space in which they wielded the power of the coin.

The bondspeople appeared to enjoy the marketplace's frenetic energy, as they haggled and bartered, yelled and conversed with all who entered into the marketplace. The black vendors surely appreciated the comaraderie of fellow bondspeople, and perhaps the comaraderie with free blacks as well. However, they merely tolerated the white consumers. One traveler, British sociologist Harriet Martineau, remarked, "They enjoy the fun and bustle of the market, and look with complacency on any white customers who will attend it."[4] Martineau meandered through the marketplace, watching with curiosity at the exchanges that were taking place. Perhaps she witnessed enslaved marketers pocketing their hard-earned money after a vigorous back-and-forth with white patrons. Maybe she watched enslaved women engage in verbal banter with customers over the merchandise they worked so hard to bring to the market.

Martineau's companions remarked that enslaved peoples' apparent enjoyment proved that they were content with their lives in bondage. "Their activity and merriment at market," Martineau observed, "were pointed out to me as an assurance of their satisfaction with their condition, their conviction that their present position is the one they were made for, and in which their true happiness is to be found."[5] However, she was not convinced. Martineau noticed that she and her guides came to different conclusions about the enslaved marketers' source of enjoyment. Her guides believed the enslaved people who worked as hucksters in the Charleston marketplace enjoyed "the fun and bustle of the market," and that this open display of amusement belied their general satisfaction in life. Martineau was more introspective. She believed that the bondspeople enjoyed, above all, the opportunity to keep the profits of their labor. For enslaved marketers, engaging in the revelry of the marketplace symbolized a rare sense of satisfaction that perhaps offered them an escape from everyday forms of violence that defined their experiences as bondspeople. They protected this long-held practice—namely, the social aspect of marketing in the city's public marketplace—to defend against the horrors of their enslavement.

Bondspeople understood the marketplace. It took on a variety of meanings in their lives. It was a site of trauma, where slave traders forcefully separated enslaved families, with enslaved people being shackled, often stripped nude, humiliated, and auctioned off to enslavers seeking to extract as much capital from their bodies as possible.[6] John Andrew Jackson described its gruesome detail:

> On one occasion there was a sale of slaves near, and a man came to the auction to purchase a slave girl. He fixed on one who pleased him, and took her into a neighboring barn and stripped her *stark naked*, for the purpose of examining her, as he would a horse, previous to buying her. The father and mother of the girl were looking through the window and keyhole and various crevices, with many other slaves, who saw all that passed. He ultimately purchased her for his own vile purposes, and when he had had several children by her, sold both her and her children.[7]

The marketplace came to represent all the ways in which physical and emotional violence shaped enslaved peoples' lives. Yet as much as the marketplace shaped their experiences in bondage, enslaved people also understood that marketplaces could be spaces of community. They could connect with enslaved and free people through the shared tradition of haggling, bartering, and selling their goods. Enslaved people attempted to use the marketplace—a site of such anguish—for their own purposes.

They tried to use the market to protect themselves from the traumas of their enslavement.

Enslaved people recognized the ways in which a different marketplace could be a space to express their economic aspirations publicly. They experimented with the most effective strategies to receive the highest prices for their goods. Since the colonial period, they had enjoyed the customary right to push back against white power and influence. Enslaved women and men strove to wield economic control in their exchanges with white consumers, temporarily attempting to loosen the shackles of their bonded status. But enslaved marketers did not fill formal and informal marketplaces only to trade with whites. They also reveled in the opportunity to fellowship with other enslaved and free black people. The marketers used their positions as vendors in public marketplaces as a valve to release the physical, mental, and emotional pressure of their enslavement. However, few enslaved people entered the marketplace earning more than a bit of money to secure material goods for themselves and their families. They instead wielded the modicum of economic power that they possessed to ease the burden of being enslaved.[8]

In the two decades before the outbreak of the Civil War, however, these types of economic pursuits took on new significance. The ever-increasing pressure put onto enslaved people by their enslavers to raise their levels of productivity meant that they had to make extra efforts to improve their material lives. By the 1840s and 1850s, bondspeople struggled to come to terms with the limits of their economic ambitions. Though they continued to buy goods, sell commodities, and earn wages for their labor, they realized that they would not be able to earn and save enough to buy themselves out of slavery. Instead, the slaves' economy was merely a tool that enslaved people used to ensure their survival, as much as they could. It was clear to slaves that participation in networks of commodity exchange and wage labor could not bring them out of slavery. While they may have gained a psychic boost from negotiating in the marketplace with white consumers or earning money to buy goods that they wanted, as historian Lawrence McDonnell has contended, few bondspeople had the opportunity to use market activities to buy themselves out of slavery.[9] Enslaved people therefore invested their meager free time and energies to ensure that their economic pursuits produced tangible results, be it money or goods that they desired.

Enslaved peoples' exchanges with white customers, as demonstrated in Charleston's Centre Market during the summer of 1835, continued to prompt resistance from whites opposed to enslaved peoples' commercial practices during the late antebellum era. Some whites believed that the "evils of Negro trading" had gone on for long enough, a sentiment that Darlington District residents expressed in 1857.[10] Yet the past continued to foretell the future. Since the late seventeenth century, their cries were not loud enough to drown out the expansion or the sheer prevalence of the slaves' economy. Despite the ways in which enslaved people and those with whom they traded wove enslaved peoples' networks of commerce into the very fabric of life in South Carolina, vocal groups of whites strongly opposed the visibility of enslaved people with access to money and property. They expressed their opposition more vehemently in the late antebellum era, making the slaves' economy a political issue. But in this period, their complaints took on a more impatient tone. Ultimately, as enslaved people strove to make their lives better through commodity exchange, property accumulation, and waged labor, these activities became an issue in the landscape of late-antebellum South Carolina politics.

One of the common complaints that white citizens made concerned enslaved peoples' open access to a marketplace of goods and customers for their products—and white South Carolinians, both slaveholding and nonslaveholding, supported such behavior. Enslaved peoples' networks of enterprise proved to be a highly controversial political issue during 1840s and 1850, which fomented intraracial contention among whites. Some white South Carolinians argued more vociferously that enterprising enslaved people threatened not only the culture of slavery, but also the security of life for whites in the state. In this period all arenas of the slaves' economy were put on public display, with enslavers accommodating the trade, nonslaveholding whites propping up enslaved peoples' entrepreneurial ambitions, and enslaved people protecting their property rights. But there had always been groups of white residents unwilling to accept slaves' economic autonomy—whites at every rung of society.

Furthermore, enslavers invested in a particular type of capitalist enterprise in the 1840s and 1850s. They expanded their predatory economic behavior, extracting as much labor and profit from enslaved people as possible. They preyed on the economic interests of enslaved people while undermining the economic prospect of poor and nonpropertied whites. In this way the slaves' economy widened political fractures between white South Carolinians in the years before the state's charge for secession in December 1860. The racial fissures that revolved around enslaved peoples' economic interests were a reflection of white South Carolinians' disagreements about the role of the marketplace and capitalist behavior in the lives of enslaved people in South Carolina.

In February 1846, Prince, Frank, and William decided to make a tradeoff: subsistence for liquor. The three enslaved men elected to forgo a weekly allowance of corn in exchange for whiskey. They probably believed that the trade was equitable when they entered in an informal agreement with Thomas P. Chandler, the overseer of the Charleston District plantation on which they were enslaved. Once the trade was complete, each leaving the exchange with the goods they desired, Chandler was arrested and subsequently indicted for violating the law. Chandler defied the Act of 1817, which forbade anyone from trading with a slave without written permission from the bondsperson's owner. But the issue at hand was not only that Prince, Frank, and William illegally acquired whiskey. In fact, Justice Francis Wardlaw argued, "It is a great abuse for an overseer to corrupt slaves, by selling liquor to them; *but* sometimes it may be commendable for an overseer to let the slaves confided to him have liquor, an even to stimulate their industry by affording them this gratification in exchange for what their labor has produced in the time allowed to them."[11] Wardlaw suggested that Prince, Frank, and William deserved to have whiskey because the drink would "stimulate their industry"—encourage their productivity—and give them a sense of "gratification."[12] He may have thought that the enslaved men deserved to enjoy the momentary sensory dullness that liquor provided in order to endure the brutality that characterized their lives as bondsmen. Yet the real issue at the center of this case revolved around not the enslaved men's possession of alcohol, but the legality of the trade. Did Chandler, as an overseer, have the legal right to trade with enslaved people? According the judges, he did not.

Networks of economic exchange involving enslaved people and white citizens were as old as the slaves' economy in South Carolina itself. But it had become a hot-button political issue by the 1840s. A faction of white South Carolinians—namely nonslaveholding whites and even a few slaveholders, who had historically been on the forefront of political discourses about the dangers of the slaves' trade—banded together to oppose the slaves' economy more vocally. Enslaved people such as Prince, William, and Frank and whites such as Thomas Chandler were on the receiving end of complaints from white South Carolinians who saw the slaves' trade as the ultimate threat to white supremacy. In 1848, white citizens from the Abbeville District sought formal permission from the General Assembly to detect, compel, publicly flog, and prosecute whites caught trading illegally with enslaved people. They were connecting bondspeoples' ability to buy liquor and other commodities to enslaved peoples' increased sense of autonomy, which they believed threatened white racial hegemony. Moreover, the petitioners wanted legislative consent to expose white residents who had been profiting from selling liquor illicitly to the enslaved. The committee responsible for responding to the petition deliberated on the residents' request. They offered a direct answer. Lawmakers did not support the Abbeville residents' request to publicly ridicule whites caught illegally trading with slaves. A revision of that magnitude, they argued, would be "dangerous." The committee concluded, in a foreboding tone, that it was "highly inexpedient to alter the law as proposed" because of "the consequences of which the committee cannot undertake to anticipate."[13]

Why, in 1848, did enslaved peoples' marketing efforts emerge as an issue of such concern to the Abbeville residents? And why did state lawmakers dismiss the complaint? Lawmakers wrote that they believed that the laws regulating trade between black slaves and whites were sufficient as written. More importantly, they realized the danger of not only legislating the master–slave relationship, but also antagonizing white citizens. They hesitated to strengthen laws that would have intervened in the dominion of enslavers over their slaves. If enslavers were permitting slaves to act economically, then no law could intercede. Enslavers—and therefore lawmakers—held this rule sacrosanct and for this reason lawmakers declined the Abbeville residents' plea, despite the fact that the petitioners were asking them to reinforce what they believed were weak slave regulations.[14]

Furthermore, it is not insignificant that seven of the eight legislators owned slaves, which surely influenced their perspective on blocking slave activities that other slaveholders condoned.[15] The lawmakers were acting in their own best interests. As long as enslaved people had their enslaver's permission to buy goods, even liquor, and as long as enslaved people were not stealing their enslavers' goods, then there was little that lawmakers *wanted* to do to block such trade. Therefore, lawmakers foresaw that imposing such harsh penalties on white residents for trading illicitly with enslaved people would be imprudent. Legislators, in the end, decided that they would allow enslaved peoples' continued visibility in the Abbeville marketplace, perhaps in order to protect what had become an important aspect of enslavers' property rights and to protect the economic interests of enslavers like themselves.

It is clear that enslaved people in the Abbeville District had been accustomed to navigating their own informal networks of trade, and it was not uncommon for these networks to include white members of Abbeville's elite class of enslavers and local merchants. It is possible that the white Abbeville petitioners were reacting to the ways in which enslaved people of Abbeville District enslaver Lewis Perrin were behaving. Bondspeople on the Perrin plantation had been regular participants in their community's economic life. They purchased items ranging from clothing and sugar, to tickets allowing travel outside plantation boundaries. In August 1856, nineteen bondspeople purchased tickets from Perrin for travel to a nearby religious meeting. Each ticket cost $0.40 and Perrin maintained an accounting of each enslaved person's economic activity, docking each bondsperson's account for purchases that they made and money they were accumulating.[16]

The spending habits of enslaved people on the Perrin plantation reveal that enslavers had become more adept at commodifying many aspects of bondspeoples' lives. Enslavers had become more focused at exploiting their slaves' interest in purchasing items or experiences that they desired to have. Nineteen bondspeople on the Perrin plantation committed themselves to extra work in an effort to purchase tickets for travel to a religious meeting. The bondspeople surely gained psychic and spiritual benefits from such an experience. Indeed, travel to the religious gathering may have provided them with a vital mental escape from the privations of plantation life. It is also probable that Perrin monetized enslaved peoples' willingness to complete extra work in order to purchase a ticket to a meeting. Perrin manufactured the expense and the enslaved people spent their free time and their earnings on a ticket that in the end benefited him financially.[17]

The visibility of enslaved people in Abbeville engaged in commodity exchange in the 1840s and 1850s extended to their trade with local merchants. In addition to trading directly with the Perrin family, enslaved people on Perrin's Abbeville District plantation also traded with a local merchant. Providence Elmore ran a local general store that serviced whites and blacks alike. Between 1851 and 1860, enslaved people owned by Perrin went to Elmore to purchase coffee, molasses, and wheat. In exchange they sold Elmore their excess cotton, with each transaction approved by Perrin. In December 1857 Perrin received three letters from Elmore, stipulating how much cotton each slave had and the compensation each bondsperson received. Ben, Mal, and Billy sold over a combined 2,650 pounds of cotton to Elmore—an amount in excess of the amount that they harvested that went to Perrin. In exchange, Elmore wrote that he compensated Ben, Mal, and Billy with a variety of items including wheat, molasses, and lard. Ben bought three pecks of wheat and two gallons of molasses, while Mal, who sold Elmore 1,500 pounds of cotton, received one pound and three pecks of wheat, one and a half gallons of molasses, and one pound of lard. Billy, who harvested 1,150 pounds of cotton, bought one pound and three pecks of wheat, one and a half gallons of molasses, and two pounds of lard. In exchange for harvesting over 2,650 extra pounds cotton, the three enslaved people in 1857 only received a few pecks wheat, several gallons of molasses, and a couple pounds of lard.[18]

As Mal, Ben, and Billy's experiences demonstrate, there was no informality or hint of illicitness about their transactions with Elmore. Other than enslaved people not receiving the full value of their cotton harvests, the mere fact that Elmore and Perrin communicated in formal ways about the extra work that enslaved people completed reveals the extent to which businesspeople profited off of enslaved peoples' labor in the late antebellum era. Even though a few of the enslaved people on the Perrin plantation had personal accounts through Perrin with local merchants, the accounting of enslaved peoples' transactions was not meant to protect them. Instead, the accounting was meant to help enslavers and merchants keep track of their profits. In an unspecified year, enslaver Thomas Perrin received a letter alerting him to his slaves' account status. Eighteen of Perrin's bondspeople held accounts at the family's local general store in Abbeville. The amounts held in each slave account ranged from Ben with $2.26 to Shack who had $25.52.[19] The letter stated: "Dear Sir, the above is a list of your Negro acts [accounts] with us. Fearing you might make a settlement with them and not know the amount they owe us we send you the above you will please save it for us and very much oblige."[20] On another occasion, Thomas Perrin received a letter from Cathran Perrin titled "A List of debts due C. Perrin by Negroes of T. C. Perrin Esq." In the letter, C. Perrin listed twenty of Thomas Perrin's slaves who owed a combined amount of $226.85. Jeff held the largest debt with $25.89, and Harry held the smallest amount with $2.51. At the end of the letter, C. Perrin stated that the correspondence represented a "lone statement of amts due" by each account-holding bondsperson and requested that Thomas Perrin promptly pay the balance due.[21]

Enslaved peoples' networks of enterprise in the Abbeville District in the 1840s and 1850s—and the political pushback that such trade generated—is a microcosm of the larger landscape of enslaved enterprise in South Carolina. The slaves' economy persisted as enslaved men and women took advantage of opportunities to trade with a wider swath of people. As the slaves' economy endured, so too did political debates about the threat of bondspeople with money, goods, and property to the racial hierarchies inherent in South Carolina's culture of slavery.

The persistence of the slaves' trade converged with the escalating political tensions in South Carolina during the antebellum era. The question at the heart of these debates was: Did enslaved peoples' access to money, wages, and property threaten the foundation of slavery and white supremacy? For the majority of the slaveholding elite, the answer was a resounding "no." Middle-class, laboring-class, and even poor whites, though, were not monolithic in their perspectives on the slaves' economy in the 1840s and 1850s.

For members of South Carolina's slaveholding elite, enslaved enterprise and entrepreneurship was—and had always been—a component of their approaches to slaveholding mastery. It was grounded in the idea that the relationship between enslavers and the enslaved was a private one. Enslavers had been expressing this idea more openly and with more frequency beginning in the 1830s. In an essay read before the Agricultural Society of St. John's Colleton in 1834, South Carolina Lieutenant Governor Whitemarsh Seabrook examined this paternalist ethos, and in the process, offered a way to understand how the slaves' economy fit into enslavers' paternalist imagination. Seabrook articulated the idea that plantations in the slaveholding South were guided by enslavers' visions of justice and order. He declared, "Every plantation represents a little community differing from its chief in colour, habits and general character. The members of this community are his lawful property."[22] As an enslaver, Seabrook envisioned himself as lord and protector of his human property as he exercised "executive, legislative, and judicial powers" over enslaved peoples' lives.[23] Seabrook voiced the maxim that individual plantations were little communities, each unique in their own way, and guided by each slaveholder's individual vision. Above all, as an enslaver, he argued that South Carolina's laws protected the master–slave relationship from outside intervention. This protection allowed enslavers to dictate how they managed their slaves' lives, including the extent to which they supported—and controlled—the slaves' trade and other wage-earning pursuits.[24]

The experiences of poor whites, however, presents a different story about the place of the slaves' economy in antebellum South Carolina's culture of slavery. The historian Keri Leigh Merritt has proposed that the poorest whites in the late-antebellum South lived closer in material lifestyle to enslaved people than propertied and elite whites.[25] It was not uncommon for the poorest whites to rely on the illegal trade with enslaved people for their own survival. This was particularly true for poor and single white women. On December 12, 1853, two poor white women, Jemina and Sarah Woodward, traded with an enslaved woman named Bet for "flour and some meat."[26] A year later, on August 21, 1854, Mary Lawson, a widow, bought a piece of beef from an enslaved man named Sam.[27] Surely the white women would not have conducted the transactions with Bet and Sam if not out of necessity and perhaps proximity. The reality of poverty for both enslaved people and poor whites complicates the political discourse taking place around the slaves' economy in South Carolina culture. The poorest whites were consistently looking to enslaved people as trading partners, to buy or barter for necessary commodities such as food. Perhaps for the Woodwards and Lawson, the trade with enslaved people was the difference between satiation and hunger.

Merchants and storekeepers—members of the southern middle class—also benefitted from their trade with bondspeople in the 1840s and 1850s. They maintained a consistent flow of enslaved customers, with enslaved people looking to make as much as possible from their illicit trades.[28] On December 21, 1841, Matthew Hartford sold three and a half pints of whiskey to an enslaved man named Joe. Joe brought thirty-two pounds of cotton to Hartford's shop under the cover of darkness, presumably to shroud their illicit dealing. Then a negotiation took place. Hartford offered Joe $2.00 for his cotton, but the money would be in store credit. Joe objected. He wanted something tangible for the cotton that he brought illegally to Hartford's store. Instead, Joe told Hartford that in addition to store credit, he wanted whiskey and tobacco. Hartford agreed and Joe left Hartford's store with whiskey and tobacco in hand.[29] Hartford undersold the value of Joe's cotton, gaining between $4.00 and $7.00 in the exchange. With cotton selling from 2.6 cents to nearly 3.4 cents per pound in December 1842, Joe's cotton could have fetched much more than he received in store, credit, whiskey, and tobacco from Hartford.[30] Hartford, as a businessman, would not have wanted lawmakers to further limit what had surely become a lucrative source of profit that provided his business with economic buoyancy. Even though Joe might have sold Hartford stolen cotton, it is possible that Joe believed that he was well within his right to sell a product that he cultivated. Hartford was happy to oblige.

Merchants were eager to sell to and barter with enslaved people, and in the process, thumbed their noses at fellow white citizens who opposed their trade with slaves. One Union District storekeeper was notorious. Joshua Petty was infamous for his ongoing illicit trade with the region's bondspeople. On no less than three occasions between 1845 and 1853, he was indicted by the Union District criminal court for "Negro trading," specifically buying corn from enslaved people in exchange for whiskey and cotton cloth.[31] Though there is no evidence of the enslaved people being charged with a crime, the threat of jail and fines did not deter Petty. The frequency of his appearance before local magistrates suggests that he believed that illegal commodity exchange with slaves was worth the cost.

It was within this context of poor and middling whites trading with bondspeople that there was no singular white perspective on the slaves' trade. Yet groups of white citizens bombarded lawmakers with complaints about the trade in the late antebellum era. They levied a variety of criticisms, from the mundane to the grandiose. Charleston District residents complained in 1852 about the "unlawful traffic with slaves," which included whites who seduced enslaved people into "crimes and practices, calculated to destroy them."[32] In 1849, citizens of the Lexington District brought attention to not only "illicit trading with slaves," but also whites and enslaved blacks gambling.[33] The main concern of voters in the Union District in 1857 was for lawmakers to "suppress the illicit trafficking, trading and dealing with slaves and free persons of color, and for selling them spirituous liquors."[34] White citizens, including mechanics groups and members of local agricultural societies, sent a total of forty-one requests to state lawmakers between 1840 and 1860, asking them to make the laws to regulate the slaves' trade stronger. But in their correspondences, the petitioners revealed that they were struggling with two competing ideas. Either the legal instruments created by lawmakers—and supported by enslavers—beginning in the colonial period to regulate the slaves' economy were ineffective, or they worked as they were designed to. And it is clear that there were sections of the white populace who were eager to ensure that the slaves' trade would remain intact.

In the midst of the ongoing political debates about enslaved enterprise, enslaver control, and whites enabling "Negro trading," the slaves' economy persisted. Enslaved people sought out opportunities to engage in commodity exchange and self-hire with such frequency that one could assume that they were not concerned with the ramifications—from their enslavers or from other whites emboldened to challenge their economic endeavors. The best evidence available from the 1840s and 1850s comes from district court records, and the best records available are from the Anderson District. Between 1840 and 1860, out of the 318 cases brought before the Anderson District Court of Magistrates and Freeholders, 245 cases—or 77 percent—involved economic crimes such as theft, illegal trading, or gambling. The records show that the slave's trade continued to flourish. From an enslaved man named Jesse selling whiskey to another bondsman in 1856 to enslaved men Charles, Carter, Ned and Aaron in 1844 selling stolen liquor at a religious meeting, enslaved people were adept at creating avenues through which to engage as active participants in their local economies.[35]

For whites who opposed enslaved peoples' market ambitions, however, they believed that the slaves' economy would not only continue to threaten, but would ultimately destroy, the foundation of white supremacy in southern slave society. They posited that when bondspeople had access to money and property, then bondspeople would also have access to power. In 1840, 168 residents of the Union District wanted the passage of a law that would have prohibiting whites from bequeathing property to enslaved people in wills. "Give the slave money or property, which is its equivalent and you place it in the power at once to place himself beyond the reach of servitude—'money is power' and none need live in servitude who can command it."[36] The petitioners urged lawmakers to prevent enslaved people from inheriting property, a move that they believed would prevent bondspeople from attaining too much power and perhaps too much influence within South Carolina slave society. While the petitioners were making an argument that may have resonated with whites who believed in the equivalence between money and power, enslaved people—and enslavers as well—had a fundamentally different understanding of the connections between money, property, and real power. By the antebellum era enslavers had come to recognize the economic benefits of enslaved peoples' economic ambitions. The slaves' economy had fully become part of their investments in slavery. Enslaved people, however, understood that their economies of commodity exchange and wage labor were part of a larger system designed to keep them subservient and enslaved.

Enslaved women and men had come to terms with the bounds of their investments of time and energy into their own economic endeavors. They understood what their economic activities could and could not do for them. Commodity exchange, overwork, and even self-hire could give them the purchasing power to buy bacon, tobacco, liquor, clothing, and shoes. However, more than anyone else within South Carolina's slave society, enslaved people grasped that money did not equal power. Former bondsman Henry Ryan noted that as an enslaved boy, he and other bondspeople enslaved on Judge Pickens Butler's Edgefield District plantation used Saturday afternoons to tend their "patches of ground" during the time that they had free from plantation work. According to Ryan, "Judge Butler used to give us a little money, too, before freedom came, for our work."[37] With the money, he would purchase clothing "and things we had to have."[38] Ryan's earnings were limited, however. As a young boy of five or six years old at the outbreak of the Civil War, he could only earn enough from Butler to buy necessities, not his own liberation. Access to money and goods could only do so much for enslaved people, especially the small amounts that they received in wages. Though they had access to a modicum of money, they did not possess the social, economic, or legal power necessary to buy themselves out of slavery. What they had access to was consumer goods and items that they needed to live.[39] For bondspeople, having economic rights did not translate into legal rights or freedom.

What enslaved people could gain through their enterprising and entrepreneurial pursuits was mobility. They exploited opportunities to move around as freely as possible, and in the process, they understood that freedom of movement could be commodified as well. Enslaved people cultivated a familiarity with the various riverways and roadways, especially in the Lowcountry. They would construct roughly hewn boats and in their free time, transport goods and people along the interconnected river system that characterized the Lowcountry landscape. Runaway bondsman John Andrew Jackson described how he paid twenty cents to another enslaved man to transport him and his horse cross the Santee River. He revealed, "The negro who kept that ferry, was allowed to keep for himself all the money he took on Christmas day, and as this was Christmas day, he was only too glad to get my money and ask no questions; so I paid twenty cents, and he put me and my pony across the main gulf of the river."[40] The enslaved man fulfilled a niche and in the process earned money by transporting anyone—even runaway slaves—across the river.

White residents of St. James Santee responded to the types of economic extracurricular activities described by John Andrew Jackson. In May 1840, a group of "owners, agents, and consignees o [*sic*] boats and vessels navigating the Santee River and its branches" asked their local magistrate, C. C. Pinckney, to publish a public request in the *Camden Journal*, a Kershaw District newspaper. Though Pinckney expressed a different perspective on enslaved peoples' trading activities with other enslavers, he complied with the request of the white residents that he represented. The white boat owners who regularly navigated the local river systems wanted to prevent enslaved people from conducting their independent business on the rivers.[41] Perhaps the boat owners understood that enslaved people were using the intricate river systems to usher one another closer to freedom.

Local agricultural societies also began highlighting local failures to limit bondspeoples' engagement in trade and local failures to prosecute whites who openly traded with bondspeople.[42] One such organization was the Monticello Planter's Society, founded by a group of Fairfield District planters in 1837. Their goals were threefold. The Society's first objective was to "put down the illicit traffic of white persons with negroes."[43] Above all, the Society's concerns revolved around convincing Fairfield District planters to regulate interracial trade. The second goal was to "arrest all immoral practices hostile to our slave interests, and secure that quietude and harmony in their government most conducive to their happiness and our welfare."[44] Third, they hoped to rally public and private support for "experiments on agricultural products."[45]

In the three years after the founding of the Monticello Planters' Society, the organization moved away from their primary objective of regulating trade between whites and blacks. Their attempts to curb "illicit traffic in cotton, corn . . . between several white persons and our slaves" had, in their words, proved successful.[46] Instead, the Society shifted their efforts toward lobbying state legislators on behalf of planters' agricultural interests. Perhaps enslavers' influence in this organization—and the suspicion planters harbored regarding interlopers' attempts to regulate the master–slave relationship—caused a shift in the Society's mission.

In similar fashion, white residents of the Edgefield and Barnwell Districts established the Savannah River Anti-Slave Traffick Association in

1846. The association's primary goal was the extralegal regulation of interactions between black slaves and whites. The members believed that enslaved people residing in their districts had undergone a "visible change" in the years leading up to the association's founding. Before this pivotal period, they believed that enslaved people understood their role within the slaveholding "family." From their perspective, they maintained:

> Formerly, slaves were essentially members of the family to which they belonged, and the reciprocal interest and attachment existing between them, their relations were simple, agreeable, easily maintained, and mutually beneficial: But now masters and slaves are beginning to look upon each other as natural enemies, and the result is mutual distrust, harsh yet efficient discipline on the one hand, sullenness, discontent, and growing depravity on the other.[47]

This change in enslaved peoples' behavior, they declared, threatened to upend the social stability that existed between whites and blacks that had become the foundation of South Carolina's culture of slavery. With politician and planter James Henry Hammond at the helm, they argued that social "evils resulted from two causes": enslaver negligence in controlling the behavior and actions of bondspeople and the increased trade in "spirituous liquors" between enslaved people and white vendors. The association's primary aims evolve to including curtailing the "unlawful negro trading" and to provide extralegal reinforcements for the regulation of such trade.[48]

The Savannah River Anti-Slave Traffick Association members asserted that enslaved people engaged in their own trade neglected their primary work responsibilities, which in turn threatened enslavers' profits. Members believed that when enslavers gave enslaved women and men the latitude to engage in entrepreneurial pursuits, enslaved people were less productive because they were not dedicated to their enslaver's work. They asserted that when enslaved people worked for themselves, with their enslaver's permission, they were "seriously impaired in physical qualities" and their minds were "fatally corrupted."[49] The association, therefore, made enslavers culpable and pointed to their lax outlook regarding the regulation of their enslaved labor force. In this criticism, they shifted blame to enslavers whose negligence ultimately legitimized enslaved enterprises, thereby threatening the safety of whites. These dissatisfied residents publicly fulminated against whites who purchased illegal goods from bondspeople, and bondspeople who earned money selling goods to whites and hiring out their own time.

The Savannah River Anti-Traffick Association struggled, however, to garner public support for their ambitious plan to rid the district of so-called illicit trafficking. It is possible that enslaved peoples' trading networks were so expansive, and had become such a crucial aspect of economic life for whites in the Savannah River area, that few people willingly supported their proposals. Three years after the association was founded, members of the Committee of Safety and Vigilance for the Edgefield District held a public meeting on April 19, 1849 to discuss the recent string of enslaved peoples' display of insubordination. In an overly paternalistic tone, the Committee's representative wrote in the *Edgefield Advertiser* that enslavers had been failing to govern and discipline their slaves for reckless exhibitions of autonomy. "'Spare the rod and you spoil your negroes," this representative asserted as a call to action. Enslaved people had been openly participating in illegal networks of trade and traffick and members of the Committee believed that such economic behavior, if continued, it would lead to more serious crimes committed by enslaved people, including murder and insurrection.[50] Members of vigilance societies were responding to the public display of economic activity that enslaved people and whites had undertaken in the 1840s and 1850s. If the levels of white support for the slaves' economy from the top-down and from the bottom-up were any indication, then they had a very difficult time convincing a wide swath of white South Carolinians that enslaved enterprise was unnecessary and pernicious.

During the antebellum period enslaved people were influenced by enslavers' sense of the growing economic and political tensions brewing in not only the state, but in the country as a whole. Enslavers used such tensions to think more critically about maintaining their financial interests in slavery through a supposedly gentler form of slaveholding. The discourse of slaveholders' mastery over enslaved people slowly shifted in the antebellum period as enslavers began adopting the language of paternalism and domestication to argue for a more ameliorative form of slave control.[51] In 1838, one Darlington enslaver wrote that he understood the importance of slave management to his plantation's fiscal success. In a departure from enslavers of previous generations, he claimed to have recognized that "the management of negroes is a matter of much higher importance than is generally understood or practiced."[52] In an effort to enjoy the economic and social benefits of their planter status—and to push back against abolitionist calls about their inhumanity—enslavers began "reconfiguring," as historian Lacy Ford has claimed, their ideological stance on mastery and slaveholding.

Yet just because enslavers were revising their ideas about the relationship between mastery and the slaves' economy did not mean that enslaved people were not on the receiving end of enslaver violence. In these instances, it was violence cloaked in a velvet glove of money and coercion. Enslavers wielded ultimate control over enslaved peoples' market ambitions as they encouraged bondspeople to find productive ways to use their limited free time—usually in a way that ultimately benefited enslavers themselves. As a bondsman, Richard Jones and his fellow bondspeople would sell their independently produced corn to their enslaver, Jim Gist, who owned sixteen plantations around the Union District. He detailed, "We made corn and sold it to our master for whatever he give us fer it."[53] They received money from Gist for their independently cultivated corn and the bondspeople used the money to buy a variety of goods. "All de use we had fer money," Jones disclosed, "was to buy fish hooks, barlows, juice harps and marbles."[54] Not only did Jones and the other enslaved people receive money from Gist for their corn, but Gist would give enslaved people money as gifts three times per year, at Thanksgiving, Christmas, and the Fourth of July. Jones noted that Gist would throw coins to the enslaved children, while he flung five- and ten-dollar bills to the enslaved adults. "I ain't never seed [*sic*] so much money," he recalled, "since my marster been gone."[55] What Jones does not explore was how his experience with Gist's seeming largess may have been a result of Gist's efforts to control the enslaved people that he owned. Jones's enslaver might have used a small sum of money to buy enslaved peoples' compliance and to discourage them from running away. It was a relatively small investment for a larger payoff. After all, five- and ten-dollar bills alone could not secure for enslaved people what they desired above all: protection, security, and freedom.

Access alone did not provide enslaved people a path to freedom. Bondspeople had access to cash through their trades with whites and their exchange with enslavers. Enslaved people on the Cedar Grove plantation sold their independently grown corn to enslaver John Willson and Willson began recording the exchanges in October 1848. Forty-two bondspeople received compensation from Willson, more than half of the enslaved population on Cedar Grove. Between 1848 and 1858, they sold foodstuff such as corn and potatoes and bacon from pigs that they tended to Willson on numerous occasions. In return Willson compensated them not in goods, but in cash. In 1849 an enslaved woman, Winter, collected $3.00 from Willson in addition to receiving a cash advance of $20.00. In 1850, Winter received another cash advance in the amount of $5.00. Furthermore, eleven enslaved people traveled to Charleston with between $0.62 and $8.81, presumably to spend as they pleased in the city. In addition to corn, bondspeople sold Willson a variety of foodstuff. They cultivated potatoes and maintained livestock such as hogs and sheep. In 1858, eight bondspeople—two women and six men—sold their sheep to Willson for $1.50 each.[56] Though Willson kept an accounting of the trade and enslaved people procured goods from him on credit, the forty-two enslaved people had to continue the arduous and backbreaking pace of extra work to earn even a modicum of money for their labor.

Bondspeople were also aware of how the cycles of credit and debt influenced their lives, as historian Bonnie Martin has considered.[57] Not only did they understand that their bodies and their lives were being mortgaged by enslavers and slave traders, but they also came to understand how they could use the credit and debt cycle on a smaller scale, to their own advantage. Enslaved people in the Newberry District patronized a local merchant to fulfill their material wants and needs in the late 1850s. An enslaved man named Edward made several purchases between 1857 and 1859. On May 30, 1857, Edward used cash to purchase a pair of shoes, a hat, and molasses from this merchant. He also obtained a bucket, coffee, and sugar. But to procure these items, he did not present money at this exchange. Instead, he received these goods on credit. Between July and November 1857 Edward bought tobacco, candles, cloth, and a handkerchief. At the end of the year his purchase totaled $32.45, including a

$1.55 interest charge. Edward's buying trend continued in 1858 and 1859. He bought tobacco, coffee, shoes, clothing, ginger, and sugar over the three-year period. Edward sometimes paid in cash, and other times obtained these items on credit.[58]

Enslaved people learned the lesson that access to credit, money, and property did not equal freedom early in their lives. They were inculcated quickly into the daily life of American capitalism, absorbing lessons about money and work from their interactions with enslavers. Aaron Ford's first memory of work was holding mules and hauling away goods for his enslaver. "If people wanted any haulin done," he recalled, "he told me to help dem en collect for it."[59] Ford also used the time at his disposal to complete work on his own, for compensation. His enslaver did not ask if anyone paid him for his services and Ford never surrendered that information. His enslaver let him keep any money that he earned. With his earnings he bought cloth and he bought a girl that he liked $0.10 worth of candy.[60] Ford, however, must have understood that the small amount of money that he was making would never allow him to buy anything other than small trinkets or candy. His enslaver relied on this mindset.

While enslavers relied on enslaved peoples' overwork to bring them more cotton and other exchangeable commodities in the antebellum period, enslaved people attempted to take advantage of this reliance to earn money and buy goods through enslavers' systems of incentives.[61] On the Mars Bluff plantation in the Darlington District, enslaved people sold goods to enslaver Peter Bacot, who tracked this trade his plantation's "Negro account" book. The account book outlined bondspeoples' names, the items purchased, the goods they sold to Bacot, and slaves' yearly account balances. In 1860, enslaved man Abram sold forty-seven pounds of cotton to Bacot. In exchange, Abram received a mere $1.00. In the Charleston marketplace in 1860, short-staple cotton sold for between $0.10 and $0.12 per pound. This meant that Abram's cotton could have fetched between a total of $4.70 to $5.52.[62] Between 1858 and 1860, Bacot paid Abram for his abundant cotton harvesting efforts, and with this compensation, Abram purchased a pair of "sundry shoes" for $1.75 in September 1858 and other pieces of clothing later that year.[63]

In the 1840s and 1850s, some enslaved people were becoming accustomed to the ways in which accounting worked in their own lives.

Bondspeople on Mars Bluff grew accustomed to selling their livestock to Bacot and in turn, Bacot maintained an account with Charles & Milling, a local Darlington general store. This financial relationship between the slaves and Bacot transferred to Charles & Milling. Bondspeoples' patronage of this local store supported the local merchants and Bacot acquired livestock at reasonable prices from his slaves. Bondspeople purchased a variety of items from Charles & Milling, including flour, shoes, slave cloth, molasses, coffee, and tobacco. A few enslaved people even procured liquor. A July 16, 1859 entry detailed that Jack paid cash for a quart of whiskey. In exchange, Bacot "bought a sow from Jack for $5.00," for which he paid Jack $3.00. Presumably, Jack's whiskey cost him $2.00 and his sow settled the liquor's expense. Despite laws that prohibited slaves from possessing alcoholic beverages—and forbade whites from selling such items to them—bondspeople exploited the few tools at their disposal to procure unlawful goods. Jack utilized his economic relationship with Bacot to procure an illicit substance.[64]

Though bondspeople at Mars Bluff decided to purchase luxury items, such as whiskey or tobacco, others used their purchasing power to buy everyday material necessities. In 1858 an enslaved woman, Abbey, purchased six yards of cotton oznaburg for $0.75. In exchange, Abbey sold Bacot six chickens for $0.75. Similarly, Gus utilized Bacot's accounting system frequently between 1856 and 1860. In 1856, Gus purchased one pair of women's shoes for $1.40 and one pair of pants in 1857 for $2.50. In 1860, he bought two pairs of shoes for himself and a pair for his wife. In 1857, Gus received $2.50 in compensation for his crop.[65]

As demonstrated with Abbey and Gus, enslaved people obtained items that slaveholders did not regularly provide for them. The most common items that bondspeople acquired were clothing and shoes. Second to garments were food products such as sugar and molasses. Though many enslavers purchased and handed out clothing to enslaved people on a yearly basis, most slave clothing was made of "Negro cloth," a course and low-grade woolen manufactured in New England factories that historian Seth Rockman reveals rarely protected its wearers against the harsh summer or winter temperatures. Similarly, most enslavers distributed subsistence rations weekly.[66] Bacot's trade with Abbey and Gus suggests that he did not fully provide material necessities for his slaves. One could surmise that Bacot intentionally short-changed slaves with whom he traded to reap the pecuniary benefits of bartering with those who had no legal recourse against him.

When one considers the price at which the enslaved people owned by Bacot were compensated, it is clear that he did not pay them market value for their cotton. For example, in 1860 Bacot paid Colón $12.20 for picking 488 pounds of cotton. Colon received approximately $0.02 per pound. By contrast, in 1860, South Carolina short-staple cotton sold for between $0.10 and $0.20 per pound in Columbia and Charleston.[67] Therefore, Bacot earned between $0.08 and $0.18 per extra pound of cotton harvested by his slaves. Enslavers like Bacot continued to exploit enslaved peoples' interest in earning even meager remuneration to increase their own profits.

Ultimately, enslaved people valued specific items and used their free time to purchase material goods that planters were not providing. Bondspeople owned by Darlington District rice planter Thomas Cassels Law worked to purchase goods that they needed. In 1859 and 1860, twenty-seven bondspeople sold cotton to Law and, in turn, bought goods from him. Hannah, for example, sold Law 540 pounds of cotton and in return Law paid her $5.40. She then purchased a list of goods with her earnings, including sugar and molasses, as well as a pot, calico, homespun, thread, and handkerchiefs.[68]

Many enslavers emphasized their efforts to prevent temptation and mischief among enslaved people as a reason for encouraging (and coercing) bondsmen and women to spend their free time dedicated to economically productive pursuits. Yet some enslavers struggled with articulating their ideas about enslaved peoples' independent economic work because when they conveyed their support of slave economies, they often related slaves' industriousness in self-serving activities as a benefit to the slaveholder. Of course, this logic revolved around enslaver profits through enslaved peoples' productivity. An example of this rationale can be found in an 1852 speech before the Darlington Agricultural Association given by Thomas Law, in which he maintained that "strict discipline" and work in moderation would keep slaves productive. On the other hand, he did not believe that moderating slaves' work schedules and discipline were mutually exclusive. Law stated that he allowed his slaves to "have a small crop," and that he would always purchase what his slaves had to sell because such practices kept slaves happy, safe, and above all else, productive. This practice, Law explained, prevented slaves from "trading with unprincipled men" and "getting into mischief" while enjoying their unscheduled free time.

Law echoed fellow planters who agreed to purchase his slaves' goods at "the highest market price," whether he needed the goods or not. He believed that this system encouraged enslaved people to trust that their masters were "doing them justice."[69] Despite the fears that Law expressed about the connection between slave mischief and free time, he ultimately supported a system of plantation management that privileged his own economic well-being over the physical and emotional well-being of enslaved people on his plantations. He echoed the paternalist language of his fellow enslavers, one that included protecting enslaved people from corrupt merchants while shunning market principles to purchase enslaved peoples' independent produced goods at fair market price. In espousing these ideas, Law overshadows the harsh realities that defined enslaved peoples' lived experiences in antebellum South Carolina and the ways in which he constantly profited from his slaves' labor, even their independent economic pursuits.[70]

In a departure from enslavers of generations past, enslavers in the late antebellum era used enslaved peoples' engagement in small-scale market activities to prove to northern abolitionists that they approached slave management in a thoughtful way. Enslaver Ben Sparkman shrouded his profit-making intentions in rhetoric against northern agitators. In a March 1858 letter to fellow Lowcountrty planter Benjamin Allston, Sparkman claimed that northerners had been intent on mischaracterizing the ways in which Southern slaveholders treated enslaved people. Sparkman declared, "Such questions have repeatedly been propounded to me at the North by persons whose general acquirements and intelligence are noted but who really have fancied Slavery such a monster that no ordinary declaration of humanity and kindness and happiness etc. at the South will be received with any credulity whatever."[71]

At one point, Sparkman described how the task system functioned: how work and material allowances made for pregnant slaves; the way in which enslaved peoples' typical food and clothing allowances were allocated; how slave houses were manufactured; and the medical attention that sick slaves received from doctors. Sparkman used opportunities to present formalized ideas about plantation and slave management to communicate to other enslavers and northern abolitionist firebrands about his "benevolent" approach to running a productive plantation. The comforts that enslaved people enjoyed, according to Sparkman, revolved around the latitude that he gave them to sell goods. In the previous year, enslaved people had sold him approximately $130 in goods such as hogs, eggs, poultry, and provisions. In return, the enslaved people received a variety of items, including handkerchiefs, sugar, molasses, cloth, and hats. Sparkman's explanation—that he encouraged exchange between himself and bondspeople—suggests that he adopted a perspective of slave productivity that revolved around mutual dependence; he depended on enslaved people for their independent production and the bondspeople relied on the money earned from this production to purchase their own goods.

Yet one must question if Sparkman considered the idea of fair price and fair value. Sparkman does not mention if he offered market price for slave-produced goods. He does articulate that he engaged in this type of trade as a way to compel slave productivity and prevent enslaved people from absconding. Both were problems that proved expensive for Sparkman—or any slaveholder for that matter—to remedy.[72] After all, his primary goal was to protect his investment in slaves. He did not see the slaves' economy as being at odds with his standing as a member of the enslaving elite. Rather, he believed that if allowing enslaved people he owned to trade would accomplish his financial goals, then he would do it.

As Sparkman corresponded with Benjamin Allston about the economic benefits of internal plantation trade between enslavers and enslaved people, so too did Benjamin Allston's father with a fellow acquaintance. In March 1858, Robert F. W. Allston, Georgetown District's Chicora Wood rice plantation proprietor, received a letter from itinerant physician Dr. J. W. Gibbs, in which Gibbs relayed to the then-South Carolina governor his "experience in relation to the economy and medical management of plantations in the neighborhood of Columbia."[73] Gibbs revealed that the most prosperous and productive plantations shared common features, one of which was the sale of commodities by enslaved people to their enslavers. He argued that in addition to receiving weekly rations of bacon, molasses, and potatoes, the most "industrious" bondspeople maintained gardens as well as livestock, which proved to be "sources of comforts as well as profit."[74] Dr. Gibbs noted, "Eggs and chickens are supplied by them in large numbers to their owners, who pay them their full value, or to neighbors."[75] Gibbs even affirmed that one enslaved man earned $150 in one year from selling corn and fodder to his enslaver. All of this economic activity proved to him that "there is no class of working people in the world better cared for than the Southern slave."[76] While Gibbs wrote about the ways in which enslavers kept enslaved people productive, what he observed was a system in which enslavers forced enslaved people to behave as capitalists to survive.

Robert Allston took Gibbs's ideas into consideration, and in 1859 enslaved people on Allston's Lowcountry rice plantation began trading with him. During his two-year absence from Chicora Wood, during which time he served as South Carolina's governor, he believed that enslaved people had "taken possession" of his prized stock of hogs. This meant that enslaved people on Chicora Wood had been tending to, caring for, and killing the hogs for their own consumption. Allston therefore decided to embark on an experiment: allowing his slaves to raise and sell the hogs to him. Every head of family would be allowed to keep one hog. And for every one hundred pounds the enslaved head of family would receive $5, which constituted $0.05 per pound. However, Allston included a caveat in this arrangement. Enslaved people were not permitted to sell any hogs to any purchaser outside of the plantation without the written consent from Allston himself or the overseer. Any bondsperson who violated this agreement would forfeit the privilege of earning money and be subjected to punishment.[77] Two enslaved people on Chicora Wood did in fact receive payment from Allston, as his agreement stipulated. In December 1859, Jacky earned $7 and in early 1860, Boston, received $11.00 for a 220 pound "fat hog."[78] In the end, the enslaved people on Chicora Wood lost the privilege of selecting their trading partners and Allston benefited from relying on his slaves for livestock at reasonable prices.

Even as many enslavers increased their dedication to trade with enslaved people, in this environment other slaveholders expressed ideas about the slaves' economy that diverged from their counterparts. In 1854, members of the Agricultural Society of St. Paul's Parish expressed their concerns over the "inefficiency of the Law against hireing [*sic*] without the assent or Knowledge of the Owners." The members who signed onto the petition were Lowcountry slaveholders, including J. B. Grimbal,

William Brisbane, George Morris, and J. Mathews Sr. Each signer owned large-scale rice or cotton plantations with Mathews leading the group, owning 270 slaves.[79] The agricultural society members believed that the laws failed to regulate slave hiring and were not successful at prosecuting people harboring runaways in their parish.[80] To persuade lawmakers, the members provided three examples to further illuminate the social problems involving slaves that they sought to restrict.

The first example described an experience of one of their members, William Westcoat. An enslaved man belonging to Westcoat absconded to Charleston in the spring of that year, boarded a vessel, and never returned. Later that fall, a bondsman with skills as a carpenter fled for Charleston and boarded a ship to Europe. In both instances, the enslaved men had hired themselves out to free people of color with no official documentation from Westcoat substantiating the terms of their employment. Westcoat brought both cases before local magistrates. However, the magistrates responded that Westcoat did not prove "that the person hiring was aware that his slaves were runaways."[81] Therefore, he did not find the legal redress for which he had hoped.

Enslaver and agricultural society member J. Fraser Mathews provided the second vignette. Mathews, a rice and cotton planter from St. Bartholomew's parish, traveled to Charleston in 1852 to capture an enslaved woman and her two children. The woman escaped with her children three years prior and had been living in Charleston under the auspices of being hired out by Mathews. A free woman of color had employed her during her five-year absence from Mathews's plantation. A local jury tried the unnamed free woman of color and, according to Mathews, the presiding magistrate told the jury that they could not convict her if they believed that she was unaware that the enslaved woman was a runaway. The jury acquitted the free woman of color, an outcome that failed to satisfy Mathews.[82]

Finally, planter John Berkeley Grimbal included an anecdote of his own. He relayed a story of white ship captains cruising the Pon Pon River, picking up enslaved blacks and paying them to load gravel purchased in Charleston upon their ships. All this, he added, took place without enslavers' knowledge or permission. Such activities proved to be "a laborious task," and the time that slaves spent making money for themselves "[ought] to be devoted to rest."[83] Grimbal offered this anecdote as a warning to lawmakers. He was conveying that without lawmakers' intervention, enslaved people would continue seeking out opportunities to make money. The problem was not enslaved peoples' search for trading partners, he contended. After all, bondspeople had been negotiating with their masters for such privileges since the colonial period. The problem, as Grimbal perceived it, was when enslaved people engaged in trading activities without their master's permission. Such endeavors negatively influenced slaveholders' profits because when slaves engaged in unsanctioned work for profit, they failed to be productive for their enslavers.

The St. Paul's Agricultural Society did not make a direct request for lawmakers to revise state statutes that regulated slave hiring. Nor did they ask for stronger institutional support to find runaway slaves and prosecute those that offered them protection. In a departure from other petitioners, the agricultural society members simply asked lawmakers to consider their specific cases in hopes that legislative intervention would offer better results than had local magistrates.

Ardent fire-eater and *Charleston Mercury* owner Robert Barnwell Rhett, however, took a different route. Rhett dedicated an editorial in November 1859 to condemning the "two great evils" that plagued Southern states: enslaved people engaged in illicit trafficking, and abolition. In an essay titled "Measures of Securing Southern Safety," Rhett argued that an "efficient police and the vigilance of slave owners" would be the only way to suppress slaves' search for people with whom to trade. Ultimately, he connected enslaved peoples' economic independence to an abolitionist ideology that threatened the very existence of Southerners' way of life.[84]

Journalist Frederick Law Olmsted observed the prevalence of trade between bondspeople and enslavers during his travels to the slaveholding South in 1853. Olmsted, with a hint of surprise, witnessed enslaved peoples' dedication to accumulating small amounts of money through selling their independently produced goods to their enslavers. "They are at liberty to sell whatever they choose from the products of their own garden and to make what they can by keeping swine and fowls," Olmsted revealed of enslaved people on a Lowcountry rice plantation.[85] "Mr. X.'s family have no other supply of poultry and eggs than what is obtained by purchase from his own negroes; they frequently, also, purchase game from them." In this excerpt from *A Journey in the Seaboard States*, Olmsted recognized that the economic relationships between enslaved people and slave owners in South Carolina were symbiotic, and that enslaved people earned money from selling subsistence goods to their enslavers. However, Olmsted also depicted the ways in which slaveholders exploited slaves' need to cultivate their own food. By purchasing goods from enslaved people that he owned, Mr. X relieved himself of the financial burden of providing them with subsistence.[86] The economic activity that Olmsted witnessed had become such an entangled part of the culture of slavery in South Carolina that the subjects of his observation, Mr. X and the enslaved people, appeared to normalize the behavior.

The persistence of trade between bondspeople and their enslavers in the 1840s and 1850s, as exemplified by Mr. X's nonchalance about buying goods from enslaved people, demonstrates that bondspeople were an important part of an unending economic loop in which their labor was co-opted and exploited by those who wanted to extract as much profit from them as possible. When enslaved people spent their so-called leisure time engaged in additional labor, they did so to procure goods they were not receiving from their enslavers. Enslaved people spent their time cultivating food to fill nutritional voids not fulfilled by their masters' provisions, raised livestock for themselves or to sell, and completed extra work for remuneration from their masters or others within their vicinity willing to flout the laws for their own economic benefit.[87]

Meanwhile, by the late 1850s, it was clear that at times, enslaved people acted as capitalists. Bondspeople sold goods in public marketplaces. They engaged in self-hire and competed with white workers for employment. These pursuits were intimately connected to how enslaved people understood their lives in bondage. The reality of how bondspeople approached their economic lives defined how they interacted with their enslavers and how their enslavers interacted with them. Indeed, enslavers expressed few concerns about enslaved peoples' economic activities. They understood that they could further dominate and subjugate enslaved people through controlling their economic enterprises. Despite calls from groups of white South Carolinians who opposed enslaved peoples' economically productive ventures, enslavers and whites who profited from their trade with bondspeople realized that they could protect their investments through incorporating enslaved enterprise into their overall economic plans. Enslavers brought this knowledge with them when South Carolina brought the nation to the brink of war in 1860—and so too did enslaved people.

CONCLUSION

"Freedom Ain't Nothin'": Capitalism and Freedom in the Shadow of Slavery

By the end of December 1860, the enslaved people on the Milling family plantation in Camden must have wondered what South Carolina's declaration of secession meant for them. Specifically, would they receive the money that they had worked for and were owed? On December 18, 1860, their enslaver, Mary Milling, wrote to her husband, James Milling, about money that his father owed to the enslaved people. The elder Milling, David, was in debt for $20 to the bondspeople and she wanted to know when she would receive their money.[1] The enslaved people may have been thinking about their compensation when, on December 20, "the people of South Carolina" declared "that the State of South Carolina has resumed her position among the nations of the world, as a separate and independent State," seceding from the Union, triggering the sectional conflict, and thereafter, the Civil War.[2] It is unknown whether the enslaved people received their payments from the Millings. But by the end of 1860, they must have wondered what the declaration of secession meant for not only the money due to them, but for their livelihoods in general.

Considering the ways in which enslaved peoples' economic activities had been inextricably woven into the culture of slavery in South Carolina, it should not be surprising that during the Civil War, enslaved women and men continued creating economic opportunities for themselves. Perhaps the war made enslaved people and the people with whom they traded even more dependent on bondspeoples' networks of exchange and enterprise because of the economic instabilities wrought by the country's split into Union and Confederate factions. Even as the sectional conflict heated up in 1861 and 1862, enslaved people continued to deploy their economic and trading skills to survive. In August 1862, Abe, an enslaved man in the Union District, sold ten pounds of cotton to Jacob Guyton, a white freeholder, for $1. Abe did not bring a ticket to the transaction with Guyton, but despite the ambiguous legality of the exchange, both parties completed the transaction and went their separate ways.[3] Perhaps Abe used his earnings to buy food or clothing for himself or his family, using the money to protect against wartime unpredictability, acquiring items that would allow him to endure the vagaries of war.

Compelled by their need to survive, enslaved people found avenues through which to continue to invest in their own entrepreneurial and capitalist activities. Though such pursuits provided enslaved men and women with small material benefits, during the Civil War, the slaves' economy took on new meaning. Enslaved people used their networks of exchange to survive the uncertainty and in particular the violence of war. As the Civil War raged on, enslaved people made decisions about their futures based on what they experienced in their pasts. Former bondsman John Franklin detailed that in 1862, "there was such a shortage of food and clothes" that everyone around him experienced deprivation and hunger.[4] In the next year, after the Emancipation Proclamation freed enslaved people in rebellious states, his father left to fight for the Union, leaving him and his mother to remain on their enslaver's plantation. Soon thereafter, his mother decided to claim for herself what Lincoln proclaimed. She took Franklin and left, abandoning their enslaver in the process. They traveled ten miles to his grandfather's home where they subsisted on a variety of food and livestock, while selling what they did not consume. "I was ten years old that year," he recounted, "and we raise[d] corn, beans, 'taters and chickens for ourselves and to sell, when we could go to Columbia and sell it and buy coffee and other things that we could not raise at home."[5] Franklin's mother understood that their survival depended on their ability to successfully provide for themselves through cultivating goods and through selling their products at a profit.

Despite the challenges that the transition from slavery to freedom posed for African Americans, it is important not to underestimate how even the prospect of freedom from bondage must have felt for the formerly enslaved. African Americans gained the autonomy to negotiate contracts and earn real wages, with the hopes of purchasing land and living independently with their families. There was a glimmer of hope in the months before the end of the Civil War. On January 16, 1865, Union General William T. Sherman issued Special Field Order No. 15, which allocated a thirty-mile strip of land from Charleston to St. John's, Florida, "for the settlement of the negroes now made free by the acts of war and the proclamation of the President of the United States."[6] This order had the potential to shift approximately 400,000 acres of land, formerly owned by Confederate slaveholders, to former slaves. The land was divided into forty-acre parcels to be distributed to African American families. Almost immediately, African Americans in the Lowcountry swarmed the coastal regions of the state, eager to claim land for themselves.

However, Sherman's order, and African American's ownership of the land, was short lived. By July 1865, President Andrew Johnson overturned Sherman's directive, returning the land to its former slaveholding Confederate owners.[7] When Johnson rescinded the order, he also destroyed a potential economic boost to African Americans who had enriched their enslavers with their labor, their bodies, and their lives.

Though President Johnson quashed African Americans' property rights, they found other ways to exercise the privileges of their emancipated status. In January 1866, Freedman's Bureau agent Erastus Everson remarked that recently emancipated African Americans in the Lowcountry were willing to work, but only for themselves, for their own subsistence. In fact, they did not want to enter into labor contracts. "I have found generally, that the Freedman upon James, Johns, and Wadmalow Islands," he noted, "are not willing to contract, under any circumstances."[8] The African Americans that Everson encountered in the Lowcountry understood that they did not have to enter into work agreements. Perhaps they were unsure about the federal government's role in divesting them from land that they claimed belonged to them. Their experiences in slavery surely shaped their approach to subsistence farming and provided them with an understanding of their labor's value. Recently emancipated African Americans were inclined to be selective about where and for whom they would work.

Despite these efforts, for formerly enslaved African Americans freedom, or even the prospect of freedom, continued to be fraught. Yes, they went in search of their families and legalized their marriages.[9] They controlled for whom they worked because they wanted to gain full financial benefits from their labor. But what did freedom mean in practice after the end of legal slavery? When the formerly enslaved eighty-three-year-old Ezra Adams of Columbia, South Carolina was interviewed about his experience as an enslaved boy in 1936, he offered unadulterated remarks about the Civil War, about slavery, and about the problem of freedom. Freedpeople, he recalled, "found out dat freedom ain't nothin', 'less you is got somethin' to live on and a place to call home."[10] For some African Americans, the idea of freedom and the reality of freedom were two different experiences. For Adams, because African Americans did not have access to the essential building blocks of wealth in the United States—property and capital—it would be an uphill battle to fully realize the privileges of American citizenship.

According to Adams, African Americans in 1936 were still living with the everyday vestiges of slavery. Despite the ratification of the Thirteenth, Fourteenth, and Fifteenth Amendments—which ended legal slavery, extended American citizenship to African Americans, and gave black men the right to vote—African Americans such as Adams remained skeptical about the privileges of legal freedom.[11] Adams quipped, "Dis livin' on liberty is lak young folks livin' on love after they gits married. It just don't work."[12] Yes, the end of slavery meant that African Americans were legally free from bondage. If the formerly enslaved did not have access to the privileges of American citizenship *and* did not possess governmentally protected rights to build real wealth, then how could they fully exercise the advantages of freedom? According to Adams, freedom for African Americans was overrated. Perhaps Adams had a pessimistic view of freedom because the federal government had not done enough to ensure that African Americans transitioned from slavery to freedom with a full arsenal of federally protected civil and economic rights.[13]

Enslaved men and women learned over the generations the importance of maintaining economic autonomy. Yet they lived in a culture where people within it held ambivalent ideas about enslaved peoples' assertion of economic independence. In the colonial period, African slaves sold goods in Charleston's public marketplace and marketed their wares to anyone willing to purchase them. After the American Revolution, bondspeoples' engagement in trading, selling, buying, and hiring became an important facet of enslavers' involvement in slavery and other capitalist endeavors. As enslavers shifted toward cotton monoculture in the nineteenth century, they tethered enslaved peoples' independent cultivation and trade to the growth of their investments in slavery. This connection between enslavers' exploitative interest in profits and bondspeoples' entrepreneurial activities—even on a small scale—made the slaves' economy an aspect of the growth of the American plantation economy. Enslaved peoples' economic activities, however, remained a tool in their efforts to survive the traumas of bondage.

Whites were complicit economic actors, as enslaved enterprises persisted and evolved in the nineteenth century. Whites traded with, bartered with, and sold goods to local enslaved people. They hired enslaved labors as mechanics and blacksmiths, compensating them in money, often paying them less than similarly skilled white workers. Enslaved enterprises and enslaved peoples' economic interactions with whites were as much a part of the fabric of slavery as rice and cotton. Manipulated by enslavers and merchants who gained financial advantages from their independent economic endeavors, enslaved people traded, sold goods, and earned money for a variety of reasons. However, the most important reason for enslaved peoples' dedication to their own systems of trade and commerce was survival. Bondspeople developed their own economic networks because they wanted to take control of a valuable aspect of their lives. They attempted to provide for themselves and their families within a system that flourished off of their labor. Unfortunately, their economic activities rarely resulted in freedom.

The experience of Isiah Jeffries is an example. Jeffries was ten years old at the start of the Civil War. Before South Carolina seceded from the Union in December 1860, Jeffries lived as an enslaved boy on a cotton plantation in the state's Upcountry. The child of an enslaved woman and her white enslaver, Jeffries grew up taking care of other children on the plantation, then working his way to chopping cotton. His childhood also included waged work and tasks that he completed for his father/enslaver. Jeffries revealed, "I worked fer him to git my first money and he would give me a quarter fer a whole day's work."[14] In those days, he related, "a quarter was a lot of money."[15] As a child, he spent the money on chewing tobacco, a luxury that made him feel like a man. He believed that his compensation was worth the work because during the period of slavery "you did not need much money."[16] Jeffries argued that during the days of legal slavery, everything was provided for enslaved people by their enslavers. Jeffries's experience with earning money for what he may have considered small extravagances such as tobacco surely shaped his memory as an enslaved child. Missing from Jeffries revelation, however, were the ways in which his waged labor kept him tethered to not only his enslaver and father, but to his status as a bondsperson.

Yet if success equals economic freedom through engagement in market enterprises, then enslaved people did not attain either. Even though bondspeople earned small amounts of money and obtained material goods, these were not successes within the structure of American slavery. Simply having the *ability* to earn money and act as consumers did not free enslaved people. Though they may have made their lives a bit better through acquiring goods, the slaves' economy remained a visible aspect of South Carolina's culture of slavery *because* enslaved people could not buy themselves out of slavery. Bondswomen and bondsmen were confined to the exploitative system that defined their daily experiences. Enslavers understood this. They used enslaved peoples' dedication to their own economies to their own advantage. As enslavers allocated an increasing amount of land and capital to cotton cultivation, enslaved people found that their goods were in high demand both from slaveholders and nonslaveholders alike. Thus, enslaved enterprises became more entangled in South Carolina's economy of slavery as enslavers sought to extract as much labor from enslaved people as possible. Though enslaved women and men participated in the economic and consumerist culture that defined eighteenth- and nineteenth-century America, they could rarely transform their economic activity into freedom.

African Americans' place within the American economy has a long history. The intellectual genealogy of racial and economic inequality in America shows that African Americans have had a complicated association with American capitalism, as participants in the economy and as property. The popular notion that Americans can liberate themselves through their dedication to capitalism is fraught. If we look at generations of enslaved people, it is clear that this was not the case.

The economic interactions between enslaved people and enslavers was the precursor to other exploitative labor regimes under which African Americans worked after the end of legal slavery. These experiences shaped how they approached the economic elements of their newly gained freedoms. From sharecropping to prison contract leasing, white capitalists continued to profit off of African Americans' labor. Ultimately, lurking underneath the promise of freedom for African Americans was the reality of continued economic exploitation. The twin engines of racial and economic inequality influenced former bondspeoples' experiences in the period after the Civil War. African Americans understood and had lifetimes' worth of personal experiences with how whites exploited them. They entered the period of legal freedom with fully formed ideas about the limits of their engagement in the American economy. They invested their hard-earned wages into financial institutions such as the Freedman's Bank and Trust, only to have their lives' savings mismanaged by white bankers. Mechanisms created, in theory, to help usher African Americans into the fullness of American life as citizens became the arbiters of African Americans' enduring economic struggles.[17]

The connections between capitalism and freedom have always been tenuous for African Americans. Wages and money alone were not going to solve the social, legal, and economic hurdles that African Americans faced. It is in this way that the vestiges of slavery lingered long after the institution's end. Even though the formerly enslaved brought with them concrete knowledge about how to engage as actors in America's capitalist economy, they had to fight for what they believed rightfully belonged to them. They entered Reconstruction with no capital and no wealth. Despite their eagerness to live with full citizenship, with the hopes of taking advantage of all that American citizenship had to offer, their economic prospects were grim.

Too often, it is easy to connect capitalism to the democratic ideals of economic and political freedom. But if we interrogate the history of both slavery and capitalism, then a different message about both emerges. It becomes clear that enslaved peoples' slow loss of economic autonomy coincided with the capitalist evolution of slavery. If we consider the ways in which enslaved people struggled to survive within an increasingly capitalist economic system and still failed to attain economic or political freedom, then we need to explore how the end of slavery changed African Americans' lives. Moreover, to fully understand why the intersection of racism and capitalism continues to emerge in American discourses about economic inequality, it is important to focus not only on the late nineteenth or twentieth centuries, but on the period of legal slavery, during which the foundations of economic and racial inequality were forged.

NOTES

INTRODUCTION: CAPITALISM IN THE ECONOMIC LIVES OF ENSLAVED PEOPLE

1. *Federal Writers' Project: Slave Narrative Project, Vol. 14, South Carolina, Part 2, Eddington-Hunter*, 1936, manuscript/mixed material, https://www.loc.gov/item/mesn142/. The Federal Writers' Project (FWP) was created in 1935 under the umbrella of the Works Project Administration under the New Deal. The FWP employed writers, teachers, and historians to collect the life stories of Americans from myriad backgrounds, including the formerly enslaved. The FWP interviewers spoke with over 2,000 former slaves between 1936 and 1938. See John W. Blassingame, "Using the Testimony of Ex-Slaves: Approaches and Problems," *Journal of Southern History* 41, no. 4 (1975): 473–492; Jerrold Hirsch, *Portrait of America: A Cultural History of the Federal Writers' Project* (Chapel Hill: University of North Carolina Press, 2003).
2. *Federal Writers' Project: Slave Narrative Project, Vol. 14, South Carolina, Part 2.*
3. I use the terms "slave," "enslaved people," and "bondspeople" interchangeably.
4. Ira Berlin and Philip D. Morgan, *The Slaves' Economy: Independent Production by Slaves in the Americas* (London: Frank Cass, 1991); Ira Berlin and Philip D. Morgan, *Cultivation and Culture: Labor and the Shaping of Slave Life in the Americas* (Charlottesville: University Press of Virginia, 1993); John Campbell, "As 'a Kind of Freeman'? Slaves' Market-Related Activities in the South Carolina Upcountry, 1800–1860," *Slavery & Abolition* 12, no. 1 (1991): 131–169; Jeff Forret, *Race Relations at the Margins: Slaves and Poor Whites in the Antebellum Southern Countryside* (Baton Rouge: Louisiana State University Press, 2006); Kathleen M. Hilliard, *Masters, Slaves, and Exchange: Power's Purchase in the Old South* (New York: Cambridge University Press, 2013); Larry E. Hudson Jr., *To Have and to Hold: Slave Work and Family Life in Antebellum South Carolina* (Athens: University of Georgia Press, 1997); Larry E. Hudson,

"'All That Cash': Work and Status in the Slave Quarters," in *Working Toward Freedom: Slave Society and Domestic Economy in the American South*, ed. Larry E. Hudson Jr. (Rochester, N.Y.: University of Rochester Press, 1994), 77–94; Timothy Lockley, "Trading Encounters Between Non-Elite Whites and African Americans in Savannah, 1790–1860," *Journal of Southern History* 66, no. 1 (2000): 25–48; Lawrence T. McDonnell, "Money Knows No Master: Market Relations and the American Slave Community," in *Developing Dixie: Modernization in a Traditional Society*, ed. Winfred B. Moore Jr., Joseph F. Tripp, and Lyon G. Tyler Jr. (Westport, Conn.: Greenwood 1988), 31–44; Roderick McDonald, *The Economy and Material Culture of Slaves: Goods and Chattels on the Sugar Plantations of Jamaica and Louisiana* (Baton Rouge: Louisiana State University Press, 1993); Philip D. Morgan, *Slave Counterpoint: Black Culture in the Eighteenth-Century Chesapeake and Lowcountry* (Chapel Hill: University of North Carolina Press, 1998); Robert Olwell, *Masters, Slaves, and Subjects: The Culture of Power in the South Carolina Lowcountry, 1740–1790* (Ithaca, N.Y.: Cornell University Press, 1998); Dylan C. Penningroth, *The Claims of Kinfolk: African American Property and Community in the Nineteenth-Century South* (Chapel Hill: University of North Carolina Press, 2003); Loren Schweninger, "Slave Independence and Enterprise in South Carolina, 1782–1865," *South Carolina Historical Magazine* 93 (April 1992): 101–125; Betty Wood, *Women's Work, Men's Work: The Informal Slave Economies of Lowcountry Georgia* (Athens: University of Georgia Press, 1995).

5. *Federal Writers' Project: Slave Narrative Project, Vol. 14, South Carolina, Part 2, Eddington-Hunter.*
6. *Federal Writers' Project: Slave Narrative Project, Vol. 14, South Carolina, Part 2, Eddington-Hunter.*
7. *Federal Writers' Project: Slave Narrative Project, Vol. 14, South Carolina, Part 1, Abrams-Durant*, 1936, manuscript/mixed material, https://www.loc.gov/item/mesn142/.
8. For a discussion of enslaved peoples' lives after the Civil War, especially how sickness and illness affected former slaves, see Jim Downs, *Sick from Freedom: African-American Illness and Suffering During the Civil War and Reconstruction* (New York: Oxford University Press, 2012).
9. In recent years, historians have considered the role of slave traders in the spread and financialization of the domestic slave trade. See Adam Rothman, *Slave Country: American Expansion and the Origins of the Deep South* (Cambridge, Mass.: Harvard University Press, 2007); Calvin Schermerhorn, *The Business of Slavery and the Rise of American Capitalism, 1815–1860* (New Haven, Conn.: Yale University Press, 2015).
10. Enslaved people transformed themselves into "survivalist entrepreneurs," in what the sociologist Robert L. Boyd describes as "persons who start small businesses in response to the need to find an independent means of livelihood." The historian LaShawn Harris also argues that informal work shaped the ways in which African American women in New York City necessarily embraced survivalist entrepreneurship when they created their own underground economies. Though Boyd and Harris examine African American communities in the early twentieth century, their ideas about the informal economy and entrepreneurship can be applied to people of African

descent during the period of legal slavery. Robert L. Boyd, "Survivalist Entrepreneurship Among Urban Blacks During the Great Depression: A Test of the Disadvantage Theory of Business Enterprise," *Social Science Quarterly* 81, no. 4 (2000): 972; LaShawn Harris, *Sex Workers, Psychics, and Numbers Runners: Black Women in New York City's Underground Economy* (Urbana: University of Illinois Press, 2016), 35.

11. See, for example, Robert Fogel and Stanley Engerman, *Time on the Cross: The Economics of American Negro Slavery* (Boston: Little, Brown, 1974); Robert Fogel, *Without Consent or Contract: The Rise and Fall of American Slavery* (New York: Norton, 1989). Fogel and Engerman's economic analysis on the value of slave labor in the antebellum South has remained relevant within the more modern economic history of antebellum slavery. Their arguments about the social and cultural developments in the slaveholding South, namely their claims about slave breeding and sexual exploitation, have been rebutted, often forcefully, by historians. See Herbert Gutman, *Slavery and the Numbers Game: A Critique of Time on the Cross* (Urbana: University of Illinois Press, 1975). The more modern focus on the unpredictability of capitalism as the dominant economic system in the western world offers historians of slavery a useful lens through which to understand the lived experiences of African-descended slaves in the Americas. However, the connections between the history of capitalism and the history of slavery are not new. The historian Eric Williams published his groundbreaking book *Capitalism and Slavery* in 1944. Williams argued, controversially, that slavery in the British sugar islands funded the Industrial Revolution in Britain and that slavery was abolished not for moral reasons, but because the profitability of plantation slavery in the British island colonies of the West Indies had declined. Williams was the first historian to propose a connection between the rise of industrial capitalism and slavery. See Eric Williams, *Capitalism and Slavery* (Chapel Hill: University of North Carolina Press, 1944).
12. For one of the more controversial analyses of the relationship between capitalism and principles of freedom, see Milton Friedman, *Capitalism and Freedom* (Chicago: University of Chicago Press, 1962).
13. Scholars have been shifting their understanding of how ideas of freedom influenced enslaved peoples' daily lives. Instead, historians have become more nuanced in their interpretations of how everyday survival techniques may have been more important to enslaved people than ideas of freedom. For an analysis that locates enslaved peoples' struggles to survive the violence of Atlantic slavery, see Randy M. Browne, *Surviving Slavery in the British Caribbean* (Philadelphia: University of Pennsylvania Press, 2017).
14. Social scientists Louis A. Ferman, Stuart Henry, and Michele Hoyman have argued that these terms may not be useful in helping us understand the scope of the informal economy. Though they were not exploring informal economies in historical context, they do wonder if "distinguishing between the activity and something else is useful. What is gained in clarification may be lost by artificially separating those that are inextricably intertwined." They also contend that the various adjectives to describe the informal economy, even the term "informal," may separate the informal economy

from the formal economy. They suggest that the formal economy and informal economy may be interwoven in important ways. See Louis A. Ferman, Stuart Henry, and Michele Hoyman, "Issues and Prospects for the Study of Informal Economies: Concepts, Research Strategies, and Policy," *Annals of the American Academy of Political and Social Science* 493 (1987): 157.

15. Juliet E. K. Walker was one of the first historians to argue for shifting our perspective on the economic lives of enslaved people in the United States. Walker located African Americans within American business history. She contends, "Blacks, both slave and free, participated in America's antebellum economy as entrepreneurs within the condition of creative capitalists." Juliet E. K. Walker, "Racism, Slavery, and Free Enterprise: Black Entrepreneurship in the United States before the Civil War," *Business History Review* 60, no. 3 (1986): 343. See also Juliet E. K. Walker, *The History of Black Business in America: Capitalism, Race, Entrepreneurship* (Chapel Hill: University of North Carolina Press, 2009).
16. *South Carolina Gazette* (hereafter *SCG*), November 20, 1755.
17. *SCG*, August 12, 1756. "Charlestown" became "Charleston" in 1783, after the Treaty of Paris ended the Revolutionary War. For consistency purposes, I will be using "Charleston" in reference to Charlestown and Charles Town during the period before 1783.
18. *SCG*, August 10, 1765.
19. Ellen Hartigan-O'Connor, *The Ties That Buy: Women and Commerce in Revolutionary America* (Philadelphia: University of Pennsylvania Press, 2009), 46–47.
20. *SCG*, August 10, 1765. For a discussion of enslaved women seeking freedom and refuge in public marketplaces in Jamaica, see Shauna Sweeney, "Market Marronage: Fugitive Women and the Internal Marketing System in Jamaica, 1781–1834," *William and Mary Quarterly* 76, no. 2 (April 2019): 197–222.
21. Walker, "Racism, Slavery, and Free Enterprise," 345.
22. Free blacks in South Carolina were disproportionately located in Charleston and Columbia, especially in the nineteenth century. Moreover, African Americans did appear in the census as slave owners, especially in Charleston during the nineteenth century. Historians such as Larry Koger suggest that a notable percentage "owned" members of their family and that former slaves bought their freedom after the end of the American Revolution. Larry Koger, *Black Slaveowners: Free Black Slave Masters in South Carolina, 1790–1860* (Jefferson, N.C.: McFarland, 1985), 33–36. For a discussion of free blacks in South Carolina, see Ira Berlin, *Slaves Without Masters: The Free Negro in the Antebellum South* (New York: Pantheon, 1974); Michael Johnson and James L. Roark, *Black Masters: A Free Family of Color in the Old South* (New York: Norton, 1984); Bernard Powers, *Black Charlestonians: A Social History, 1822–1885* (Fayetteville: University of Arkansas Press, 1994); David O. Stowell, "The Free Black Population of Columbia, South Carolina in 1860: A Snapshot of Occupation and Personal Wealth," *South Carolina Historical Magazine* 104, no. 1 (2003): 6–24.
23. My argument about enslaved people working within the increasingly capitalist economy of South Carolina is in alignment with Cedric Robinson's idea of "racial capitalism." The slaves' economy evolved in tandem with the South Carolina economy.

Moreover, enslaved peoples' labor was the engine that drove the capitalist development of the South Carolina economy, with enslaved people also working as economic agents within this economy. Robinson contends, "The development, organization, and expansion of capitalist society pursued essentially racialist directions, so too did social ideology. As a material force, then, it could be expected that racialism would inevitably permeate the social structure of emergent capitalism. I have used the term 'racial capitalism' to refer to this development and to the subsequent structure as a historical agency." Cedric J. Robinson, *Black Marxism: The Making of the Black Radical Tradition* (Chapel Hill: University of North Carolina Press, 2000), 2.

24. The pioneering work on the slaves' economy by anthropologists Sidney Mintz and Douglas Hall suggests that the slaves' economy in Jamaica was informal and internal, but influenced the experiences of slaves in important ways. See Sidney Mintz and Douglas Hall, *The Origins of the Jamaican Internal Marketing System*, Yale University Publications in Anthropology, No. 57 (New Haven, Conn.: Yale University, 1960). See also Hilary McD. Beckles, *Natural Rebels: A Social History of Enslaved Women in Barbados* (New Brunswick, N.J.: Rutgers University Press, 1989); Barbara Bush, *Slave Women in Caribbean Society, 1650–1838* (Kingston, Jamaica: Heinemann Caribbean; Bloomington: Indiana University Press, 1990); Lucille Mathurin Mair, *A Historical Study of Women in Jamaica, 1655–1844*, ed. Hilary McD. Beckles and Verene A. Shepherd (Kingston, Jamaica: University of the West Indies Press, 2006); Jennifer L. Morgan, *Laboring Women: Reproduction and Gender in New World Slavery* (Philadelphia: University of Pennsylvania Press, 2004).
25. Peter Wood, *Black Majority: Negroes in Colonial South Carolina from 1670 Through the Stono Rebellion* (New York: Knopf, 1974).
26. U.S. Bureau of the Census, *Historical Statistics of the United States, Colonial Times to 1957* (Washington, D.C., 1960), 13.
27. Max Farrand, *The Records of the Federal Convention of 1787*, 4 vols. (New Haven, Conn.: Yale University Press, 1911), II: 364–365. See also David Brion Davis, *The Problem of Slavery in the Age of Revolution, 1770–1823* (Ithaca, N.Y.: Cornell University Press, 1975), 104–131; Don E. Fehrenbacher and Ward M. McAfee, *The Slaveholding Republic: An Account of the United States Government's Relations to Slavery* (New York: Oxford University Press, 2001), 26–38; David Waldstreitcher, *Slavery's Constitution: From Revolution to Ratification* (New York: Hill and Wang, 2009); Jeffrey Robert Young, *Domesticating Slavery: The Master Class in Georgia and South Carolina, 1670–1837* (Chapel Hill: University of North Carolina Press, 1999), 93–98.
28. For a discussion of South Carolina planter politicians and their outspokenness in the antebellum era, see William W. Freehling, *Prelude to Civil War: The Nullification Controversy in South Carolina, 1816–1836* (Oxford: Oxford University Press, 1992); Manisha Sinha, *The Counterrevolution of Slavery: Politics and Ideology in Antebellum South Carolina* (Chapel Hill: University of North Carolina Press, 2000).
29. For an examination about the ways in which the institution of slavery varied across place and time, see Ira Berlin, *Many Thousands Gone: The First Two Centuries of Slavery in North America* (Cambridge, Mass.: Harvard University Press, 1998).

30. Over the last decade, historians have pushed the relationship between the history of slavery and the rise of capitalism in the United States to the fore. Scholars' overarching perspective is this: Slavery as an institution was not only profitable but thrived, especially in the six decades before the Civil War. Historians have come to terms with how enslaved peoples' labor supported the growth of American capitalism after the American Revolution. This new literature builds on and sometimes challenges earlier work by historians, economic historians in particular, to understand how the expansion of slavery and the introduction of short-staple cotton influenced the American economy. Economic historians of the 1970s and 1980s, such as Robert Fogel and Stanley Engerman, used large-scale economic analysis to argue that antebellum slavery was as efficient as it was profitable. See Edward Baptist, *The Half Has Never Been Told: Slavery and the Making of American Capitalism* (New York: Basic Books, 2014); Sven Beckert, *Empire of Cotton: A Global History* (New York: Vintage Books, 2014); Sven Beckert and Seth Rockman, eds., *Slavery's Capitalism: A New History of American Economic Development* (Philadelphia: University of Pennsylvania Press, 2016); Daina Ramey Berry, *The Price for Their Pound of Flesh: The Value of the Enslaved, from Womb to Grave, in the Building of a Nation* (Boston: Beacon Press, 2017); Walter Johnson, *River of Dark Dreams: Slavery and Empire in the Cotton Kingdom* (Cambridge, Mass.: Harvard University Press, 2013); Sharon Ann Murphy, *Investing in Life: Insurance in Antebellum America* (Baltimore, Md.: Johns Hopkins University Press, 2010); Seth Rockman, *Scraping By: Wage Labor, Slavery, and Survival in Early Baltimore* (Baltimore, Md.: Johns Hopkins University Press, 2009); Caitlin Rosenthal, *Accounting for Slavery: Masters and Management* (Cambridge, Mass.: Harvard University Press, 2018); Calvin Schermerhorn, *The Business of Slavery and the Rise of American Capitalism, 1815–1860* (New Haven, Conn.: Yale University Press, 2015).
31. The sociologist Sudhir Venkatesh argues that because of the illicit and often invisible nature of underground economies, gathering a full accounting of clandestine and informal economic activity is impossible. He contends, "Even for a particular activity . . . it is doubtful that one could put together an exhaustive accounting on how many goods are being traded or how much money is being earned in a given neighborhood." Though Venkatesh explores the underground illicit economies of Southside Chicago between 1995 and 2003, his observation about the difficulty in quantifying the informal economy applies to my exploration of the slaves' economy. See Sudhir Venkatesh, *Off the Books: The Underground Economy of the Urban Poor* (Cambridge, Mass.: Harvard University Press, 2009), 10.
32. Recently, historians have interrogated the ways in which Southern legal culture was rife with complexity and was often unpredictable. See Loren Schweninger, *Appealing for Liberty: Freedom Suits in the South* (New York: Oxford University Press, 2018); Kimberly M. Welsh, *Black Litigants in the Antebellum American South* (Chapel Hill: University of North Carolina Press, 2018).
33. For an analysis of the rise of consumerism in the United States, see T. H. Breen, *The Marketplace of Revolution: How Consumer Politics Shaped American Independence* (New York: Oxford University Press, 2005); Joanna Cohen, *Luxurious Citizens: The*

Politics of Consumption in Nineteenth-Century America (Philadelphia: University of Pennsylvania Press, 2017).

34. Berlin and Morgan, *Cultivation and Culture*, 3.
35. Shennette Garrett-Scott, *Banking on Freedom: Black Women in U.S. Finance Before the New Deal* (New York: Columbia University Press, 2019), 1–12; Walter Johnson, "Clerks All! Or Slaves with Cash," *Journal of the Early Republic* 26, no. 4 (2006): 641–651; Penningroth, *Claims of Kinfolk*, 45–78.
36. Penningroth, *Claims of Kinfolk*, 78.

1. "NEGROES PUBLICKLY CABALING IN THE STREETS": THE ENSLAVED ECONOMY AND THE CULTURE OF SLAVERY IN COLONIAL SOUTH CAROLINA

1. Laurens's brother-in-law, Elias Ball, died in 1751 and Laurens was named the executor of Ball's estate, of which the Ashepoo Plantation was a part. Ball, a wealthy South Carolina slaveholder and merchant, owned several Lowcountry plantations. Laurens kept Wiggins employed as an overseer on Ashepoo during the eighteenth century because of his "knowledge & where the Negroes are employed." However, Wiggins was also known as a stern and sometimes violent overseer. In March 1766, Laurens received a copy of a letter sent from a neighboring planter to Wiggins, in which Wiggins's brutality was put on display. Planter John Jackson wrote, "I am informed what a fine parcel of Company you keep, & must whip Wenches till they miscarry . . . Keep a still tongue & and mind your business." It is possible that Laurens was aware of Wiggin's violent proclivities and wanted to ensure that the African slaves did not rebel against him or Wiggins. See George G. Rogers Jr. et al., *The Papers of Henry Laurens, Volume 5: Sept. 1, 1765–July 31, 1768* (Columbia: University of South Carolina Press, 1968), 10, 95. Emphasis added. Overseers played an important role in colonial America's burgeoning plantation complex. Specifically, as the historian Tristan Stubbs explores, overseers meted out violence on behalf of enslavers. See Tristan Stubbs, *Masters of Violence: The Plantation Overseers of Eighteenth-Century Virginia, South Carolina, and Georgia* (Columbia: University of South Carolina Press, 2018).
2. This idea—of Laurens recognizing enslaved peoples' property rights—is consistent with what the historian Jeffrey Robert Young has argued, that Laurens had an evolving perspective on slaveholding, one that included an increasingly "humanitarian concern" for his slaves. Laurens even wrote in 1776, in a letter to his son John Laurens, "You know, my dear son, I abhor slavery." According to Young, Laurens believed that he should have treated his bondspeople humanely. Young also contends that Laurens attempted to run his plantations in a way that recognized the humanity of the enslaved people who labored on them, which was perhaps an early demonstration of the paternalist ideology that emerged more publicly in the nineteenth century. See Henry Laurens, *Correspondence of Henry Laurens: of South Carolina* (New York: Printed for the Zenger Club, 1861), 20; Jeffrey Robert Young, *Domesticating Slavery: The Master Class*

in Georgia and South Carolina, 1670–1837 (Chapel Hill: University of North Carolina Press, 1999), 44–45.

3. The historian S. Max Edelson has argued that the "controlled experiences of exchange" reinforced the patriarchal master–slave relationship. See S. Max Edelson, *Plantation Enterprise in Colonial South Carolina* (Cambridge, Mass.: Harvard University Press, 2006), 231.
4. For one of the first scholarly investigations of the Sunday market and the internal slave economy in the Atlantic world, see Sidney Mintz, "The Jamaican Internal Marketing System: Some Notes and Hypotheses," *Social and Economic Studies* 4, no. 1 (March 1955): 95–103.
5. For an analysis of the slaves' economy in colonial South Carolina, see Ira Berlin, *Generations of Captivity: A History of African American Slaves* (Cambridge, Mass.: Harvard University Press, 2003), 116–117; Philip D. Morgan, "Work and Culture: The Task System and the World of Lowcountry Blacks, 1700–1880," *William and Mary Quarterly* 39, no. 4 (October 1982): 563–599; Philip D. Morgan, "The Ownership of Property by Slaves in the Mid-Nineteenth-Century Low Country," *Journal of Southern History* 49, no. 3 (August 1983): 399–420; Philip Morgan, *Slave Counterpoint: Black Culture in the Eighteenth-Century Chesapeake and Lowcountry* (Chapel Hill: University of North Carolina Press, 1998), 358–376; Robert Olwell, *Masters, Slaves, and Subjects: The Culture of Power in the South Carolina Low Country, 1740–1790* (Ithaca, N.Y.: Cornell University Press, 1998), 141–180; Betty Wood, "'White Society' and the 'Informal' Slave Economies of Lowcountry Georgia, c. 1730–1830," *Slavery & Abolition* 11, no. 3 (December 1990): 313–331.
6. For connections between slavery and emerging forms of capitalist enterprise in colonial Charleston, see Gregory O'Malley, "Slavery's Converging Ground: Charleston's Slave Trade as the Black Heart of the Lowcountry," *William and Mary Quarterly* 74, no. 2 (April 2017): 271–302.
7. The rapid growth of the Barbadian sugar industry pushed emerging planters out of the island colony in the 1660s. Designed initially as a satellite colony of Barbados, Carolina's first residents were enslaved Africans and according to Peter Coclanis, white colonists "from groups at the bottom of the seventeenth-century social hierarchy." See Peter A. Coclanis, *Shadow of a Dream: Economic Life and Death in the South Carolina Lowcountry, 1670–1920* (New York: Oxford University Press, 1989), 22. The legal culture of slavery in South Carolina mirrored what existed in Barbados. See Bradley J. Nicholson, "Legal Borrowing and the Origins of Slave Law in the British Colonies," *American Journal of Legal History* 38, no. 1 (January 1994): 38–54.
8. Jack P. Greene, "Colonial South Carolina and the Caribbean Connection," *South Carolina Historical Magazine* 88, no. 4 (October. 1987): 197.
9. *Acts, passed in the island of Barbados* (London: Printed for Richard Hall, 1974), 51.
10. Hilary McD. Beckles, *Natural Rebels: A Social History of Enslaved Black Women in Barbados* (New Brunswick, N.J.: Rutgers University Press, 1989), 72–89; Hilary McD. Beckles, "An Economic Life of Their Own: Slaves as Commodity Producers and Distributors in Barbados," in *The Slaves' Economy: Independent Production by Slaves in*

the Americas, ed. Ira Berlin and Philip D. Morgan (London: Frank Cass & Co., 1991), 31–47; Richard S. Dunn, *Sugar and Slaves: The Rise of the Planter Class in the English West Indies: 1642–1723* (Chapel Hill: University of North Carolina Press, 1972), 240–241; Simon P. Newman, *A New World of Labor: The Development of Plantation Slavery in the British Atlantic* (Philadelphia: University of Pennsylvania Press, 2013), 57–64; Edward B. Rugemer, *Slave Law and the Politics of Resistance in the Early Atlantic World* (Cambridge, Mass.: Harvard University Press, 2018), 26–34.

11. John J. Navin, *The Grim Years: Settling South Carolina, 1670–1720* (Columbia: University of South Carolina Press, 2019), 106–108; Peter Wood, *Black Majority: Negroes in Colonial South Carolina from 1670 Through the Stono Rebellion* (New York: Norton, 1974), 95–130. According to the historian Ryan A. Quintana, enslaved Africans helped to construct the infrastructure of the colony, including the building of roads. Colonial administrators co-opted enslaved people from their enslavers in these efforts. See Ryan A. Quintana, *Making a Slave State: Political Development in Early South Carolina* (Chapel Hill: University of North Carolina, 2018), 15–47.
12. It is important to note that enslaved people were at the receiving end of enslaver violence. Enslavers may have integrated the slaves' trade into their ideas about slaveholding and mastery, but violence was an ever-present aspect of enslaved peoples' experiences in the Lowcountry during the colonial era. See Edelson, *Plantation Enterprise in Colonial South Carolina*, 83.
13. Johann Martin Bolzius, "Reliable Answer to Some Submitted Questions Concerning the Land Carolina," *William and Mary Quarterly* 14, no. 2 (April 1957): 259. See also S. Max Edelson, "Affiliation Without Affinity: Skilled Slaves in Eighteenth Century South Carolina," in *Money, Trade, and Power: The Evolution of Colonial South Carolina's Plantation Society*, ed. Jack P. Greene, Rosemary Brana-Shute, and Randy J. Sparks (Columbia: University of South Carolina Press, 2001), 219. For a discussion of rice culture in colonial South Carolina, see Judith Carney, *Black Rice: The African Origins of Rice Cultivation in the Americas* (Cambridge, Mass.: Harvard University Press, 2001); S. Max Edelson, *Plantation Enterprise in Colonial South Carolina* (Cambridge, Mass.: Harvard University Press, 2006); Daniel Littlefield, *Rice and Slaves: Ethnicity and the Slave Trade in Colonial South Carolina* (Baton Rouge: Louisiana State University Press, 1981). Peter Wood first introduced the idea that enslaved Africans may have contributed to the development of South Carolina's rice culture. He argued, "In the establishment of rice cultivation, as in numerous other areas, historians have ignored the possibility that Afro-Americans could have contributed anything more than menial labor to South Carolina's early development. Yet the Negro slave, faced with limited food supplies before 1700, and encouraged to raise their own subsistence, could readily have succeeded in nurturing rice where their masters had failed." See Wood, *Black Majority*, 62. But this idea, of the African origins of South Carolina's rice culture, has been challenged by a number of historians who believe that scholars need to take a more analytical approach to understanding African slaves' role in the development of rice culture in South Carolina. See S. Max Edelson, "Beyond *Black Rice*: Reconstruction Material and Cultural Contexts for Early Plantation

Agriculture," *American Historical Review* 115, no. 1 (February 2010): 125–135; David Eltis, Philip Morgan, and David Richardson, "Agency and Diaspora in Atlantic History: Reassessing the African Contribution to Rice Cultivation in the Americas," *American Historical Review* 112, no. 5 (December 2007): 1329–1358.

14. Wood, *Black Majority*, 62. The historian Ira Berlin also argues that slaveholders in South Carolina may have "jump-started the slaves' economy in the new settlement." See Ira Berlin, *Many Thousands Gone: The First Two Centuries of Slavery in North America* (Cambridge, Mass.: Belknap Press of Harvard University Press, 1998), 68.
15. Bolzius, "Reliable Answer to Some Submitted Questions Concerning the Land Carolina," 259–260.
16. Johann Martin Bolzius, "Reliable Answer to Some Submitted Questions Concerning the Land Carolina," *William and Mary Quarterly* 14, no. 2 (April 1957), 236.
17. Wood, *Black Majority*, 62.
18. Enslaved people may not have had access to money in the early colonial period because of the scarcity of hard money in the colonies. Rather, they may have been involved in bartering arrangements with the people with whom they traded. It is also possible that they dealt in credit. In 1750 a German Lutheran minister, Rev. John Martin Bolzius, published a pamphlet in which he encouraged German emigration to South Carolina and Georgia. In the pamphlet Bolzius wrote, "Cash is very rare in the land, and it is to be feared that one would not receive money for goods from the merchants in Carolina and Georgia . . . The granting of credit or borrowing of goods is a common thing in Carolina and Georgia, and a merchant would be able to sell little if he did not give his goods out on credit for 6 and more months." See Bolzius, "Reliable Answer," 251–252.
19. David J. McCord, *Statutes at Large of South Carolina: Acts from 1682 to 1716* (Columbia, S. C.: A. S. Johnson, 1837), 22–23; David J. McCord, *Statutes at Large of South Carolina: Acts relating to Charleston, Courts, Slaves and Rivers* (Columbia, S. C.: A. S. Johnson, 1840), 380–408. For an analysis of the Barbadian influence on South Carolina laws of slavery, see Sally E. Hadden, *Slave Patrols: Law and Violence in Virginia and the Carolinas* (Cambridge, Mass.: Harvard University Press, 2001), 10–14; H. M. Henry, "Police Control of the Slave in South Carolina" (PhD diss., Vanderbilt University, 1914), 4–5; Thomas J. Little, "The South Carolina Slave Laws Reconsidered, 1670–1700," *South Carolina Historical Magazine* 94, no. 2 (April 1993): 86–101; M. Eugene Sirmans, "The Legal Status of the Slave in South Carolina, 1670–1740," *Journal of Southern History* 28, no. 4 (November 1962): 464–465; Tomlins, *Freedom Bound*, 428–452.
20. McCord, *Statutes at Large of South Carolina: Acts from 1682 to 1716*, 22–23.
21. Thomas Cooper, *The Statutes at Large of South Carolina: Acts from 1682 to 1716* (Columbia, S.C.: A. S. Johnson, 1837), 22.
22. Cooper, *The Statutes at Large of South Carolina: Acts from 1682 to 1716*, 22.
23. Cooper, *The Statutes at Large of South Carolina: Acts from 1682 to 1716*, 22.
24. Legal historians suggest that because slavery, as an institution, was not recognized within the canon of English jurisprudence when English colonies began using slave labor in the seventeenth century, laws of slavery emerged piecemeal. For this reason,

according to the historian Jonathan A. Bush, remedies to legal concerns regarding slaves "came not in the form of systematic codes or treatises, genres peripheral to the common law tradition, but in a large quantity of local case law and statutes." Jonathan A. Bush, "Free to Enslave: The Foundation of Colonial American Slave Law," *Yale Journal of Law and the Humanities* 5, no. 2 (1993): 425. See also Sally E. Hadden, "The Fragmented Laws of Slavery in the Colonial and Revolutionary Eras," in *Cambridge History of Law in America*, Christopher Tomlins and Michael Grossberg, ed. (Cambridge: Cambridge University Press, 2008), 273.

25. Ira Berlin and Philip D. Morgan, eds., *The Slaves' Economy: Independent Production by Slaves in the Americas* (London: Frank Cass & Co., 1991); Ira Berlin and Philip D. Morgan, eds., *Cultivation and Culture: Labor and the Shaping of Slave Life in the Americas* (Charlottesville: University of Virginia Press, 1993).
26. Wood, *Black Majority*, 62.
27. Ira Berlin and Philip D. Morgan, eds., "Introduction," in *The Slaves' Economy*, 1–28; Ira Berlin and Philip D. Morgan, eds., "Introduction: Labor and the Shaping of Slave Life in the Americas," in *Cultivation and Culture: Labor and the Shaping of Slave Life in the Americas* (Charlottesville: University of Virginia Press, 1993), 26–27.
28. Bolzius, "Reliable Answer to Some Submitted Questions Concerning the Land Carolina," 260.
29. The failure of the 1686 law to regulate slaves' marketing activities mirrored the outcome of the Barbadian law. The historian Sally Hadden argues, "The continued reenactment of legislation might, in fact, suggest precisely the opposite, that slaves were able to flee or engage in other acts of resistance and that only a concerted effort could restrain them." See Sally Hadden, *Slave Patrols: Law and Violence in Virginia and the Carolinas* (Cambridge, Mass.: Harvard University Press, 2001), 12–13.
30. U.S. Bureau of the Census, *Historical Statistics of the United States*, 756.
31. Lawmakers did not want to "hinder any person from letting their negroes or slaves to hire" because doing so would have weakened enslavers' authority over enslaved Africans. Instead, the statute allowed enslaved people to engage in self-hire for up to a year if the slave was under the "care and direction of the master, or some other person by his order instructed with the slave." Therefore, enslaved people could legally participate in self-hire and hiring out their own time with their master's explicit permission. Enslavers were in favor of slave hiring if they benefitted economically from the practice. Enslaved people sought to benefit economically as well. See McCord, *Statutes at Large of South Carolina: Acts Relating to Charleston, Courts, Slaves and Rivers*, 363.
32. According to demographic records, enslaved people reached a majority of the South Carolina population in 1720. U.S. Bureau of the Census, *Historical Statistics of the United States*, 1960, 756.
33. Philip D. Morgan, "Work and Culture: The Task System and the World of Lowcountry Blacks, 1700–1880," *William and Mary Quarterly* 39, no. 4 (October 1982): 563–599.
34. Edelson, *Plantation Enterprise in Colonial South Carolina*, 157–158.
35. Edward Ball, *Slaves in the Family* (New York: FSG, 1998), 136–137. See also Morgan, "Work and Culture," 572.

36. For a discussion of slave hiring practices in eighteenth-century Charleston, see Emma Hart, *Building Charleston: Town and Society in Eighteenth-Century British Atlantic World* (Charlottesville: University of Virginia Press, 2010), 111–112; Jonathan Martin, *Divided Mastery: Slave Hiring in the American South* (Cambridge, Mass.: Harvard University Press, 2004), 20–27. See also Ira Berlin and Herbert Gutman, "Natives and Immigrants, Free Men and Slaves: Urban Workingmen in the Antebellum American South," *American Historical Review* 88, no. 5 (December 1983): 1185–1186; Wood, *Black Majority*. Some historians have described instances of slaves' self-hire as "illicit," "illegal," or "extralegal." However, according to South Carolina statute, slaveholder approval of slaves hiring out and self-hire made such activities legal. The majority of the literature on this phenomenon is situated in the early national and antebellum periods. See Loren Schweninger, "The Underside of Slavery: The Internal Economy, Self-Hire, and Quasi-Freedom in Virginia, 1780–1865," *Slavery & Abolition* 12, no. 2 (September 1991): 2; Loren Schweninger, "Slave Independence and Enterprise in South Carolinas," *South Carolina Historical Magazine* 93 (April 1992): 101–125.
37. *SCG*, March 4, 1732.
38. Mabel L. Webber, "Presentment of the Grand Jury, March 1733/34," *South Carolina Historical and Genealogical Magazine* 25, no. 4 (October 1924): 193–195.
39. *SCG*, March 30, 1734.
40. *SCG*, March 30, 1734.
41. *SCG*, December 29, 1737.
42. *SCG*, March 11, 1734.
43. *SCG*, May 23, 1738. In 1738, the General Assembly sought to further discourage not only enslaved Africans but also petty hawkers and peddlers from illegally "trading with indented Servants, Overseers, Negroes and other Slaves."
44. *SCG*, November 5, 1737.
45. *SCG*, April 6, 1734. For an analysis of illicit commerce in colonial through antebellum Charleston, see Michael D. Thompson, "'Some Rascally Business': Thieving Slaves, Unscrupulous Whites, and Charleston's Illicit Waterfront Trade," in *Capitalism by Gaslight: Illuminating the Economy of Nineteenth-Century America*, ed. Brian P. Luskey and Wendy A. Woloson (Philadelphia: University of Pennsylvania Press, 2015), 150–167.
46. *SCG*, September 10, 1737.
47. There is not a consensus among historians about the catalyst for the Stono Rebellion in 1739. Some historians believe it was fomented by colonists in Spanish Florida, to the immediate south of South Carolina. For example, Ira Berlin has argued that Spanish officials made an offer of freedom to African slaves who were willing to flee South Carolina for freedom in Spanish Florida. See Ira Berlin, *Generations of Captivity: A History of African-American Slaves* (Cambridge, Mass.: Harvard University Press, 2003), 45–47. For the literature on the Stono Rebellion of 1739, see Peter Charles Hoffer, *Cry Liberty: The Great Stono River Slave Rebellion of 1739* (New York: Oxford University Press, 2010); Mark M. Smith, "Remembering Mary, Shaping Revolt: Reconsidering the Stono Rebellion," *Journal of Southern History* 67, no. 3 (August 2001): 513–534; Jack

Shuler, *Calling Out Liberty: The Stono Slave Rebellion and the Universal Struggle for Human Rights* (Jackson: University of Mississippi Press, 2009); John K. Thornton, "African Dimensions of the Stono Rebellion," *American Historical Review* 96, no. 4 (October 1991), 1101–1113; Wood, *Black Majority*, 309–326.

48. Cynthia Kennedy, *Braided Relations, Entwined Lives: The Women of Charleston's Urban Slave Society* (Bloomington: Indiana University Press, 2005), 25.
49. McCord, *Statutes at Large of South Carolina: Acts relating to Charleston, Courts, Slaves and Rivers*, 397–417.
50. *SCG*, July 9, 1750; *SCG*, May 13, 1751; Edelson, "Affiliation Without Affinity," 217–255.
51. *SCG*, November 5, 1744.
52. George Fenwick Jones, "John Martin Boltzius' Trip to Charleston, October 1742," *South Carolina Historical Magazine* 82, no. 2 (April 1981): 104. See also Morgan, *Slave Counterpoint*, 358–359.
53. Ravenel family. Ravenel family papers, 1695–1925. (1171.00) South Carolina Historical Society, Charleston, SC.
54. *SCG*, November 1, 1746.
55. *SCG*, November 1, 1746.
56. *SCG*, July 7, 1767.
57. *SCG*, May 31, 1770.
58. Sweeney, "Market Marronage," 197–222.
59. Beckles, *Natural Rebels*, 72–89, Beckles, "An Economic Life of Their Own," 31–47; Russell R. Menard, *Sweet Negotiations: Sugar, Slavery, and Plantation Agriculture in Early Barbados* (Charlottesville: University of Virginia Press, 2006), 99–101. "Market women" were enslaved women who brought goods including produce, textiles, and livestock to sell in the marketplace in regions of the slaveholding Atlantic world. For a discussion of market women in early Barbados, see Judith Carney, *In the Shadow of Slavery: Africa's Botanical Legacy in the Atlantic World* (Berkeley: University of California Press, 2009), 182–185; Jennifer L. Morgan, *Laboring Women: Reproduction and Gender in New World Slavery* (Philadelphia: University of Pennsylvania Press, 2004), 62–63.
60. For the literature on enslaved market women in the Atlantic word, see Barbara Bush, *Slave Women in Caribbean Society: 1650–1832* (Bloomington: Indiana University Press, 1990), 48–50; Mary C. Karasch, "Suppliers, Sellers, Servants, and Slaves," in *Cities and Societies in Colonial Latin America*, ed. Louisa S. Hoberman and Susan Socolow (Albuquerque: University of New Mexico Press, 1986), 251–283; Bernard Moitt, *Women and Slavery in the French Antilles, 1635–1848* (Bloomington: Indiana University Press, 2001), 34–56; Morgan, *Laboring Women*, 62–63; Robert Olwell, *Masters, Slaves, and Subjects: The Culture of Power in the South Carolina Lowcountry, 1740–1790* (Ithaca, N.Y.: Cornell University Press, 1998), 141–180.
61. Olwell, *Masters, Slaves, and Subjects*, 168.
62. *SCG*, September 24, 1772. For a discussion of market women in colonial Charleston, see Cynthia Kennedy, *Braided Relations, Entwined Live*, 24–26.
63. Edward A. Pearson, *Stono: Documenting and Interpreting a Southern Slave Revolt* (Columbia: University of South Carolina Press, 2005), 89–90.

64. *SCG*, September 24, 1772. For an analysis of the ways in which enslaved people influenced the culinary culture of Charleston in the early national and antebellum eras, see Kelly Kean Sharp, "Planters' Plots to Backlot Stewpots: Food, Race, and Labor in Charleston, South Carolina, 1780–1850," PhD diss. (University of California, Davis, 2018).
65. *SCG*, September 24, 1772.
66. *SCG*, February 1, 1768; *SCG*, April 27, 1771.
67. *South Carolina and American General Gazette* (*SCAGG*), August 12, 1771.
68. *South Carolina Gazette and Country Journal* (hereafter *SCGCJ*), September 17, 1771.
69. Jonathan Mercantini, "The Great Carolina Hurricane of 1752," *South Carolina Historical Magazine* 102, no. 4 (October 2002): 351–365.
70. *SCG*, September 19, 1752.
71. *SCG*, November 22, 1763.
72. *SCG*, November 22, 1763.
73. *SCG*, April 7, 1760; *SCG*, March 28, 1761.
74. *SCG*, October 22, 1763.
75. George G. Rogers Jr. et al., *The Papers of Henry Laurens, Volume 5: Sept. 1, 1765–July 31, 1768* (Columbia: University of South Carolina Press, 1968), 57.
76. According to Johann Bolzius, "cash is very rare in the land," which suggests that enslaved people, most often traded or bartered for goods because of the rarity of cash on hand in the Southern English colonies. See Bolzius, "Reliable Answer," 251.
77. *SCG*, May 11, 1767.
78. *SCG*, November 11, 1770.
79. *SCG*, April 10, 1762; *SCGCJ*, January 29, 1768; *SCGCJ*, May 13, 1768; *SCGCJ*, June 1, 1773; *SCG*, March 2, 1773; *SCG*, May 24, 1773; *SCGCJ*, May 27, 1774; *SCG*, October 31, 1774; *SCAGG*, June 16, 1775; *SCG*, May 19, 1777.
80. *SCG*, January 25, 1770. The "magistrates" are a reference to the Court of Magistrates and Freeholders, the local judicial body that decided court cases involving enslaved people. Josiah Quincy Jr., a lawyer from New England, traveled to Charleston in spring 1775 and commented on the "Curious laws and policy" of South Carolina. He observed that "any two justices and three freeholders might and very often did *instanter* upon view or complaint try a negro for any crime, and might and did often award execution of death—issue their warrant and it was done forthwith . . . This law too was for *free* as well as *slave* negroes and mulattoes." Jennie Holton Fant, ed., *The Travelers' Charleston: Accounts of Charleston and Lowcountry South Carolina, 1666–1861* (Columbia: University of South Carolina Press, 2016), 30. For a discussion of the history of the Court of Magistrates and Freeholders in South Carolina, see also Terry W. Lipscomb and Theresa Jacobs, "The Magistrates and Freeholders Court," *South Carolina Historical Magazine* 77, no. 1 (January 1976): 62–65.
81. *SCG*, January 25, 1770.
82. *SCG*, January 29, 1768.
83. Rogers et al., *The Papers of Henry Laurens, Volume Five*, n80–81.
84. *SCG*, December 19, 1761.

85. *SCG*, January 10, 1771.
86. *SCGCJ*, December 21, 1773.
87. *SCGCJ*, December 13, 1774.
88. U.S. Bureau of the Census, *Historical Statistics of the United States, Colonial Times to 1957* (Washington, D.C., 1960), 767–768.
89. O'Malley, "Slavery's Converging Ground," 276.

2. "THIS INFAMOUS TRAFFICK": THE SLAVES' TRADE IN THE AGE OF REVOLUTION

1. For a discussion of the British capture of Charleston in May 1780 and how the confiscation of enslaved people as property factored into British military strategies, see Lauren Duval, "Mastering Charleston: Property and Patriarchy in British-Occupied Charleston, 1780–1782," *William and Mary Quarterly* 75, no. 4 (October 2018), 589–622; Alexander R. Stoesen, "The British Occupation of Charleston, 1780–1782," in *South Carolina Historical Magazine* 63, no. 2 (April 1962), 71–82.
2. Charles Cotesworth Pinckney (1746–1825) to Eliza Lucas Pinckney, September 7, 1780, in *The Papers of Eliza Lucas Pinckney and Harriott Pinckney Horry Digital Edition*, ed. Constance Schulz (Charlottesville: University of Virginia Press, 2012), http://rotunda.upress.virginia.edu/PinckneyHorry/ELP0255 (accessed November 19, 2019).
3. According to Timothy Lockley, between 1779 and 1782, approximately 85 percent of runaway slaves were male, many of whom may have fled to maroon communities. Timothy James Lockley, *Maroon Communities in South Carolina: A Documentary Record* (Columbia: University of South Carolina Press, 2009), 40.
4. Eliza Lucas Pinckney to Rebecca Raven Evance (Mrs. Branfill), September 25, 1780, in *The Papers of Eliza Lucas Pinckney and Harriott Pinckney Horry Digital Edition*, ed. Schulz.
5. Charles Cotesworth Pinckney, (1746–1825) to Eliza Lucas Pinckney, November 23, 1780, in *The Papers of Eliza Lucas Pinckney and Harriott Pinckney Horry Digital Edition*, ed. Schulz.
6. Sylvia Frey, *Water from the Rock: Black Resistance in a Revolutionary Age* (Princeton, N.J.: Princeton University Press, 1991), 113–114; Gary Nash, *The Unknown American Revolution: The Unruly Birth of Democracy and the Struggle to Create America* (New York: Viking, 2005), 330–332; Robert Olwell, *Masters, Slaves, and Subjects: The Culture of Power in the South Carolina Low Country, 1740–1790* (Ithaca, N.Y.: Cornell University Press, 199), 299; Alexander R. Stoesen, "The British Occupation of Charleston," 80.
7. Elizabeth A. Fenn, *Pox Americana: The Great Smallpox Epidemic of 1775–1782* (New York: Hill & Wang, 2001), 104–134; Gary Sellick, "'Undistinguished Destruction': The Effects of Smallpox on British Emancipation Policy in the Revolutionary War," *Journal of American Studies* 51, no. 3 (August 2017): 865–885.
8. For analyses of slavery and the making of American constitution, see George Van Cleve, *A Slaveholders' Union: Slavery, Politics, and the Constitution in the Early*

American Republic (Chicago: University of Chicago Press, 2010); David Waldstreicher, *Slavery's Constitution: From Revolution to Ratification* (New York: Hill and Wang, 2009).

9. Joyce E. Chaplin, "Creating a Cotton South in Georgia and South Carolina, 1760–1815," *Journal of Southern History* 57, no. 2 (May 1991), 181–182; U.S. Bureau of the Census, *Historical Statistics of the United States, Colonial Times to 1957* (Washington, D.C., 1960), 756; Tim Lockley and David Doddington, "Maroon and Slave Communities in South Carolina Before 1865," *South Carolina Historical Magazine* 113, no. 2 (April 2012): 130.
10. Lockley and Doddington, "Maroon and Slave Communities," 126. The historian Sylviane Diouf has argued that during the American Revolution, it is difficult to ascertain which numbers of enslaved people were fleeing to the British, and how many fled to maroon communities, with the intention of living with other runaway slaves. She contends that marronage and running to the British were two different decisions that enslaved people made during the War. See Sylviane Diouf, *Slavery's Exiles: The Story of American Maroons* (New York: New York University Press, 2014), 33–36.
11. Douglas Egerton, *Death or Liberty: African Americans and Revolutionary America* (New York: Oxford University Press, 2009), 151–152; Benjamin Quarles, *Negro in the American Revolution* (Chapel Hill: University of North Carolina Press, 1961), 141–144.
12. George G. Rogers Jr. et al., *The Papers of Henry Laurens, Volume 11: Jan. 5, 1776–Nov. 1, 1777* (Columbia: University of South Carolina Press, 1988), 350.
13. Sylvia Frey, *Water from the Rock: Black Resistance in a Revolutionary Age* (Princeton, N.J.: Princeton University Press, 1991), 118; Robert A, Olwell, "'Domestick Enemies': Slavery and Political Independence in South Carolina, May 1775–March 1776," *Journal of Southern History* 55, no. 1 (February 1989): 21–48; Olwell, *Masters, Slaves, and Subjects*, 221–270.
14. SCAGG, February 19, 1778. See also Cynthia M. Kennedy, *Braided Relations, Entwined Lives: The Women's of Charleston's Urban Slave Society* (Bloomington: Indiana University Press, 2005), 38.
15. Robert Olwell, "'Loose, Idle and Disorderly': Slave Women in the Eighteenth-Century Charleston Marketplace," in *More than Chattel: Black Women and Slavery in the Americas*, ed. David Barry Gaspar and Darlene Clark Hine (Bloomington: Indiana University Press, 1996), 106.
16. Kennedy, *Braided Relations*, 38.
17. *SCGGA*, November 8, 1783.
18. Enslavers feared that enslaved people would take advantage of instabilities caused by the war to abscond, take up arms, or simply refuse to work. They dreaded a second revolution, one that enslaved people waged internally to destroy the foundation of slaveholding life in the colony. See Alan Gilbert, *Black Patriots and Loyalists: Fighting for Emancipation in the War for Independence* (Chicago: University of Chicago Press, 2012), 15–45; Olwell, *Masters, Slaves, and Subjects*, 225–226.
19. Quoted in Gary B. Nash, *The Unknown American Revolution: The Unruly Birth of Democracy and The Struggle to Create America* (New York: Penguin, 2005), 330–331.

20. Extracts from the Journal of Mrs. Gabriel (Ann Ashby) Manigault, 1754–1781, quoted in Carl P. Borick, *A Gallant Defense: The Siege of Charleston, 1780* (Columbia: University of South Carolina Press, 2003), 32.
21. Alan Taylor, *American Revolutions: A Continental History, 1750–1804* (New York: Norton, 2017), 228–229.
22. Chaplin, "Creating a Cotton South," 181–182; Olwell, *Masters, Slaves, and Subjects*, 260–261.
23. Peter Horry Papers, South Caroliniana Library, University of South Carolina. See also Chaplin, "Creating a Cotton South," 182.
24. Eliza Lucas Pinckney to Rebecca Raven Evance (Mrs. Branfill), September 25, 1780, in *The Papers of Eliza Lucas Pinckney and Harriott Pinckney Horry Digital Edition*, ed. Schulz.
25. Robert Gibbes (1857), *Documentary History of the American Revolution* (Carlisle, Mass.: Applewood Books, 2009), 215–216.
26. Robert Gibbes (1857), *Documentary History of the American Revolution* (Carlisle, Mass.: Applewood Books, 2009), 215–216.
27. Joyce E. Chaplin, *An Anxious Pursuit: Agricultural Innovation and Modernity in the Lower South, 1730–1815* (Chapel Hill: University of North Carolina Press, 1993), 157–158; Egerton, *Death or Liberty*, 160–161; Frey, *Water from the Rock*, 211–213.
28. Frey, *Water from the Rock*, 208–209; Morgan, "Work and Culture," 576; U.S. Bureau of the Census, *Historical Statistics of the United States, Colonial Times to 1957* (Washington, D.C., 1960), 768.
29. Peter Coclanis, *Shadow of a Dream: Economic Life and Death in the South Carolina Lowcountry, 1670–1920* (New York: Oxford University Press, 1989), 113–115.
30. Thomas Pinckney to Eliza Lucas Pinckney, May 17, 1779, in *The Papers of Eliza Lucas Pinckney and Harriott Pinckney Horry Digital Edition*, ed. Schultz.
31. Thomas Pinckney to Eliza Lucas Pinckney, May 17, 1779.
32. Adele Stanton Edwards, ed., *Journals of the Privy Council, 1783–1789* (Columbia: South Carolina Department of Archives and History, 1971), 132.
33. Ryan A. Quintana, *Making a Slave State: Political Development in Early South Carolina* (Chapel Hill: University of North Carolina, 2018), 48–88.
34. Eliza Lucas Pinckney to Alexander Garden, May 14, 1782, in *The Papers of Eliza Lucas Pinckney and Harriott Pinckney Horry Digital Edition*, ed. Schultz.
35. Koger also contends that a significant percentage of these manumissions may have been a result of slave owners freeing trusted enslaved people after the Revolution and enslavers being influenced by the "revolutionary rhetoric" of the era. See Larry Koger, *Black Slaveowners: Free Black Slave Masters in South Carolina, 1790–1860* (Jefferson, N.C.: McFarland, 1985), 34–35; See "Head of Families at the First Census, 1790," https://www2.census.gov/prod2/decennial/documents/1790m-02.pdf.
36. John J. Zaborney, *Slaves for Hire: Renting Enslaved Laborers in Antebellum Virginia* (Baton Rouge: Louisiana State University Press, 2012), 5.
37. Jonathan D. Martin, *Divided Mastery: Slave Hiring in the American South* (Cambridge, Mass.: Harvard University Press, 2004), 17–43.

38. O. Nigel Bolland, "Proto-Proletarians? Slave Wages in the Americas," in *From Chattel Slaves to Wage Slaves: The Dynamics of Labour Bargaining in the Americas*, ed. Mary Turner (London: James Currey; Bloomington: Indiana University Press, 1995), 129–131; Loren Schweninger, "Slave Independence and Enterprise in South Carolina, 1780–1865," *South Carolina Historical Magazine* 93 (April 1992): 101–125; Stephanie M. H. Camp, *Closer to Freedom: Enslaved Women and Everyday Resistance in the Plantation South* (Chapel Hill: University of North Carolina Press, 2004), 139; Kennedy, *Braided Relations, Entwined Lives*, 36–39, 148–153; Loren Schweninger, *Black Property Owners in the South* (Urbana: University of Illinois Press, 1990), 38–43. For a discussion of runaway slaves passing as self-hired slaves to secure money and security, see John Hope Franklin and Loren Schweninger, *Runaway Slaves: Rebels on the Plantation* (New York: Oxford University Press, 1999), 134–136. For hiring out practices outside of South Carolina, see John V. Zaborney, *Slaves for Hire: Renting Enslaved Laborers in Antebellum Virginia* (Baton Rouge: Louisiana State University Press, 2012).
39. Johann David Schoepf, "After the Revolution," in *The Travelers' Charleston: Accounts of Charleston and Lowcountry, South Carolina, 1666–1861*, ed. Jennie Holton Fant (Columbia: University of South Carolina Press, 2016), 51. The idea of enslaved people as investments and slave hiring as a way for enslavers to reap the financial benefits of slavery through slave hiring grows in the early republican period. "'The historian Seth Rockman explores the ways in which enslavers in early national Baltimore approached slaveholding as an investment and used enslaved men and women as "investment property." See Rockman, *Scraping By*, 57–66.
40. Johann David Schoepf, "After the Revolution," 51–52.
41. Records of the General Assembly, 1783, #159, South Carolina Department of Archives and History, Columbia, SC (hereafter SCDAH). See also *South Carolina Weekly Gazette* (hereafter *SCWG*), November 28, 1783.
42. Records of the General Assembly, 1783, #159, South Carolina Department of Archives and History, Columbia, SCDAH. See also Frey, *Water from the Rock*, 224–225.
43. *SCWG*, November 28, 1783.
44. *SCWG*, November 28, 1783.; Harlan Greene and Harry S. Hutchins Jr., *Slave Badges and the Slave-Hire System in Charleston, 1783–1865* (Jefferson, N.C.: McFarland & Company, 2004), 25–27.
45. *SCWG*, November 28, 1783.
46. *SCWG*, November 28, 1783.
47. *South-Carolina Gazette and General Advertiser*, October 14, 1783.
48. Philip D. Morgan, "Black Society in the Lowcountry, 1760–1810," in *Slavery and Freedom in the Age of the American Revolution*, ed. Ira Berlin and Ronald Hoffman (Urbana: United States Capitol Historical Society by the University of Illinois Press, 1983), 108.
49. *The Columbian Herald*, October 21, 1785; *Charleston Evening Gazette*, February 23, 1786.
50. The historian Jennifer L. Goloboy has argued that Charleston merchants in the early national period were particularly corrupt and often ignored laws that attempted to

regulate their retail businesses. An extension of their renegade business dealings was perhaps their illicit dealings with enslaved people, a tradition that continued into the nineteenth century. Jennifer L. Goloboy, "Strangers in the South: Charleston's Merchants and Middle-Class Values in the Early Republic," in *The Southern Middle Class in the Long Nineteenth Century*, ed. Jonathan Daniel Wells and Jennifer R. Green (Baton Rouge: Louisiana State University Press, 2011), 47. See also Jennifer L. Goloboy, *Charleston and the Emergence of Middle-Class Culture in the Revolutionary Era* (Athens: The University of Georgia Press, 2016).

51. *SCWG*, July 27, 1786.
52. *SCWG*, July 27, 1786.
53. *Ordinances of the City of Charleston*, 65–68. The 1789 revisions did not end Charleston administrators' wavering about slave hire. Only a year later, the city council amended the 1789 ordinance, which stipulated, "no negro or other slave" would be allowed to "buy, sell, trade, traffic, deal, barter, or use commerce" on their own account. The council excluded licensed fishermen from the restrictions and this provision created to manage enslaved fisherman presented the council with an unprecedented problem. The problem seemed to be particularly acute among slave fishermen, who until 1790 enjoyed more autonomy than other skilled slaves. The Charleston city council began making exemptions for enslaved fisherman in 1783. Yet presumably between June 1789 and March 1790, the enslaved fisherman of Charleston determined that they could continue their trade freely without fear of prosecution. The council admitted that the exception for fishermen gave them a privilege "to a much greater extent than was meant and intended by the said ordinance." The city council revisited the ordinance and extended restrictions on the slaves' trade to encompass enslaved fisherman as well. See *The City Gazette*, November 13, 1790.
54. *The City Gazette*, August 17, 1791.
55. Records of the General Assembly, 1783, #159, SDCAH; Records of the General Assembly, 1783, #258, SDCAH; Records of the General Assembly, 1785, #100, SDCAH; Records of the General Assembly, 1790, #19, SDCAH; Records of the General Assembly, 1790, #28, SDCAH; Records of the General Assembly, 1790, #6, SDCAH; Records of the General Assembly, 1791, #78, SDCAH; Records of the General Assembly, 1790, #65, SDCAH; Records of the General Assembly, 1793, #64, SDCAH; Records of the General Assembly, 1796, #8, SDCAH; Records of the General Assembly, 1799, #4, SDCAH.
56. Joyce E. Chaplin, "Tidal Rice Cultivation and the Problem of Slavery in South Carolina and Georgia, 1760–1815," *William and Mary Quarterly* 49 (January 1992): 29–61. See also William Dusinberre, *Them Dark Days: Slavery in the American Rice Swamps* (New York: Oxford University Press, 1996).
57. Morgan, "Work and Culture," 563–599.
58. Morgan, "Work and Culture," 565–566.
59. Kennedy, *Braided Relations*, 138–140; Thomas Cooper and David J. McCord, *Statutes at Large of South Carolina: Acts, 1787–1814* (Columbia, S. C.: A. S. Johnson, 1839), 21–22.
60. Cooper and McCord, *Statutes at Large of South Carolina: Acts, 1787–1814*, 21–22.

61. Records of the General Assembly, 1790, #28, SCDAH; Records of the General Assembly, 1789, #144, SCDAH.
62. Olwell, *Masters, Slaves, and Subjects*, 165.
63. *Guardian of Sally, a Negro v. Beaty*, 1 Bay 260, 262 (S.C. 1792).
64. *Guardian of Sally, a Negro v. Beaty.*
65. James Haw and M. Leigh Harrison have argued that Chief Justice John Rutledge exerted considerable sway in convincing the jury to rule in favor of Sally. See James Haw, *John and Edward Rutledge of South Carolina* (Athens: University of Georgia Press, 1996), 226; M. Leigh Harrison, "A Study of the Earliest Reported Decisions of the South Carolina Court of Law," *American Journal of Legal History* 16, no. 1 (January 1972): 63.
66. *Guardian of Sally, a Negro v. Beaty*, 1 Bay 260, 262 (S.C. 1792).
67. Andrew Fede, *People Without Rights: An Interpretation of the Fundamentals of the Law of Slavery in the U.S. South* (New York: Garland Publishing, 1992), 148–149; Haw, *John and Edward Rutledge of South Carolina*, 226; Kennedy, *Braided Relations*, 151–152; Thomas Morris, *Southern Slavery and the Law*, 49–50, 381; Donald J. Senese, "The Free Negro and the South Carolina Courts, 1790–1860," *South Carolina Historical Magazine* 63, no. 3 (July 1967): 141–142.
68. Sally Hadden, "The Fragmented Laws of Slavery," 253–287. Legal historian Laura Edwards has investigated how in the post-Revolutionary and nineteenth-century South, enslaved people influenced the ways in which legal culture evolved. See Laura F. Edwards, "Enslaved Women and the Law: Paradoxes of Subordination in the Post-Revolutionary Carolinas," *Slavery & Abolition* 26, no. 2 (2005): 305–323; Laura F. Edwards, "Status Without Rights: African Americans and the Tangled History of Law and Governance in the Nineteenth-Century U.S. South," *American Historical Review* 112, no. 2 (April 2007): 365–393.
69. A dram shop was a tavern or bar where alcoholic beverages were sold.
70. Records of the General Assembly, 1792, #3, SCDAH.
71. Sally Hadden, "South Carolina's Grand Jury Presentments: The Eighteenth-Century Experience," in *Signposts: New Directions in Southern Legal History*, ed. Sally Hadden and Patricia Hagler Minter (Athens: University of Georgia Press, 2013), 91. The historian Gregory A. Mark has suggested that petitioning was a "peculiar quasi-judicial mechanism" and that petitions presented "sound bites" wherein citizens revealed their social and legislative concerns. See Gregory A. Mark, "The Vestigial Constitution: The History and Significance of the Right to Petition," *Fordham Law Review* 66, no. 6 (1998): 2153–2231.
72. Ruth Bogin, "Petitioning and the New Moral Economy in Post-Revolutionary America," *William and Mary Quarterly* 45, no. 3 (July 1998): 391–425; David A. Frederick, "John Quincy Adams, Slavery, and the Right of Petition," *Law and History Review* 9, no. 1 (Spring 1999): 113–155; Mark, "The Vestigial Constitution," 2197–2198.
73. Records of the General Assembly, 1793, #63–64, SCDAH.
74. Records of the General Assembly, 1793, #63–64, SCDAH; *Columbian Herald*, November 9, 1793; *The City Gazette and Daily Advertiser*, December 14, 1793. See also Olwell, *Masters, Slaves, and Subjects*, 141–180.

75. Records of the General Assembly, 1793, #63–64, SCDAH; Michael P. Johnson and James Roark, *Black Masters: A Free Family of Color in the Old South* (New York: Norton, 1984), 174–176. In the early national era, white artisans expressed growing frustrations with enslaved artisans and skilled workers. See Michele Gillespie, *Free Labor in an Unfree World: White Artisans in Slaveholding Georgia, 1789–1860* (Athens: University of Georgia Press, 2000); Seth Rockman, *Scraping By: Wage Labor, Slavery, and Survival in Early Baltimore* (Baltimore, Md.: Johns Hopkins University Press, 2009); Michael D. Thompson, *Working on the Dock of the Bay: Labor and Enterprise in an Antebellum Southern Port* (Columbia: University of South Carolina Press, 2015).
76. *The City Gazette and Daily Advertiser*, Charleston, SC, November 23, 1793.
77. *Supplement to the City Gazette*, 12/4/1793; "Charleston District, Presentment Concerning the Condition of the Court House, Road Taxes in St. Philips and St. Michael's Parishes, The Condition of the Gaol, The Provision of Entertainment Houses by Ferry Owners, and The Rights of Slave Mechanics to Perform Other Trades," Records of the General Assembly, 1795, #2–3, SCDAH. For a discussion of white Charleston mechanics in the 1760s and 1770s, see Richard Walsh, "The Charleston Mechanics: A Brief Study, 1760–1776," *South Carolina Historical Magazine* 60, no. 3 (July 1959): 123–144.
78. "An Ordinance to Prohibit Slaves from Carrying on any Mechanic or Handicraft Trade, and for other Purposes Therein Mentioned," *City Gazette and Daily Advertiser*, September 3, 1796.
79. "An Ordinance to Prohibit Slaves from Carrying on any Mechanic or Handicraft Trade, and for other Purposes Therein Mentioned," *City Gazette and Daily Advertiser*, September 3, 1796.
80. Thomas Cooper and David McCord, *Statutes at Large of South Carolina: Acts relating to Charleston, Courts, Slaves, and Rivers* (Columbia, S. C.: A. S. Johnston, 1840), 434–435.
81. Philip D. Morgan, "Black Society in the Lowcountry, 1760–1810," in *Slavery and Freedom in the Age of the American Revolution*, ed. Ira Berlin and Ronald Hoffman (Charlottesville: University of Virginia Press, 1983), 84–85.
82. "Presentments of Edgefield County for October Term 1798," Records of the General Assembly, 1798, #3, SCDAH.
83. *City Gazette and Daily Advertiser*, July 19, 1800.
84. *City Gazette and Daily Advertiser*, July 19, 1800.
85. *City Gazette and Daily Advertiser*, July 19, 1800; Johnson and Roark, *Black Masters*, 175–176.
86. *City Gazette and Daily Advertiser*, May 2, 1801.
87. *City Gazette and Daily Advertiser*, May 2, 1801.
88. *City Gazette and Daily Advertiser*, September 18, 1804.
89. *City Gazette and Daily Advertiser*, April 13, 1804.
90. *City Gazette and Daily Advertiser*, June 6, 1801.
91. It is worth noting, however, that even private manumission did not dramatically increase the proportion of emancipated enslaved people in South Carolina between 1790 and 1800. In 1790, there were 1,801 free people of color in South Carolina,

.72 percent of the population. In 1800, the number of free people of color rose to 3,185, .92 percent of the population. See "Head of Families at the First Census, 1790," https://www2.census.gov/prod2/decennial/documents/1790m-02.pdf; "Thirteenth Census of the United States Taken in 1910," https://www2.census.gov/prod2/decennial/documents/41033935v35-41ch6.pdf.

92. David J. McCord, *The Statutes at Large of South Carolina* (Columbia, S. C.: A. S. Johnston, 1840), 440. The statute also made it more difficult for enslaved people held illegally in bondage to secure their freedom. See Loren Schweninger, *Appealing for Liberty: Freedom Suits in the South* (New York: Oxford University Press, 2018), 30–31.
93. McCord, *The Statutes at Large of South Carolina*, 442. For more on the experiences of enslaved people in old age, see Alix Lerner, "Aging in Bondage: Slavery, Debility, and the Problem of Dependency in the Old South" (PhD diss., Princeton University, 2016).
94. McCord, *The Statutes at Large of South Carolina*, 443.

3. "A DANGEROUS AND GROWING PRACTICE": ENSLAVED ENTREPRENEURSHIP AND THE COTTON ECONOMY IN THE NEW NATION

1. John Davis, "The Woods of South Carolina," in *The Travelers' Charleston: Accounts of Charleston and Lowcountry, South Carolina, 1666–1861*, ed. Jennie Holton Fant (Columbia: University of South Carolina Press, 2016), 75.
2. Walter Edgar, *South Carolina: A History* (Columbia: University of South Carolina Press, 1998), 270.
3. Peter A. Coclanis, *Shadow of a Dream: Economic Life and Death in the South Carolina Lowcountry, 1670–1920* (New York: Oxford University Press, 1989), 27–47.
4. John Dayton, *A View of South Carolina, as Respects her Natural and Civil Concerns* (Charleston, S.C., 1802), 27–128.
5. Charles Ball, *Slavery in the United States: A Narrative of the Life and Adventures of Charles Ball, A Black Man* (New York: John S. Taylor, 1837), https://docsouth.unc.edu/neh/ballslavery/ball.html.
6. Ball, *Slavery in the United States*, 81.
7. Ball, *Slavery in the United States*, 81.
8. Angela Lakwete, *Inventing the Cotton Gin: Machine and Myth in Antebellum America* (Baltimore, Md.: Johns Hopkins University Press, 2003); Walter Edgar, *South Carolina: A History*, 271.
9. Drayton, *A View of South Carolina*, 128.
10. Drayton, *A View of South Carolina*, 128.
11. Lacy K. Ford, "Self-Sufficiency, Cotton, and Economic Development in the South Carolina Upcountry, 1800–1860," *Journal of Economic History* 45, no. 2 (June 1985): 262–263.
12. Ford, "Self-Sufficiency, Cotton, and Economic Development in the South Carolina Upcountry," 262–263. William Freehling explores the ways in which the political

power of Upcountry planters challenged the hegemonic influence of Lowcountry planters within the state's political landscape as short-staple cotton came to define the state's economy. See William H. Freehling, *The Road to Disunion: Secessionists at Bay, 1776–1854: Volume 1* (New York: Oxford University Press, 1990), 220–222.

13. Ball, *Slavery in the United States,* 82.
14. Ball, *Slavery in the United States,* 43–44.
15. Ball, *Slavery in the United States,* 108.
16. Ball, *Slavery in the United States,* 187.
17. Ball, *Slavery in the United States,* 190.
18. Ball, *Slavery in the United States,* 190.
19. Ball, *Slavery in the United States,* 108.
20. Ball, *Slavery in the United States,* 192.
21. Union District Criminal Case Files, #56, 1805, SCDAH. Surprisingly, there is a visible blank space in the court documents where the enslaved person's name should have been recorded.
22. Ryan A. Quintana, *Making a Slave State: Political Development in Early South Carolina.* Chapel Hill: University of North Carolina, 2018, 89–115.
23. *State v. Nancy Edwards,* Union District Criminal Court, #118, SCDAH.
24. *State v. Nancy Edwards.* For analyses of enslaved people in Southern courts, see Ariela Gross, *Double Character: Slavery and Mastery in the Antebellum Southern Courtroom* (Princeton, N.J.: Princeton University Press, 2000); Kimberly Welsh, *Black Litigants in the Antebellum American South* (Chapel Hill: University of North Carolina Press, 2018). For a discussion of slaves in local courts in the colonial period, see A. Leon Higginbotham, *In the Matter of Color: Race and the American Legal Process, The Colonial Period* (New York: Oxford University Press, 1978), 179–181; Peter Wood, *Black Majority: Negroes in Colonial South Carolina from 1670 Through the Stono Rebellion* (New York: Norton, 1974), 308–326.
25. For a discussion of white women's legal rights in the early national period, see Marylynn Salmon, *Women and the Law of Property in Early America* (Chapel Hill: University of North Carolina Press, 2016).
26. Jeff Forret, *Race Relations at the Margins: Slaves and Poor Whites in the Antebellum Southern Countryside* (Baton Rouge: Louisiana State University Press, 2006), 77–78. See also Keri Leigh Merritt, *Masterless Men: Poor Whites and Slavery in the Antebellum South* (New York: Cambridge University Press, 2017), 206–209.
27. 1800 Federal Census, Union District, South Carolina. There is no extant census information on Bird Bluford for the 1810 census. The appearance of Bluford and Suckey in the historical record coincides with the cotton boom experienced in Upcountry South Carolina at the beginning of the nineteenth century.
28. The ways in which the market activities of the enslaved appear in the historical record during the early national period is significant. The informal exchanges that occurred between enslaved people and their trading partners appear with startling frequency in early nineteenth-century local court records. There were myriad cases that involved not only enslaved people trading with whites of every social class, but enslaved people

accused of trading with other bondspeople, and of gambling or stealing. Each case offers insight into not only the logistics of enslaved peoples' networks of exchange, but also the sheer scope of the goods traded, the individuals involved, and how the introduction of new products shaped the relationship between slaves' networks of enterprise and South Carolina's economy of slavery in the early nineteenth century.

29. For an analysis of the economic and social development of South Carolina's upper piedmont, see W. J. Megginson, *African American Life in South Carolina's Upper Piedmont, 1780–1900* (Columbia: University of South Carolina Press, 2006), 19–29.
30. Ford, "Self-Sufficiency, Cotton, and Economic Development in the South Carolina Upcountry," 261–267.
31. The historian W. J. Megginson argues that enslaved people in upstate South Carolina interacted more frequently with white people than their Lowcountry counterparts. He contends that whites in the Upcountry region of the state feared blacks less than whites in the Lowcountry and they "feared rebellion less and operated in a more relaxed atmosphere than did Lowcountry owners." For this reason, enslaved people had "some latitude in their daily lives, including local travel and contacts." See Megginson, *African-American Life in South Carolina's Upper Piedmont*, 9.
32. Lacy K. Ford, *Origins of Southern Radicalism: The South Carolina Upcountry, 1800–1860* (New York: Oxford University Press, 1988), 6–8.
33. Ball, *Slavery in the United States*, 130.
34. Ball, *Slavery in the United States*, 130.
35. David E. Peterson, "Slavery, Slaves, and Cash in a Georgia Village, 1825–1865," *Journal of Southern History* 75, no. 4 (November 2009): 880.
36. "Petition of the Inhabitants and Wardens and others of Columbia praying that owners of slaves may be prohibited by law from hiring to their slaves their own time," 1819, #97, SCDAH; Richland District petition, #494, 1819, SCDAH; Richland District Presentment, #12, 1819, SCDAH.
37. Ball, *Slavery in the United States*, 130.
38. For a discussion of the history of whiteness, class, and capitalism in the first six decades of the nineteenth century, see Merritt, *Masterless Men*, 1–37; David Roediger, *The Wages of Whiteness: Race and the Making of the American Working Class* (London: Verso, 1991).
39. "The Petition of Sundry Inhabitants of Georgetown in the said State, and its Vicinity," Records of the General Assembly, 1810, #76, SCDAH. See also "Presentment of the Grand Jury of Georgetown District, Nov. Term 1810," Records of the General Assembly, 1810, #6, SCDAH.
40. "The Petition of Sundry Inhabitants of Georgetown in the said State, and its Vicinity," Records of the General Assembly, 1810, #76, SCDAH.
41. "Report of the Committee to whom was referred the petition of sundry inhabitants praying the establishment of the guard in Georgetown," 1810, #74, SCDAH.
42. *City Gazette and Daily Advertiser*, December 15, 1810.
43. *State v. Bob*, Kershaw District Court of Magistrates and Freeholders, #3, 1806, SCDAH. Enslaved people were summoned before the Court of Magistrates and Freeholders for

a variety of economic crimes, including larceny, retailing goods, and being in possession of stolen goods. In this period, enslaved people were most frequently brought to trial for larceny, not for illicit engagement in trade. In fact, in one Upcountry district, between 1800 and 1830, 21 percent of the cases heard by the Magistrates' court involved slaves' stealing goods or illegally trading commodities such as liquor or cotton. The other 79 percent of cases heard by the Pendleton and Anderson Court of Magistrates and Freeholders involved crimes such as harboring runaway slaves, assault and battery, and possessing firearms. Between 1800 and 1830 in the Pendleton and Anderson Districts, there are no cases that involved enslaved people illegally engaged in trade.

44. *State v. Sam*, 1817, Kershaw District Court of Magistrates and Freeholders, #25, SCDAH; *State v. Garrick*, Kershaw District Court of Magistrates and Freeholders, #27, SCDAH;

45. This analysis incorporates theft into slaves' networks of trade because as enslaved peoples' economic activities became more circumscribed in the late eighteenth and early nineteenth centuries, enslaved people used any means at their disposal to procure goods that they wanted or needed. For the literature on slaves and theft (property crimes) in the slaveholding South, see Edward Ayers, *Vengeance and Justice: Crime and Punishment in the Nineteenth-Century American South* (New York: Oxford University Press, 1984); Eugene Genovese, *Roll, Jordan, Roll: The World the Slaves Made* (New York: Vintage Books, 1974), 599–612; Lawrence Levine, *Black Culture, Black Consciousness: Afro-American Folk Thought from Slavery to Freedom* (New York: Oxford University Press, 1977), 77–78; Alex Lichtenstein, "'That Disposition to Theft, Which They Have Been Branded': Moral Economy, Slave Management, and the Law," *Journal of Southern History* 21, no. 3 (Spring 1988): 413–440; Kenneth Stamp, *The Peculiar Institution: Slavery in the Ante-Bellum South* (New York: Knopf, 1956), 125–127.

46. Ball, *Slavery in the United States*, 299.

47. Ball, *Slavery in the United States*, 301.

48. Ball, *Slavery in the United States*, 301.

49. Ball, *Slavery in the United States*, 144.

50. Lichtenstein, "'That Disposition to Theft,'" 418.

51. For a discussion of the challenge with understanding the history of enslaved people and resistance, see Walter Johnson, "On Agency," *Journal of Social History* 37, no. 1 (Autumn 2003): 113–124.

52. Stephen Mihm shows the ways in which the counterfeit economy of money was a response to the lack of a national currency between the American Revolution and the Civil War. Stephen Mihm, *A Nation of Counterfeiters: Capitalists, Con Men, and the Making of the United States* (Cambridge, Mass.: Harvard University Press, 2007).

53. Not the same women referenced earlier in the chapter.

54. *State v. Sukey, a Negro Woman*, 1812, Kershaw District Court of Magistrates and Freeholders, #9, SCDAH. See also Laura Edwards, *The People and Their Peace: Legal Culture and the Transformation of Inequality in the Post-Revolutionary South* (Chapel Hill: University of North Carolina Press, 2009), 134–136. For discussion of black

slaveholders, see Larry Koger, *Black Slaveowners: Free Black Slave Masters in South Carolina, 1790–1860* (Jefferson, N.C.: McFarland, 1985).

55. *State v. Sukey, a Negro Woman*, 1812, Kershaw District Court of Magistrates and Freeholders, #9, SCDAH.
56. For a discussion of paper money in the early national period, see Joshua R. Greenberg, *Banknotes and Shinplasters: The Rage for Paper Money in the Early Republic* (Philadelphia: University of Pennsylvania Press, 2020); Stephen Mihm, *A Nation of Counterfeiters: Capitalists, Con Men, and the Making of the United States* (Cambridge, Mass.: Harvard University Press, 2009); Sharon Ann Murphy, *Other People's Money: How Banking Worked in the Early American Republic* (Baltimore, Md.: Johns Hopkins University Press, 2017).
57. *State v. Frank, Dick, and Milton*, Court of Magistrates and Freeholders, Kershaw District, 1816, #15, SCDAH.
58. *State v. Frank, Dick, and Milton.*
59. *State v. Frank, Dick, and Milton.*
60. *State v. Frank, Dick, and Milton.*
61. *State v. Frank, Dick, and Milton.*
62. For an analysis of localism in antebellum Southern courts, see Laura Edwards, *The People and Their Peace: Legal Culture and the Transformation of Inequality in the Post-Revolutionary South* (Chapel Hill: University of North Carolina Press, 2009).
63. 1810 United States Federal Census, Kershaw County, South Carolina, Roll 62, Page 448, Image 00181, Ancestry.com.
64. 1820 United States Federal Census, Kershaw County, South Carolina, Roll M33, Page 146, Image 299, Ancestry.com.
65. Lacy Ford describes the distinction between a middling slaveholder and a planter. See Ford, *Origins of Southern Radicalism*, 59–71. For an analysis of the emergent middle class in the slaveholding South during the nineteenth century, see Jonathan Daniel Wells, *The Origins of the Southern Middle Class, 1800–1861* (Chapel Hill: University of North Carolina Press, 2004); Jonathan Daniel Wells and Jennifer R. Green, eds. *The Southern Middle Class in the Long Nineteenth Century* (Baton Rouge: Louisiana State University Press, 2011).
66. Ball, *Slavery in the United States*, 195.
67. *Camden Gazette*, April 4, 1815. See also L. Glen Inabinet, "'The Fourth of July Incident' of 1816," in *South Carolina Legal History: Proceedings of the Reynolds Conference, University of South Carolina, December 2–3, 1977*, ed. Herbert A. Johnson (Spartanburg: University of South Carolina, 1980), 209–221. Few historians have examined this alleged planned slave revolt. When scholars have referenced this incident, they almost always cite the aforementioned Inabinet paper.
68. Records of the General Assembly of South Carolina, NDoo (circa 1816), #1661, SCDAH; Records of the General Assembly of South Carolina, NDoo (circa 1816), #1816, SCDAH. See also Edwin C. Holland, *A Refutation of the Calumnies Circulated Against the Southern & Western States, Respecting the Institution and Existence of Slavery Among Them* (Charleston: A. E. Miller, 1822), 75–79.

69. "Presentment of the Grand Jury of Kershaw District, Fall Term 1816," Records of the General Assembly, 1816, #15, SCDAH.
70. "Presentment of the Grand Jury of Kershaw District, Fall Term 1816," Records of the General Assembly, 1816, #15, SCDAH. In the following year, whites from Kershaw again expressed dismay at ineffective laws that failed to curtail trade between enslaved people and white liquor vendors. See "Presentment of the Grand Jury of Kershaw District," Records of the General Assembly, 1817, #8, SCDAH.
71. "Inhabitants of the Orangeburg District, Amelia Township Petition," Records of the General Assembly of South Carolina," 1816, #321, SCDAH.
72. "Inhabitants of the Orangeburg District, Amelia Township Petition," 1816.
73. "Inhabitants of the Orangeburg District, Amelia Township Petition," 1816.
74. "Inhabitants of the Orangeburg District, Amelia Township Petition," 1816.
75. "Inhabitants of the Orangeburg District, Amelia Township Petition," 1816.
76. "Inhabitants of the Orangeburg District, Amelia Township Petition," 1816.
77. "Report of the Judiciary Committee on the Petition of Sundry Inhabitants of Amelia Township," Records of the General Assembly, 1816, #125, SCDAH.
78. David J. McCord, *Statutes at Large of South Carolina: Acts from 1814 to 1836, with an Appendix* (Columbia, S. C.: A. S. Johnston, 1839), 61.
79. Records of the General Assembly of South Carolina, NDoo (c. 1818), #1516, SCDAH.
80. Records of the General Assembly of South Carolina, NDoo (c. 1818), #1516, SCDAH.
81. House of Representatives Judiciary Committee Report on the Petition of the Mechanics of Columbia, Records of the General Assembly of South Carolina, NDoo, #718, SCDAH; Senate Judiciary Committee Report on the Petition of the Mechanics of Columbia, 1818, #66, SCDAH.
82. As a point of comparison, between 1815 and 1817, there were three complaints related to slaves trading or self-hire sent to state lawmakers.
83. Records of the General Assembly of South Carolina, NDoo, #1566, SCDAH.
84. "Presentment of the Grand Jury of Georgetown District for Term October 1818," Records of the General Assembly, 1818, #7, SCDAH; "Petition from the Mechanics of Columbia to prohibit Masters from Permitting their mechanic slaves to hire their own time and to prohibit such slaves from taking apprentices," Records of the General Assembly, NDoo (c. 1818), #1565 and #1566, SCDAH; "Presentment of the Grand Jury of Kershaw District for Nov. Term 1819," Records of the General Assembly, 1819, #5 and #6, SCDAH; "Presentment of the Grand Jury of Orangeburgh District," Records of the General Assembly, 1819, #9, #10, #11, SCDAH; "Grand Jury Presentments of Richland District," Records of the General Assembly, 1819, #12 and #13, SCDAH; "Petition of the Inhabitants and Wardens and others of Columbia praying that owners of slaves may be prohibited by law from hiring to their slaves their own time," Records of the General Assembly, 1819, #97 and #98, SCDAH.
85. Report of the Judiciary Committee on the petition of the Merchants and shopkeepers of the town of Camden, Records of the General Assembly of South Carolina, ND (c. 1818), #2599, SCDAH; Records of the General Assembly, ND (c. 1818), #1855, SCDAH.
86. *State v. Francis Anone*, 2 Nott & McCord 27 (1819).

87. It is also possible that the slaveholder held a personal grudge against Anone or that the slaveholder had already established a trading relationship with another merchant other than Anone. The trial records do not provide the name of the slaveholder.
88. *State v. Jacob Sonnerkalb.*
89. *State v. Jacob Sonnerkalb.* See also Forret, *Race Relations at the Margins*, 100–101.
90. For the Kershaw District, see *State v. Sam*, Kershaw District Court of Magistrates and Freeholder Records, #25, 1817, SCDAH; *State v. Garrick*, Kershaw District Court of Magistrates and Freeholder Records, #27, 1819, SCDAH; *State v. Jim*, Kershaw District Court of Magistrates and Freeholder Records, #28, 1819, SCDAH. For the Laurens District, see *State v. Dublin, a Negro*, Laurens District Court of Magistrates and Freeholder Records, #4, 1816, SCDAH; *State v. Jack, a Negro*, Laurens District Court of Magistrates and Freeholder Records, #6, 1816, SCDAH.
91. *State v. Washington Rainfro*, Union District Criminal Court Records, #422, 1816, SCDAH.
92. *State v. James Graham*, Union District Criminal Court Records, #506, 1820, SCDAH.

4. "THE FACILITY OF OBTAINING MONEY": VIOLENCE, FEAR, AND ACCUMULATION IN THE VESEY ERA

1. James Hamilton, 1822, *Negro Plot. An Account of the Late Intended Insurrection Among a Portion of the Blacks of the City of Charleston, South Carolina*, Documenting the American South. University Library, The University of North Carolina at Chapel Hill, 1999, 17. https://docsouth.unc.edu/church/hamilton/hamilton.html. See also Michael P. Johnson, "Telemaque's Pilgrimage? A Tale of Two Charleston Churches, Three Missionaries, and Four Ministers, 1783–1817," *South Carolina Historical Magazine* 118, no. 1 (January 2017): 4–36.
2. For a discussion of the rise of sugar production in St. Domingue, see Trevor Burnard and John Garrigus, *The Plantation Machine: Atlantic Capitalism in French Saint-Domingue and British Jamaica* (Philadelphia: University of Pennsylvania Press, 2016); Laurent DuBois, *Avengers of the New World: The Story of the Haitian Revolution* (Cambridge, Mass.: Harvard University Press, 2005).
3. Hamilton, *Negro Plot*, 17.
4. Hamilton, *Negro Plot*, 17.
5. Hamilton, *Negro Plot*, 17.
6. Hamilton, *Negro Plot*, 43–44.
7. Hamilton, *Negro Plot*, 43–44.
8. In the early national era, lotteries became an efficient way for municipalities and cities to raise money for internal improvements without directly taxing citizens. In the 1780s, South Carolina's General Assembly permitted the Charleston city administrators to hold lotteries as a way to raise funds for public improvement projects. In particular, the East Bay Street lottery collected money from participants to extend East Bay Street and protect the southernmost region of Charleston from the daily tides on

the waterfront. Christina Rae Butler, *Lowcountry at High Tide: A History of Flooding, Drainage, and Reclamation in Charleston, South Carolina* (Columbia: University of South Carolina Press, 2020), 45–47; Joyce E. Chaplin, *An Anxious Pursuit: Agricultural Innovation and Modernity in the Lower South, 1730–1815*. Chapel Hill: University of North Carolina Press, 1993), 178–182.

9. According to measuringworth.com, in terms of income value, $1,500 in 1800 is $1.081 million in income value as of 6/25/2020. See https://www.measuringworth.com/dollar valuetoday/relativevalue.php?year_source=1800&amount=1500&year_result=2019.
10. The emancipation deed stipulates that Telemaque's owner at the time of his emancipation was Mary Clodner, but Joseph Vesey did appear as a witness on December 7, 1799. The deed suggests that Vesey transferred ownership rights of Telemaque to Clodner between the time that Joseph Vesey and Telemaque arrived in Charleston and the fall of 1799. Douglas R. Egerton and Robert L. Paquette, *The Denmark Vesey Affair: A Documentary History* (Gainesville: University of Florida Press, 2017), 10. Another man, lottery commissioner Charles Core, was in attendance on December 7, 1799, when the terms of Telemaque's manumission were legalized. The historian Nic Butler suggests that Core was a witness to the signing of Telemaque's manumission papers to validate that Telemaque's winnings were in fact his and that his participation in the lottery was legitimate. See "Denmark Vesey's Winning Lottery Ticket," https://www.ccpl.org /charleston-time-machine/denmark-veseys-winning-lottery-ticket.
11. Hamilton, *Negro Plot*, 42–43.
12. Hamilton, *Negro Plot*, 2–3.
13. Douglas Egerton, *He Shall Go Free: The Lives of Denmark Vesey* (Madison, Wisc.: Madison House, 1999), 104–106.
14. Hamilton, *Negro Plot*, 4–5.
15. Hamilton, *Negro Plot*, 12.
16. The historian Kellie Carter Jackson argues that Denmark Vesey may have been inspired by not only his time enslaved in St. Domingue, but also by the violent slave rebellion in St. Domingue that began in 1791. See Kellie Carter Jackson, *Force and Free: Black Abolitionists and the Politics of Violence* (Philadelphia: University of Pennsylvania Press, 2019), 15–17.
17. Hamilton, *Negro Plot*, 30.
18. Hamilton, *Negro Plot*, 30.
19. For an analysis of conspiracy scares in regions of the slaveholding Atlantic world, see Jason T. Sharples, *The World That Fear Made: Slave Revolts and Conspiracy Scares in Early America* (Philadelphia: University of Pennsylvania Press, 2020).
20. Not all enslaved violence was directed toward whites. The historian Jeff Forret has argued that violent behavior between enslaved people was not uncommon, especially if the issues between bondspeople had to do with romantic relationships or money. See Jeff Forret, *Slave Against Slave: Plantation Violence in the Old South* (Baton Rouge: Louisiana State University Press, 2015).
21. Michael P. Johnson, "Denmark Vesey and His Co-Conspirators," *William and Mary Quarterly* 58, no. 4 (October 2001): 971.

22. Egerton and Paquette, *The Denmark Vesey Affair*, xxiii.
23. The scholarly skepticism of the Denmark Vesey plot has forced historians to contend with the propositions first made by Richard Wade in 1965 and again by Michael Johnson in 2001 that enslaved and free black Charlestonians were falsely accused, tried, and executed for an event that they never planned. The trial record does reveal, however, that white Charlestonians feared enslaved and free black residents of Charleston who exerted their political and economic independence openly. In 2001 historian Michael Johnson reviewed three works on Vesey, by Douglas Egerton, *He Shall Go Free: The Lives of Denmark Vesey* (Madison, Wisc.: Madison House, 1999) and Edward Pearson, *Designs Against Charleston: The Trial Record of the Denmark Vesey Slave Conspiracy of 1822* (Chapel Hill: University of North Carolina, 1999) and David Robertson, *Denmark Vesey: The Buried Story of America's Largest Slave Rebellion and the Man Who Led It* (New York: Knopf, 1999). In the review, he challenged the widely held notion that there was a slave revolt conspiracy led by Vesey. Instead, Johnson builds upon the argument first proposed by Richard Wade that the conspiracy was less a product of the black imagination and more a mirror of white paranoia. See Johnson, "Denmark Vesey and His Co-Conspirators," 915–976. However, there is no scholarly consensus on how to interpret the events of 1822. For an examination of Johnson's arguments in context with newer research on the Vesey plot, see James O'Neil Spady, "Power and Confession: On the Credibility of the Earliest Reports of the Denmark Vesey Slave Conspiracy," *William and Mary Quarterly* 68, no. 2 (April 2011): 287–304. For a rebuttal of the Johnson argument, see David Robertson, "Inconsistent Contextualism: The Hermeneutics of Michael Johnson," *William and Mary Quarterly* 59, no. 1 (January 2002): 153–158; James Sidbury, "Plausible Stories and Varnished Truths," *William and Mary Quarterly* 59, no. 1 (January 2002): 179–184. For a discussion of Denmark Vesey in the memory of slavery in Charleston and South Carolina, see Douglas R. Egerton, "'Why They Did Not Preach Up This Thing': Denmark Vesey and Revolutionary Theology," *South Carolina Historical Magazine* 100, no. 4 (October 1999): 298–318; Ethan J. Kytle and Blain Roberts, *Denmark Vesey's Garden: Slavery and Memory in the Cradle of the Confederacy* (New York: The New Press, 2018); John Lofton, *Denmark Vesey's Revolt: The Slave Plot That Lit a Fuse to Fort Sumter* (Kent, Ohio: Kent State University Press, 1983); Walter C. Rucker, "'I Will Gather All Nations': Resistance, Culture, and Pan-African Collaboration in Denmark Vesey's South Carolina," *Journal of Negro History* 86, no. 2 (2001): 132–147.
24. "Citizens of Columbia and vicinity, Petition to End Allowing Slaves to Hire Their Own Time," Records of the General Assembly, n.d., #2893, SCDAH.
25. "Citizens of Columbia and vicinity, Petition to End Allowing Slaves to Hire Their Own Time," Records of the General Assembly, n.d., #2893, SCDAH.
26. Denmark Vesey, approximately, Lionel Henry Kennedy, and Thomas Parker. *An official report of the trials of sundry Negroes, charged with an attempt to raise an insurrection in the state of South-Carolina: preceded by an introduction and narrative: and, in*

an appendix, a report of the trials of four white persons on indictments for attempting to excite the slaves to insurrection (Charleston, S.C.: James R. Schneck 1822), 61–79. https://www.loc.gov/item/90107205/.

27. Vesey, *An Official Report*, 27.
28. Vesey, *An Official Report*, 26.
29. *Negro Plot*, 30.
30. Vesey, *An Official Report*, 28.
31. "Newberry District Presentment," #13, 1822, Records of the South Carolina General Assembly, SCDAH.
32. "Georgetown District Presentment," #13, 1823, Records of the South Carolina General Assembly, SCDAH; "Georgetown District Presentment complaining of the practice of dueling, and of Negroes trafficking with one another," #11, 1823, Records of the South Carolina General Assembly, SCDAH. For a discussion of slave hiring in antebellum Charleston, see Michael D. Thompson, *Working on the Dock of the Bay: Labor and Enterprise in an Antebellum Southern Port* (Columbia: University of South Carolina 2011), 42–44.
33. "Presentment of the Grand Jury at Fall Term 1822, Newberry District," Records of the South Carolina General Assembly, 1822, #13, SCDAH; "Presentment of the Grand Jury of Charleston District," Records of the South Carolina General Assembly, 1822, #3, SCDAH; "Presentment of the Grand Jury from Georgetown District Made at the Fall Court in 1823," Records of the South Carolina General Assembly, 1823, #11 and #14, SCDAH; "Officers of the Edisto Island Auxiliary Association," Records of the South Carolina General Assembly, 1823, #151, SCDAH; "Black Swamp Association Petition," Records of the South Carolina General Assembly, 1823, #147, SCDAH.
34. "Citizens of Columbia and Vicinity, Petition to End Allowing Slaves to Hire Their Own Time," Records of the General Assembly, n.d., #2893, SCDAH.
35. Richard Brookes and William Darby, *Darby's Edition of Brooke's Universal Gazetteer, or a New Geographical Dictionary* (Philadelphia, 1823), 366.
36. "Citizens of Columbia and Vicinity, Petition to End Allowing Slaves to Hire Their Own Time," Records of the South Carolina General Assembly, Document ND #2893, SCDAH.
37. Henry W. DeSaussure, *A Series of Numbers Addressed to the Public in the Subject of Slaves and Free People of Colour; First Published in the South Carolina State Gazette, in the Months of September and October 1822* (Columbia, S.C.: State Gazette Office, 1822). See also Lacy K. Ford, *Deliver Us From Evil: The Slavery Question in the Old South* (New York: Oxford University Press, 2009), 240–246.
38. For a comprehensive analysis of the slave revolt in St. Domingue, see Laurent Dubois, *Avengers of the New World: The Story of the Haitian Revolution* (Cambridge, Mass.: Harvard University Press, 2009). Historians have also examined the ways in which the revolt in St. Domingue influenced enslaved people and the institution of slavery in the United States. See James Alexander Dun, *Dangerous Neighbors: Making the Haitian Revolution in Early America* (Philadelphia: University of Pennsylvania Press, 2016);

Julius Scott, *A Common Wind: Afro-American Organization in the Revolution Against Slavery* (London: Verso, 2018); Ashli White, *Encountering Revolution: Haiti and the Making of the Early Republic* (Baltimore, Md.: Johns Hopkins University Press, 2010).

39. Thomas Pinckney, *Reflections, occasioned by the late disturbances in Charleston, by Achates* (Charleston, S.C.: A. E. Miller, 1822), 6–7.
40. Pinckney, *Reflections*, 9–30.
41. "To regulate the performance of Patrol Duty on Charleston Neck," *City Gazette and Commercial Daily Advertiser*, 10/29/1822.
42. "To regulate the performance of Patrol Duty on Charleston Neck," *City Gazette and Commercial Daily Advertiser*, 10/29/1822.
43. *State v. Negro Man Slave Jim*, Kershaw District Court of Magistrates and Freeholders, #30, 1822, SCDAH.
44. *State v. Negro Man Slave Jim*, Kershaw District Court of Magistrates and Freeholders, #30, 1822, SCDAH.
45. *State v. Negro Man Slave Jim*, Kershaw District Court of Magistrates and Freeholders, #30, 1822, SCDAH.
46. ND #2059, Microfilm Reel #1, Frames 308–314, Records of the South Carolina General Assembly, SCDAH, Columbia, S.C.
47. Jonathan Martin, *Divided Mastery: Slave Hiring in the American South* (Cambridge, Mass.: Harvard University Press, 2004), 1–16.
48. Records of the General Assembly, #502, 1828, SCDAH.
49. "State v. Randolph Alexander," #600, Union District Criminal Case Files, SCDAH.
50. Walter Johnson, "Clerks All! Or, Slaves with Cash," *Journal of the Early Republic* 26, no. 4 (Winter 2006): 643.
51. David J. McCord, *Statutes at Large of South Carolina: Acts Relating to Charleston, Courts, Slaves and Rivers* (Columbia, S.C.: A. S. Johnson, 1840), 461.
52. McCord, *Statutes at Large of South Carolina: Acts Relating to Charleston, Courts, Slaves and Rivers*, 461. For a history of the South Carolina Seaman Acts, a set of statutes that regulated the lives of black seamen, see Michael A. Schoeppner, *Moral Contagion: Black Atlantic Sailors, Citizenship, and Diplomacy in Antebellum America* (New York: Cambridge University Press, 2019).
53. McCord, *Statutes at Large of South Carolina: Acts Relating to Charleston, Courts, Slaves and Rivers*, 462.
54. McCord, *Statutes at Large of South Carolina: Acts Relating to Charleston, Courts, Slaves and Rivers*, 462.
55. For a discussion of enslaved women as runaways in antebellum Charleston and their hired-out labor, see Amani T. Marshall, "'They Are Supposed to Be Lurking About the City': Enslaved Women Runaways in Antebellum Charleston," *South Carolina Historical Magazine* 110, no. 3 (July 2014): 188–212.
56. Angela Davis, "Reflections on the Black Woman's Role in the Community of Slaves," *Massachusetts Review* 13, no. 1/2 (Winter–Spring 1972): 81–100; Deborah Gray White, *Ar'n't I a Woman: Female Slaves in the Plantation South* (New York: Norton, 1985).

57. Stephanie Camp, *Closer to Freedom: Enslaved Women and Everyday Resistance in the Plantation South* (Chapel Hill: University of North Carolina Press, 2004), 36–77; Jacqueline Jones, *Labor of Love, Labor of Sorrow: Black Women, Work, and the Family from Slavery to the Present* (New York: Basic Books, 1985), 11–43; Amritra Chakrabarti Myers, *Forging Freedom: Black Women and the Pursuit of Liberty in Antebellum Charleston* (Chapel Hill: University of North Carolina Press, 2011), 77–112.
58. See, for example, *A. S. Rhodes v. Lydia Bunch, et al.* 3 McCord 66 (1825). For a discussion of trade between enslaved people and poor whites in the antebellum South, see Charles C. Bolton, *Poor Whites of the Antebellum South: Tenants and Laborers in Central North Carolina and Eastern Mississippi* (Durham, N.C.: Duke University Press, 1994), 106–108; Jeff Forret, *Race Relations at the Margins: Slaves and Poor Whites in the Antebellum Southern Countryside* (Baton Rouge: Louisiana State University Press, 2006); Kathleen Hilliard, *Masters, Slaves, and Exchange: Power's Purchase in the Old South* (New York: Cambridge University Press, 2014); Larry E. Hudson Jr., *To Have and to Hold: Slave Work and Family Life in Antebellum South Carolina* (Athens: University of Georgia Press, 1997); Timothy Lockley, "Trading Encounters Between Non-Elite Whites and African Americans in Savannah, 1790–1860," *Journal of Southern History* 66, no. 1 (February 2000): 25–48); Timothy Lockley, *Lines in the Sand: Race and Class in Lowcountry Georgia, 1750–1860* (Athens: University of Georgia Press, 2001), 57–97; Dylan C. Penningroth, *The Claims of Kinfolk: African American Property and Community in the Nineteenth-Century South* (Chapel Hill: University of North Carolina Press, 2003), 65–67.
59. *State v. Isaac*, Anderson District Court of Magistrates and Freeholders, #53, 1830, SCDAH.
60. See *State v. Solomon, A Slave*, Kershaw District Court of Magistrates and Freeholders, #35, 1824, SCDAH; *State v. Alexander, Bartlett, and Trim*, Pendleton/Anderson District Court of Magistrates and Freeholders, #7, 1824, SCDAH.
61. *State v. Thomas Spurrier*, SCDAH, Kershaw Court of Magistrates and Freeholders, #35.
62. Union District, Records of the Circuit Court, 1822, #600, SCDAH; Union District, Records of the Circuit Court, 1822, #655, SCDAH; Union District, Records of the Circuit Court, 1824, #776, SCDAH; Union District, Records of the Circuit Court, 1824, #794, SCDAH; Union District, Records of the Circuit Court, 1825, #824, SCDAH.
63. "Recollections of Slavery by a Runaway Slave," in *I Belong to South Carolina: South Carolina Slave Narratives*, ed. Susana Ashton (Columbia: University of South Carolina Press, 2010), 63.
64. *The State v. Amey*, #32, Kershaw Court of Magistrates and Freeholders, SCDAH, Columbia, South Carolina.
65. *State v. Bartlett, Trim, Alexander*, Court of Magistrates and Freeholders, Pendleton/Anderson District Trial Papers, #7, SCDAH.
66. *State v. Bartlett, Trim, Alexander*, Court of Magistrates and Freeholders, Pendleton/Anderson District Trial Papers, #7, SCDAH.

5. "THE NEGROES' ACCOUNTS": CAPITALIST INFLUENCES IN THE SLAVES' ECONOMY

1. John Andrew Jackson, *Experience of a Slave in South Carolina* (Chapel Hill: University of North Carolina Press, 2011), 7, https://docsouth.unc.edu/fpn/jackson/jackson.html.
2. Jackson, *Experience of a Slave in South Carolina*, 12–13.
3. Jackson, *Experience of a Slave in South Carolina*, 14–17. For a discussion of enslaved people, their purchase of alcohol, whiskey in particular, and enslaved peoples' consumer habits, see Kathleen Hilliard, *Masters, Slaves, and Exchange: Power's Purchase in the Old South.* (Cambridge: Cambridge University Press, 2014), 46–93.
4. For an analysis of the Panic of 1819 and its effect on the American and trans-Atlantic cotton industry, see Andrew H. Browning, *The Panic of 1819: The First American Depression* (Columbia: University of Missouri Press, 2019).
5. R. King Jr., "On the Management of the Butler Estate, and the Cultivation of Sugar Cane, by R. King Jr. addressed to William Washington, Esq.," *Southern Agriculturist* 1 (December 1828): 525.
6. King, "On the Management of the Butler Estate," 525.
7. King, "On the Management of the Butler Estate," 525.
8. For a discussion of the volatile cotton industry in the slaveholding South, see Joshua Rothman, *Flush Times and Fever Dreams: A Story of Capitalism in the Age of Jackson* (Athens: University of Georgia Press, 2012).
9. Alfred G. Smith, *The Economic Readjustment of an Old Cotton State: South Carolina, 1820–1860* (Columbia: University of South Carolina Press, 1958), 1–18. For a discussion of the cotton industry's expansion in the antebellum period, see Sven Beckert, *Empire of Cotton: A Global History* (New York: Vintage Books, 2015), 98–136; Walter Johnson, *River of Dark Dreams: Slavery and Empire in the Cotton Kingdom* (Cambridge, Mass.: Harvard University Press, 2013); Adam Rothman, *Slave Country: American Expansion and the Origins of the Deep South* (Cambridge, Mass.: Harvard University Press, 2009), 165–216. For an analysis of the Panic of 1819 and its effect on American banking, see Sharon Ann Murphy, *Other People's Money: How Banking Worked in the Early American Republic* (Baltimore, Md.: Johns Hopkins University Press, 2017), 85–90.
10. Smith, *The Economic Readjustment of South Carolina*, 220–221.
11. James Haw, "'The Problem of South Carolina' Reexamined: A Review Essay," *South Carolina Historical Magazine* 107, no. 1 (January 2006), 9–25; Charles Sydnor, *The Development of Southern Sectionalism, 1819–1848* (Baton Rouge: Louisiana State University Press, 1948), 250–252. For a discussion of the South Carolina Lowcountry specifically, see Peter A. Coclanis, *The Shadow of a Dream: Economic Life and Death in the South Carolina Lowcountry, 1670–1920* (New York: Oxford University Press, 1991), 111–158.
12. Enslaved people were under the constant threat of sale because of enslavers' risky financial investments. See Larry E. Hudson, *To Have and to Hold: Slave Work and Family Life in Antebellum South Carolina* (Athens: University of Georgia Press, 1997), 168–171.

13. Charles Ball, *Slavery in the United States: A Narrative of the Life and Adventures of Charles Ball, A Black Man* (New York: John S. Taylor, 1837). 166–167, https://docsouth.unc.edu/neh/ballslavery/ball.html.
14. Ball, *Slavery in the United States*, 166–167.
15. Peter Rousseau, "Jacksonian Monetary Policy, Specie Flows, and the Panic of 1837," *Journal of Economic History* 62 (June 2002): 457–488.
16. Daniel Feller, *The Jacksonian Promise: America, 1815–1840* (Baltimore, Md.: Johns Hopkins University Press, 1995); William W. Freehling, *The Prelude to Civil War: The Nullification Controversy in South Carolina, 1816–1836* (Oxford: Oxford University Press, 1992), 25–29; Edwin J. Perkins, "Langdon Cheves and the Panic of 1819: A Reassessment," *Journal of Economic History* 44, no. 2 (June 1984): 455–461; Samuel Rezneck, "The Depression of 1819–1822, A Social History," *American Historical Review* 39, no. 1 (October 1933): 28–47; Charles Sellers, *The Market Revolution: Jacksonian America, 1815–1846* (New York: Oxford University Press, 1991).
17. Theodore Rosengarten, "The Southern Agriculturist in an Age of Reform," in *Intellectual Life in Antebellum Charleston*, ed. Michael O'Brien and David Moltke-Hansen (Knoxville: The University of Tennessee Press, 1986), 279–281.
18. C. C. Pinckney, "The Traffic of Bond with Free," *Southern Agriculturist and Register of Rural Affairs* (June 1837), 281–284. By 1837, South Carolina statutes were ambiguous on the issue of slaves' trading. For a discussion of slave laws' ambiguity in North Carolina and South Carolina during the early national and antebellum periods, see Laura F. Edwards, *The People and Their Peace: Legal Culture and the Transformation of Inequality in the Post-Revolutionary South* (Chapel Hill: University of North Carolina Press, 2009).
19. Pinckney, "The Traffic of Bond with Free," 281–284.
20. Pinckney, "The Traffic of Bond with Free," 281–284.
21. For a discussion of enslavers' provisions to slaves, see John Blassingame, *The Slave Community: Plantation Life in the Antebellum South* (New York: Oxford University Press, 1972), 263–265; Ira Berlin, *Many Thousands Gone: The First Two Centuries of Slavery in North America* (Cambridge, Mass.: Belknap Press of Harvard University Press, 1998), 32–33; Eugene Genovese, *Roll, Jordan, Roll: The World the Slaves Made* (New York: Knopf, 1974), 535–549.
22. Records of the General Assembly, #447 and #212, 1827, SCDAH.
23. Records of the General Assembly, #447 and #212, 1827, SCDAH.
24. For a discussion of violence and capitalism in the lives of enslaved people in the antebellum South, see Baptist, *The Half Has Never Been Told*, xv–xxix.
25. *Proceedings of the Agricultural Convention and of the State Agricultural Society* (Columbia, S.C.: Summer & Carroll, 1846), 107.
26. *State vs. Matthew Hartford*, Union District Criminal Court, #1997, SCDAH. Scholar Josh Lauer has argued that in the 1840s, the expansion of credit relied on trust between lender and debtor. This idea can be extended to economic relationships between merchants and enslaved people. See Josh Lauer, *Creditworthy: A History of Consumer Surveillance and Financial Identity in America* (New York: Columbia University Press, 2017), 28.

27. According to information gathered by Alfred G. Smith, the range of short-staple cotton prices for December 1842 in Charleston was between $0.575 and $0.775 per pound. See Smith, *Economic Readjustment of South Carolina*, 222.
28. *State vs. Matthew Hartford*, Union District Criminal Court, #1997, SCDAH.
29. *State vs. Matthew Hartford*, Union District Criminal Court, #1997, SCDAH.
30. "On Plantation Gardens, and the Culture of Vegetables; by the Editor," *Southern Agriculturist and Register of Rural Affairs*, August 1830.
31. "On Plantation Gardens, and the Culture of Vegetables; by the Editor," *Southern Agriculturist and Register of Rural Affairs*, August 1830.
32. Charles Joyner, *Down By the Riverside: A South Carolina Slave Community* (Urbana: University of Illinois Press, 1984), 57–67.
33. Henry William Ravenel, "Recollections of Southern Plantation Life," *Yale Review* 25 (June 1936): 751. As quoted in Schweninger, "Slave Independence and Enterprise in South Carolina, 1782–1865," 11. Though there was no indication of how Jenny paid back her debt to Ravenel, one may assume that she tended a garden and sold Ravenel the excess of her independent horticultural efforts. Thomas Porcher Ravenel Papers, 1731–1899, "Unidentified Account Book, 1829–33," *Records of Ante-Bellum Southern Plantations*, Series B, Reel 2. See also Stanley Engerman and Richard Fogel, *Time on the Cross: The Economics of American Slavery* (Boston: Little, Brown, 1974); Lacy K. Ford, "Self-Sufficiency, Cotton, and Economic Development in the South Carolina Upcountry, 1800–1860," *Journal of Economic History* 45 (June 1985): 261–267; Brian Schoen, *Fragile Fabric of Union: Cotton, Federal Politics, and the Global Origins of the Civil War* (Baltimore, Md.: Johns Hopkins University Press, 2009).
34. "Account of the Management of Pushee, the residence of Dr. Henry Ravenel; by the Editor," *Southern Agriculturist and Register of Rural Affairs*, July 1831, 4, 6; Penningroth, *The Claims of Kinfolk*, 47; Christy Clark-Pujara, *Dark Work: The Business of Slavery in Rhode Island* (New York: NYU Press, 2016), 90–94; Seth Rockman, "Negro Cloth: Mastering the Market for Slave Clothing in Antebellum America," in *American Capitalism: New Histories*, ed. Sven Beckert and Christine Desan (New York: Columbia University Press, 2018), 170–194.
35. Leach Carrigan Papers, South Caroliniana Library, University of South Carolina, Columbia.
36. McDonnell, "Money Knows No Master," 33. For a discussion of accounting and legitimacy, see Bruce G. Carruthers and Wendy Nelson Espeland, "Accounting for Rationality: Double-Entry Bookkeeping and the Rhetoric of Rationality," *American Journal of Sociology* 97 (July 1991): 31–69. For a discussion of accounting and slavery in antebellum America, see Rosenthal, *Accounting for Slavery*, 1–8.
37. Eve Chiapello, "Accounting and the Birth of the Notion of Capitalism," *Critical Perspectives on Accounting* 3, no. 18 (March 2007): 263–296; James O. Winjum, "Accounting and the Rise of Capitalism: An Accountant's View," *Journal of Accounting Research* 2, no. 9 (Autumn 1971): 333–350.
38. Peter Miller, "Accounting as a Social and Institutional Practice: An Introduction," in *Accounting as a Social and Institutional Practice*, ed. Anthony Hopwood and Peter

Miller (New York: Cambridge University Press, 1994): 1–39. See also Richard K. Fleishman, David Oldroyd, and Thomas N. Tyson, "Plantation Accounting and Management Practices in the US and the British West Indies at the End of Their Slavery Eras," *Economic History Review* 64, no. 3 (2011): 766; Jacob Metzer, "Rational Management, Modern Business Practices, and Economies of Scale in the Ante-Bellum Southern Plantations," *Explorations in Economic History* 12, no. 2 (1975): 123–150; Louis J. Stewart, "A Contingency Theory Perspective on Management Control Systems Design Among U.S. Ante-bellum Slave Plantations," *Accounting Historians Journal* 25 (June 2010): 91–120. I choose not to use the term "accountant" because I have not found documentary evidence that the term was used in this period in South Carolina. Perhaps this fact suggests that planters maintained their own financial records. For a brief discussion of this phenomenon, see Fleishman, Oldroyd, and Tyson, "Plantation Accounting and Management," 769–769. For discussions of accounting and the Atlantic Slave Trade, see Stephanie Smallwood, *Saltwater Slavery: A Middle Passage from Africa to the American Diaspora* (Cambridge, Mass.: Harvard University Press, 2008).

39. Robin Blackburn, *The Making of New World Slavery: From the Baroque to the Modern* (London: Verso Books, 1997), 1–27; Rosenthal, *Accounting for Slavery*, 135–136.
40. Stephanie Jones-Rogers, *They Were Her Property: White Women as Slaveholders in the American South* (New Haven, Conn.: Yale University Press, 2019), 63. Slaveholders throughout the South shared information about agricultural reform in the antebellum era. From the upper South to regions of the lower South, Natchez for example, historian Anthony Kaye discusses how "like-minded men convened around short-lived periodicals and institutions." See Anthony Kay, *Joining Places: Slave Neighborhoods in the Old South* (Chapel Hill: University of North Carolina Press, 2007), 96–100.
41. "Instructions for Planting Sea-Island Cotton, as Practiced on Edisto Island; by the Hon. Whitemarsh B. Seabrook," *Southern Agriculturist and Register of Rural Affairs*, March 1830.
42. "Instructions for Planting Sea-Island Cotton, as Practiced on Edisto Island; by the Hon. Whitemarsh B. Seabrook," *Southern Agriculturist and Register of Rural Affairs*, March 1830.
43. B. McBride, "Directions for Cultivating the Various Crops Grown at Hickory Hill," *Southern Agriculturist* 3 (May 1830) (italics in original).
44. McBride, "Directions for Cultivating the Various Crops Grown at Hickory Hill."
45. For discussions of slaves' growing their own subsistence, see Timothy J. Lockley, "Trading Encounters Between Non-Elite Whites and African Americans in Savannah, 1790–1860," *Journal of Southern History* 66, no. 1 (February 2000): 27; Roderick A. McDonald, *The Economy and Material Culture of Slaves: Goods and Chattels on the Sugar Plantations of Jamaica and Louisiana* (Baton Rouge: Louisiana State University Press, 1993).
46. "On the Management of Slaves," *Southern Agriculturist* 6 (June 1833), 285.
47. "On the Management of Slaves," *Southern Agriculturist*, 285.
48. John Campbell, "As 'a Kind of Freeman'? Slaves' Market-Related Activities in the South Carolina Upcountry, 1800–1860," *Slavery & Abolition* 12, no. 1 (May 1991): 131–169.

49. For literature on slavery and liberal capitalism, see Douglas Egerton, "Markets Without a Market Revolution: Southern Planters and Capitalism," *Journal of the Early Republic* 16, no. 2 (Summer 1996): 207–221; Robert Fogel and Stanley Engerman, *Time on the Cross: The Economics of American Negro Slavery* (Boston: Little, Brown, 1974); Lacy K. Ford, *Origins of Southern Radicalism: The South Carolina Upcountry, 1800–1860* (New York: Oxford University Press, 1988); Lacy K. Ford, "Self-Sufficiency, Cotton, and Economic Development in the South Carolina Upcountry, 1800–1860," *Journal of Economic History* 45, no. 2 (June 1985): 261–267; Eugene D. Genovese, *The Political Economy of Slavery: Studies in the Economy & Society of the Slave South* (New York: Pantheon Books, 1965); Eugene D. Genovese and Elizabeth Fox-Genovese, "The Slave Economies in Political Perspective," *Journal of American History* 66, no. 1 (June 1979): 7–23; Michael Merrill, "Putting 'Capitalism' in Its Place: A Review of Recent Literature," *William and Mary Quarterly* 52, no. 2 (April 1995): 315–326.
50. "Recollections of Slavery by a Runaway Slave," in *I Belong to South Carolina: South Carolina Slave Narratives*, ed. Susana Ashton (Columbia: University of South Carolina Press, 2010), 67.
51. Alex Lichtenstein, "'That Disposition to Theft, with Which They Have Been Branded': Moral Economy, Slave Management, and the Law," *Journal of Social History* 21, no. 3 (Spring 1988): 413–440. According to historian Jeff Forret, stealing within slave communities was not uncommon, as enslaved people attempted to either use goods that they stole from other bondspeople or sell to local whites. See Forret, *Slave Against Slave: Plantation Violence in the Old South* (Baton Rouge: Louisiana State University Press, 2015), 211–229. Economic anthropologist Keith Hart argues that within informal economic sectors, theft by members of the lower classes could be understood as a means of wealth redistribution. See Keith Hart, "Informal Income Opportunities and Urban Employment in Ghana," *Journal of Modern African Studies* 11, no. 1 (March 1973): 86–87.
52. Drew Gilpin Faust, *James Henry Hammond and the Old South: A Design for Mastery* (Baton Rouge: Louisiana State University Press, 1982), 70.
53. "Silver Bluff Plantation Book, 1857–1858," Box 35 Reel 18, James Henry Hammond Papers, Library of Congress, Manuscript Division, Washington, D.C.
54. "Silver Bluff Plantation Book, 1857–1858," Box 35 Reel 18, James Henry Hammond Papers, Library of Congress, Manuscript Division, Washington, D.C.
55. "Silver Bluff Plantation Book, 1857–1858," Box 35 Reel 18, James Henry Hammond Papers, Library of Congress, Manuscript Division, Washington, D.C. See also Faust, *James Henry Hammond*, 73–100. Hammond gradually realized that in order to maintain a profitable plantation, he needed to re-evaluate his style of mastery. In the 1840s and 1850s, Hammond's ideas about plantation management evolved to include more free time for his slaves and compensation for better productivity.
56. Spartanburg District Presentment, S165015, 1831, #34, SCDAH.
57. "Report upon presentment of Grand Jury of Spartanburg Concerning laws against trading with slaves," Records of the General Assembly, 1831, #52, SCDAH.

58. Lewis Cecil Gray and Esther Katherine Thompson, *History of Agriculture in the Southern United States to 1860* (Washington, D.C.: Carnegie Institution of Washington, 1933), 1027. For literature on the Panic of 1837, see Edward Baptist, "Toxic Debt, Liar Loans, and Securitized Human Beings," *Common Place* 10 (April 2010), http://commonplace.online/article/toxic-debt-liar-loans; Bray Hammond, *Banks and Politics in America: From the Revolution to the Civil War* (Princeton, N.J.: Princeton University Press, 1957): 451–499; Daniel Walker Howe, *What Hath God Wrought: The Transformation of America* (New York: Oxford University Press, 2007): 501–508; Jessica M. Lepler, *The Many Panics of 1837: People, Politics, and the Creation of a Transatlantic Financial Crisis* (New York: Cambridge University Press, 2013); Marvin Meyers, *The Jacksonian Persuasion: Politics and Belief* (Palo Alto: Stanford University Press, 1957); Alasdair Roberts, *America's First Great Depression: Economic Crisis and Political Disorder after the Panic of 1837* (Ithaca, N.Y.: Cornell University Press, 2012); Rousseau, "Jacksonian Monetary Policy," 457–488; Peter Temin, *The Jacksonian Economy* (New York: Norton, 1969); Richard H. Timberlake Jr., "The Specie Circular and the Distribution of Surplus," *Journal of Political Economy* 68 (April 1960): 109–117; Sean Wilentz, *Rise of American Democracy: Jefferson to Lincoln* (New York: Norton, 2005): 436–446. For a discussion of antebellum banking and its effect of slavery, see Calvin Schermerhorn, *The Business of Slavery and the Rise of American Capitalism, 1815–1860* (New Haven, Conn.: Yale University Press, 2015).
59. *Federal Writers' Project: Slave Narrative Project, Part 1, Administrative Files.* 1936. Manuscript/Mixed Material. https://www.loc.gov/item/mesn001/, p. 291.
60. *Federal Writers' Project: Slave Narrative Project, Part 1, Administrative Files.* 1936. Manuscript/Mixed Material. https://www.loc.gov/item/mesn001/.
61. Ford, *Origins of Southern Radicalism*, 51–52.
62. "Proceedings of the South Carolina Agricultural Society," *Farmer's Register*, September 30, 1842.
63. William M. Dana, *The Merchants Magazine and Commercial Review* (New York, 1850), 507–508.
64. Ford, *Origins of Southern Radicalism*, 51–57; Ford, "Self-Sufficiency, Cotton, and Economic Development in the South Carolina Upcountry," 264–266; Stephanie McCurry, *Masters of Small Worlds: Yeoman Households, Gender Relations, and the Political Culture of the Antebellum South Carolina Lowcountry* (New York: Oxford University Press, 1995), 61–72. For literature on plantation self-sufficiency, see Sam Bowers Hilliard, *Hog Meat and Hoecake: Food Supply in the Old South, 1840–1860* (Athens: University of Georgia Press, 2014).
65. Samuel Porcher Gaillard Plantation Journal, *Records of Ante-Bellum Southern Plantations*, Series A, Part 2.
66. Samuel Porcher Gaillard Plantation Journal, *Records of Ante-Bellum Southern Plantations*; 1840 Federal Census. According to the 1840 Federal Census, Gaillard owned 61 enslaved people.
67. Samuel Porcher Gaillard Plantation Journal, *Records of Ante-Bellum Southern Plantations.*

68. "Charleston Market," *Charleston Courier*, 1/23/1841.
69. "To Country Merchants," *Charleston Courier*, January 25, 1841. For a discussion of enslaved women's strategies to procure fashionable items, see Stephanie Camp, *Closer to Freedom: Enslaved Women and Everyday Resistance in the Plantation South* (Chapel Hill: University of North Carolina Press, 2004), 79–82.
70. It is not surprising that enslavers made calculated risks regarding how they treated their slaves. The idea of risk and slavery emerged in the nineteenth century at a time when insurance as an industry emerged as well. For a discussion of risk and financial capitalism, see Jonathan Levy, *Freaks of Fortune: The Emerging World of Capitalism and Risk in America* (Cambridge, Mass.: Harvard University Press, 2012).

6. "A MONSTROUS NUISANCE": ENSLAVED ENTERPRISES, CLASS ANXIETIES, AND THE COMING OF THE CIVIL WAR

1. As told by Harriet Martineau in *Retrospect of Western Travel* (London: Saunders and Otley, 1838), 239–240. For a discussion of South Carolina topography, see Walter Edgar, *South Carolina: A History*, 1–9.
2. Laura F. Edwards, *The People and Their Peace: Legal Culture and the Transformation of Inequality in the Post-Revolutionary South* (Chapel Hill: University of North Carolina Press, 2009), 144–149; Dylan C. Penningroth, *The Claims of Kinfolk: African American Property and Community in the Nineteenth-Century South* (Chapel Hill: University of North Carolina Press, 2003), 79–109.
3. Martineau, *Retrospect of Western Travel*, 239–240. The basket-making tradition that enslaved people in the South Carolina Lowcountry created was an important feature of Gullah and Geechee culture. Basket-making was among the skills that bondspeople on Lowcountry rice plantations cultivated in the eighteenth and nineteenth centuries. See J. Lorand Matory, "The Illusion of Isolation: The Gullah/Geechees and the Political Economy of African Culture in the Americas," *Comparative Studies in Society and History* 50, no. 4 (2008): 949–980. For an exploration of the history of the Gullah language, see Charles Joyner, *Down By the Riverside: A South Carolina Slave Community* (Urbana: University of Illinois Press, 1984).
4. Martineau, *Retrospect of Western Travel*, 240.
5. Martineau, *Retrospect of Western Travel*, 240.
6. Anne E. Bailey, *The Weeping Time: Memory and the Largest Slave Auction in American History* (New York: Cambridge University Press, 2017); Walter Johnson, *Soul by Soul: Life Inside the Antebellum Slave Market* (Cambridge, Mass.: Harvard University Press, 1999).
7. John Andrew Jackson, "The Experience of a Slave in South Carolina," in *I Belong to South Carolina: South Carolina Slave Narratives*, ed. Susana Ashton (Columbia: University of South Carolina Press, 2010), 109.

8. Jeff Forret, *Slave Against Slave: Plantation Violence in the Old South* (Baton Rouge: Louisiana State University Press, 2015), 201–203; Douglas R. Egerton, "Markets Without a Market Revolution: Southern Planters and Capitalism," *Journal of the Early Republic* 16, no. 2 (1996): 207–221.
9. Lawrence T. McDonnell, "Money Knows No Master: Market Relations and the American Slave Community," in *Developing Dixie: Modernization in a Traditional Society*, ed. Winfred B. Moore Jr., Joseph F. Tripp, and Lyon G. Tyler Jr. (Westport, Conn.: Greenwood, 1988), 33.
10. *The Charleston Mercury*, August 17, 1857.
11. 33 S.C.L. 266,1848 WL 2431 (S.C. App.L.). Italics added for emphasis.
12. 33 S.C.L. 266,1848 WL 2431 (S.C. App.L.).
13. South Carolina General Assembly, Records of the General Assembly, "Report of the Committee on the Judiciary upon the petition of Abbeville praying an alteration of the laws in relation to the duties of grand jurors," 1848, #197, SCDAH. The Committee of the Judiciary members included Wilmot G. DeSaussure, Nelson Mitchell, J. H. Irby, Charles Macbeth, Charles C. Hay, R. L. Tillinghast, Thomas Thompson, and William R. Robertson.
14. For a discussion of Southern laws that regulated—and protected—the legal domination of enslavers over enslaved people, see Andrew Fede, *People Without Rights: An Interpretation of the Fundamentals of the Law of Slavery in the U.S. South* (New York: Garland, 1992); Eugene D. Genovese, *Roll, Jordan, Roll: The World the Slaves Made.* (New York: Pantheon Books, 1974), 25–49; Thomas Morris, *Southern Slavery and the Law: 1619–1860* (Chapel Hill: University of North Carolina Press, 1999), 262–288; Mark Tushnet, *The American Law of Slavery, 1810–1860: Considerations of Humanity and Interest* (Princeton, N.J.: Princeton University Press, 1981); Jenny Wahl, *The Bondsman's Burden: An Economic Analysis of the Common Law of Southern Slavery* (Cambridge: Cambridge University Press, 1998).
15. According to the 1850 Census, the only member of the Committee on the Judiciary who did not own slaves was Charles C. Hay. The others owned between 3 slaves (Nelson Mitchell) and 83 slaves (Thomas Thompson). 1850 United States Federal Census, South Carolina.
16. "Folder 3," Perrin Family Papers, Southern Historical Collection, The Wilson Library, University of North Carolina at Chapel Hill.
17. For a discussion of slave religion, see Albert Raboteau, *Slave Religion: The Invisible Institution in the Antebellum South* (New York, 1978).
18. Folder 3, Perrin Family Papers, Southern Historical Collection, The Wilson Library, University of North Carolina at Chapel Hill; Lewis C. Gray, *Agriculture in the Southern United States to 1860*, Vol. II (Washington, D.C.: Carnegie Institute of Washington, 1941), 697. For a discussion of bondspeople trading with white merchants, storekeepers, and yeoman farmers, see Jeff Forret, "Slaves, Poor Whites, and the Underground Economy of the Rural Carolinas," *Journal of Southern History* 70, no. 4 (November 2004): 783–824; Forret, *Race Relations at the Margins: Slaves and*

Poor Whites in the Antebellum Southern Countryside (Baton Rouge: Louisiana State University Press, 2006), 74–114; Timothy J. Lockley, "Trading Encounters Between Non-Elite Whites and African Americans in Savannah, 1790–1860," *Journal of Southern History* 66, no. 1 (February 2000): 27; Roderick A. McDonald, *The Economy and Material Culture of Slaves: Goods and Chattels Other Sugar Plantations of Jamaica and Louisiana* (Baton Rouge: Louisiana State University Press, 1993); Dylan Penningroth, *The Claims of Kinfolk: African-American Community and Property in the Nineteenth Century South* (Chapel Hill: University of North Carolina Press, 2003), 66–67.

19. Of the 18 enslaved people with accounts, 16 were men and two, Charity and Huldy, were women. Charity had $5.55 and Huldy had $3.65 in their respective accounts.
20. Folder 6—Undated, Perrin Family Papers, Southern Historical Collection, The Wilson Library, University of North Carolina at Chapel Hill.
21. Folder 6—Undated, Perrin Family Papers, Southern Historical Collection, The Wilson Library, University of North Carolina at Chapel Hill.
22. Whitemarsh Seabrook, "An Essay on the Management of Slaves, and Especially, on their Religious Instruction: Read Before the Agricultural Society of St. John's Colleton," (Charleston: A. E. Miller, 1834).
23. Seabrook, "An Essay on the Management of Slaves."
24. The most prominent articulation of slaveholders' paternalist ethos comes from the historian Eugene Genovese. See Eugene Genovese, *Roll, Jordan, Roll: The World the Slaves Made* (New York: Pantheon, 1974), 75–86. Historians have explored more nuanced interpretations of slaveholder paternalism. Jeffrey Young and Lacy Ford, in particular, have offered interpretations of the paternalism debate that addresses the criticisms expressed in the literature on capitalism and paternalism. Young rejected the use of *paternalism* in his analysis and instead opted for the term *corporate individualism*. Corporate individualism, according to Young, described domestic relations between slave owners and their slaves. Slavery represented an extension of the household economy, and therefore enslaved people were members of the slaveholders' domestic sphere. Ford favors the term *paternalism* and argues that whites accepted the paternalist ethos as a defense against abolitionist fervor. See Young, *Domesticating Slavery*, 123–160; Lucy K. Ford, "Reconfiguring the Old South: 'Solving' the Problem of Slavery, 1787–1838," *Journal of American History* 95, no. 1 (June 2008): 95–122; Lacy K. Ford, *Deliver Us from Evil: The Slavery Question in the Old South* (New York: Oxford University Press, 2009), 143–172. For rebuttals of Genovese's paternalist ideology, see James D. Anderson, "Aunt Jemima in Dialectics: Genovese on Slave Culture," *Journal of African American History* 87 (Winter 2002): 26–42; Herbert Gutman, *The Black Family in Slavery and Freedom, 1750–1925* (New York: Random House, 1976); James Oakes, *Slavery and Freedom: An Interpretation of the Old South* (New York: Knopf, 1990).
25. Merritt, *Masterless Men*, 114–142.
26. Union District Criminal Court Records, #2645, 1853, SCDAH. See also Jeff Forret, "Slaves, Poor Whites, and the Underground Economy of the Rural Carolinas," 796.

27. Union District Criminal Court Records, #2786, 1854, SCDAH.
28. Historians have begun to think more critically about the false binaries about class within the literature on the antebellum South. In the nineteenth century, we can carve out the Southern middle class as a distinct group comprised of skilled artisans, business people, and a newly skilled professional class of doctors and lawyers. See Jennifer R. Green and Jonathan Daniel Wells, eds., *The Southern Middle Class in the Long Nineteenth Century* (Baton Rouge: Louisiana State University Press, 2011); Jonathan Daniel Wells, *The Origins of the Southern Middle Class, 1800–1861* (Chapel Hill: University of North Carolina Press, 2005).
29. Union District Criminal Court Records, #1997, 1841, SCDAH.
30. Cotton price data from Alfred G. Smith, *The Economic Readjustment of an Old Cotton State: South Carolina, 1820–1860* (Columbia: University of South Carolina Press, 1958), 226.
31. Union District Criminal Court Records, #2190, 1845, SCDAH; Union District Criminal Court Records, #1982, 1843, SCDAH; Union District Criminal Court Records, #2643, 1853, SCDAH.
32. "March Term, 1852, Presentments of the Grand Jury of the Court of General Sessions and Common Pleas, of Charleston District," SCDAH.
33. Presentment of the Grandy Jury of Lexington District at Fall Term 1849," #16, 1849, Records of the General Assembly, SCDAH.
34. "Presentment of the Grand Jury of Union District, Fall Term 1857," #16, 1857, SCDAH.
35. *State v. Jesse*, Anderson District Court of Magistrates and Freeholders, #301, 1856, SCDAH; *State vs. Charles, Carter, Ned, Aaron*, Anderson District Court of Magistrates and Freeholders, #155, 1844, SCDAH. For a discussion of African American litigants in antebellum Southern courts, see Kimberly M. Welsh, *Black Litigants in the Antebellum American South* (Chapel Hill: University of North Carolina Press, 2018).
36. Records of the General Assembly, #288 and #40 (Reel #2), 1840, SCDAH. The 168 petitioners comprised .88 percent of the Union District population in 1840.
37. *Federal Writers' Project: Slave Narrative Project, Vol. 14, South Carolina, Part 1, Abrams-Durant.* 1936. Manuscript/Mixed Materials. https://www.loc.gov.item/mesn141/.
38. *Federal Writers' Project: Slave Narrative Project, Vol. 14, South Carolina, Part 1, Abrams-Durant.* 1936. Manuscript/Mixed Materials. https://www.loc.gov.item/mesn141/.
39. For an analysis of enslaved peoples' consumer habits in the antebellum South, see Kathleen Hilliard, *Masters, Slaves, and Exchange: Power's Purchase in the Old South* (Cambridge: Cambridge University Press, 2014), 46–68.
40. Jackson, "Experience of a Slave in South Carolina," 25.
41. *The Camden Journal*, May 16, 1840.
42. McDonnell, "Money Knows No Master," 36–37.
43. "Constitution of the Monticello Planter's Society," *Southern Agriculturist and Register of Rural Affairs* (June 1838), 283.
44. "Constitution of the Monticello Planter's Society," 283.
45. "Constitution of the Monticello Planter's Society," 283.

46. "Monticello Planters' Society," *Southern Agriculturist and Register of Rural Affairs* (June 1838), 281.
47. Preamble and Regulations of the Savannah River Anti-Slave Traffick Association, 3.
48. Preamble and Regulations of the Savannah River Anti-Slave Traffick Association, 3. See also Stephanie M. H. Camp, "The Pleasures of Resistance: Enslaved Women and Body Politics in the Plantation South, 1830–1861," in *New Studies the History of American Slavery*, ed. Edward Baptist and Stephanie M. H. Camp (Athens: University of Georgia, 2006), 112–114; Drew Gilpin Faust, *James Henry Hammond and the Old South: A Design for Mastery* (Baton Rouge: Louisiana State University Press, 1982), 98; Forret, *Race Relations at the Margins*, 111.
49. Preamble and Regulations of the Savannah Anti-Slave Traffick Association, 5.
50. *Edgefield Advertiser*, May 2, 1849.
51. See also Ford, "Reconfiguring the Old South," 117–119; Manisha Sinha, *The Counterrevolution of Slavery: Politics and Ideology in Antebellum South Carolina* (Chapel Hill: University of North Carolina Press, 2000), 9–32. Though the term *paternalism* is controversial within the historiography on nineteenth-century Southern slavery, I believe that the term encapsulates the ways in which slaveholders conceptualized the relationship with their slaves.
52. "The Management of Negroes," *Southern Agriculturist and Register of Rural Affairs*, October 1838.
53. *Federal Writers' Project: Slave Narrative Project, Vol. 14, South Carolina, Part 3, Jackson-Quattlebaum*. 1936. Manuscript/Mixed Material. https://www.loc.gov.item/mesn143/.
54. *Federal Writers' Project: Slave Narrative Project, Vol. 14, South Carolina, Part 3, Jackson-Quattlebaum*. 1936. Manuscript/Mixed Material. https://www.loc.gov.item/mesn143/.
55. *Federal Writers' Project: Slave Narrative Project, Vol. 14, South Carolina, Part 3, Jackson-Quattlebaum*. 1936. Manuscript/Mixed Material. https://www.loc.gov.item/mesn143/.
56. John Willson Papers, South Caroliniana Library, University of South Carolina, Columbia. According to the 1850 Federal Census, Willson owned 69 enslaved people. In addition, slaves were forced by their enslavers to be increasingly more responsible for fulfilling plantation subsistence needs during the 1850s. Enslavers such as John Willson embraced ideas of plantation self-sufficiency and slaveholders also had no qualms about swindling their slaves at the same time. Enslavers' decision to make their plantations independently functioning enterprises relied on their ability to extract as much labor from bondspeople as possible. As enslavers exploited enslaved peoples' long-held investments in their own economies to help plantations maintain their profitability, enslaved people necessarily dedicated more of their independent time toward pursuits that, in the end, buttressed slaveholders' interests in profits above all else. See, for example, "Proceedings of the South Carolina Agricultural Society," *Farmer's Register*, September 30, 1842.

57. Bonnie Martin, "Slavery's Invisible Engine: Mortgaging Human Property," *Journal of Southern History* 76, no. 4 (November 2010): 817–886.
58. *Newberry Account Book*, Newberry District, South Caroliniana Library, University of South Carolina, Columbia.
59. *Federal Writers' Project: Slave Narrative Project, Vol. 14, South Carolina, Part 2, Eddington-Hunter.* 1936. Manuscript/Mixed Material. https://www.loc.gov.item/mesn142/.
60. *Federal Writers' Project: Slave Narrative Project, Vol. 14, South Carolina, Part 2, Eddington-Hunter.* 1936. Manuscript/Mixed Material. https://www.loc.gov.item/mesn142/. For a discussion of enslaved children in the antebellum South, see Wilma King, *Stolen Childhoods: Slave Youth in Nineteenth Century America* (Bloomington: Indiana University Press, 1995).
61. Richard K. Fleishman and Thomas N. Tyson, "Accounting in Service to Racism: Monetizing Slave Property in the Antebellum South," *Critical Perspectives on Accounting* 15 no. 3 (January 2004): 391.
62. Smith, *Economic Readjustment of South Carolina*, 223.
63. "Negro Accts.," Peter Samuel Bacot Papers, South Caroliniana Library, University of South Carolina, Columbia.
64. "Negro Accts.," Peter Samuel Bacot Papers, South Caroliniana Library, University of South Carolina, Columbia.
65. "Negro Accts.," Peter Samuel Bacot Papers, South Caroliniana Library, University of South Carolina, Columbia. "Oznaburg," or osnaburg, describes a popular fabric typically used for slave clothing in the nineteenth century. The fabric was originally made in Germany and exported to regions of the slaveholding Americas. See Linda Baumgarten, *What Clothes Reveal: The Language of Clothing in Colonial and Federal America* (New Haven, Conn.: Yale University Press, 2002), 135.
66. Seth Rockman, "Negro Cloth: Mastering the Market for Slave Clothing in Antebellum America," in *American Capitalism: New Histories*, Sven Beckert and Christine Desan (New York: Columbia University Press 2018), 170–194.
67. "Negro Accts.," Peter Samuel Bacot Papers, South Caroliniana Library, University of South Carolina, Columbia; Lewis C. Gray, *Agriculture in the Southern United States to 1860*, Vol. II (Washington, D.C., 1941), 697.
68. Thomas Cassels Law Papers, Records of Antebellum Southern Plantations, Series A, Part 2; John Campbell, "'As a Kind of Freedman': Slaves' Market-Related Activities in the South Carolina Upcountry, 1800–1860," in *The Slaves' Economy: Independent Production by Slaves in the Americas*, ed. Ira Berlin and Phillip D. Morgan (London: Frank Cass, 1991), 144–145. In this record, John Campbell argues that Law offered his slaves more than the average market price for cotton. He argues that in November 1859, the average market price for ginned cotton per pound was approximately $0.10. He claims that Thomas Law paid his slaves 11.5 cents per pound for their independently produced ginned cotton. However, in my reading of the records, Law only compensated his slaves in 1859 at $0.03 per pound. See also Larry Hudson, *To Have*

and to Hold: Slave Work and Family Life in Antebellum South Carolina (Athens: University of Georgia Press, 1997).

69. "Thomas Cassels Law Papers," Records of ante-bellum Southern plantations from the Revolution through the Civil War. Series A, Selections from the South Caroliniana Library, University of South Carolina; pt. 2, Miscellaneous collections, reels 7–8. For trade between enslaved people and poor whites in the Carolinas, see Jeff Forret, "Slaves, Poor Whites, and the Underground Economy of the Rural Carolinas," 74–114.
70. Eugene G. Genovese and Elizabeth Fox-Genovese, *Fatal Self-Deception: Slaveholding Paternalism in the Old South* (Cambridge: Cambridge University Press, 2011), 1.
71. J. H. Easterby, ed., *The South Carolina Rice Plantation, As Revealed in the Papers of Robert F. W. Allston* (Chicago: University of Chicago Press, 1945), 345.
72. *The South Carolina Rice Plantation*, 349–350.
73. R. W. Gibbs, "Southern Slave Life," *DeBow's Review* 24 (April 1858): 321.
74. Gibbs, "Southern Slave Life," 324.
75. Gibbs, "Southern Slave Life," 324.
76. Gibbs, "Southern Slave Life," 323.
77. Esterby, *The South Carolina Rice Plantation*, 350.
78. Esterby, *The South Carolina Rice Plantation*, 456.
79. 1850 United States Federal Census, South Carolina, Slave Schedules.
80. David J. McCord, *Statutes at Large of South Carolina: Containing Acts relating to Corporations and the Militia* (Columbia, S. C.: A. S. Johnston, 1840), 373.
81. South Carolina General Assembly, Records of the General Assembly, "Petition of the Agricultural Society St. Paul's Parish praying that the laws in relation to the employing of slaves without the consent of their Owners and the Harboring of Runaways be so amended as more effectually to protect them against the evils complained of," 1854, #83, SCDAH; South Carolina General Assembly, "Petition of the Agricultural Society St. Paul's Parish," 1854, #83, SCDAH. See also John Hope Franklin and Loren Schweninger, *Runaway Slaves: Rebels on the Plantation* (New York: Oxford University Press, 2000), 131; Loren Schweninger, "Slave Independence and Enterprise in South Carolina, 1782–1865," *South Carolina Historical Magazine* 93, no. 2 (April 1992): 118–119.
82. South Carolina General Assembly, Records of the General Assembly, "Petition of the Agricultural Society St. Paul's Parish," 1854, #83, SCDAH.
83. South Carolina General Assembly, Records of the General Assembly, "Petition of the Agricultural Society St. Paul's Parish," 1854, #83, SCDAH.
84. South Carolina General Assembly, Records of the General Assembly, "Petition of the Agricultural Society St. Paul's Parish," 1854, #83, SCDAH; "Legislature of South Carolina," *The Charleston Mercury*, December 9, 1859; South Carolina General Assembly, Records of the General Assembly, "So Much of the Presentment of the Grand Jury of the Richland District, Fall Term 1859," 1859, #50–#51, SCDAH; "Measures of Securing Southern Society," *The Charleston Mercury*, November 23, 1859. See also Steven A.

Channing, *Crisis of Fear: Secession in South Carolina* (New York: Simon & Schuster, 1974), 26–31; Sinha, *The Counterrevolution of Slavery*, 209–216.

85. Frederick Law Olmsted, *A Journey in the Seaboard States: With Remarks on Their Economy* (New York, 1861), 439–440, (https://docsouth.unc.edu/nc/olmsted/olmsted.html).
86. Olmstead, *A Journey in the Seaboard States*, 439–440.
87. James Walvin, "Slaves, Free Time, and the Question of Leisure," *Slavery & Abolition* 16 (April 1995): 1–16.

CONCLUSION: "FREEDOM AIN'T NOTHIN": CAPITALISM AND FREEDOM IN THE SHADOW OF SLAVERY

1. Folder #5, James S. Milling Papers #3583, Southern Historical Collection, The Wilson Library, University of North Carolina at Chapel Hill.
2. *Declaration of the Immediate Causes Which Induce and Justify the Secession of South Carolina from the Federal Union; and the Ordinance of Secession* (Charleston, S.C.: Evans & Cogswell, 1860), 10.
3. *State v. Jacob Guyton*, Union District Criminal Court Records, #3546, 1863, SCDAH. Enslaved people faced the threat of punishment during the war, as magistrates and freeholders continued to try them for their economic crimes in local courts while the military conflict between Union and Confederate forces waged on. In the early 1860s, enslaved people and whites carried on their illicit trade, such as the one between Abe and Jacob Guyton, despite the social upheaval caused by the sectional conflict. Bondspeople made and spent money, through selling cotton to anyone who would purchase it, and they resorted to stealing goods for their own consumption or to sell on the open market. In the Pendleton and Anderson Districts, for example, the Court of Magistrates and Freeholders heard 71 cases between 1861 and 1865. Of the 71 cases, 55 percent involved enslaved people accused of stealing and trading illegally. And of the eighty enslaved people and free people of color tried for economic crimes during this short period, 50 percent were found guilty and faced punishments from 15 lashes to death by hanging. In comparison, between 1856 and 1860, of the 65 cases decided by the Pendleton and Anderson District magistrates court that involved 89 slaves and free people of color charged with stealing goods, selling liquor, and gambling, 62 percent were found guilty. There was only a slight dip in the number of cases and number of guilty verdicts, but not by much. The majority of enslaved people and free people of color brought to trial for their economic crimes were found guilty. See Pendleton/Anderson Court of Magistrates and Freeholders Records, #358–429, 1861–1865, SCDAH.
4. For enslaved people who fled to Union encampments, the threat of hunger and illness was ever-present. See Jim Downs, *Sick from Freedom: African-American Illness and Suffering During the Civil War and Reconstruction* (New York: Oxford University

Press, 2012); Amy Murrell Taylor, *Embattled Freedom: Journey's through the Civil War's Slave Refugee Camps* (Chapel Hill: University of North Carolina Press, 2018).

5. *Federal Writers' Project: Slave Narrative Project, Vol. 14, South Carolina, Part 2, Eddington-Hunter.* 1936. Manuscript/Mixed Material. https://www.loc.gov/item/mesn142, pp. 84–85.
6. Ira Berlin, Thavolia Glymph, Steven F. Miller, Joseph P. Reidy, Leslie S. Rowland, and Julie Saville, *Freedom: A Documentary History of Emancipation, 1861–1867: Series 1, Volume 3: The Wartime Genesis of Free Labor: The Lower South* (Cambridge: Cambridge University Press, 1990), 338.
7. Eric Foner, *Reconstruction: America's Unfinished Revolution, 1863–1877* (New York: Harper & Row, 1988), 159; Leslie A. Schwalm, *A Hard Fight for We: Women's Transition from Slavery to Freedom in South Carolina* (Urbana: University of Illinois Press, 1997), 157–158.
8. René Hayden, Anthony E. Kaye, Kate Masur, Steven F. Miller, Susan E. O'Donovan, Leslie S. Rowland, and Stephen A. West, *Freedom: A Documentary History of Emancipation, 1861–1867*: Series 3, Volume 2: *Land and Labor, 1866–1867* (Chapel Hill: University of North Carolina Press, 2013), 240.
9. Tera W. Hunter, *Bound in Wedlock: Slave and Free Black Marriage in the Nineteenth Century* (Cambridge, Mass.: Harvard University Press, 2019); Heather Andrea Williams, *Help Me Find My People: The African American Search for Family Lost in Slavery* (Chapel Hill: University of North Carolina Press, 2012).
10. Ezra Adams, *Federal Writers' Project: Slave Narrative Project, Vol. 14, South Carolina, Part 1, Adams-Durant*, 1936.
11. For an analysis of the complications of legal freedom for the formerly enslaved, see Joseph P. Reidy, *Illusions of Emancipation: The Pursuit of Freedom and Equality in the Twilight of Slavery* (Chapel Hill: University of North Carolina Press, 2019).
12. Ezra Adams, *Federal Writers' Project: Slave Narrative Project, Vol. 14, South Carolina, Part 1, Adams-Durant*, 1936.
13. For a discussion of the extension of legal slavery through incarceration, see Michelle Alexander, *The New Jim Crow* (New York: The New Press, 2010); Douglas Blackmon, *Slavery by Another Name: The Re-Enslavement of Black Americans From the Civil War to World War II* (New York: Knopf, 2008); Talitha L. LaFlouria, *Chained in Silence: Black Women and Convict Labor in the New South* (Chapel Hill: University of North Carolina Press, 2015). It is also possible that Adams was contextualizing the ways in which he and other African Americans were experiencing the economic ravages of the Great Depression. The Federal Writers' Project narratives were taken between 1936 and 1938, after a period in which African American unemployment hovered around 50 percent. See Stephanie Shaw, "Using the WPA Ex-Slave Narratives to Study the Impact of the Great Depression," *Journal of Southern History* 69, no. 3 (2003): 623–658; Catherine A. Stewart, *Long Past Slavery: Representing Race in the Federal Writers' Project* (Chapel Hill: University of North Carolina Press, 2016).
14. *Federal Writers' Project: Slave Narrative Project, Vol. 14, South Carolina, Part 3, Abrams-Durant. 1936.* Manuscript/Mixed Materials.

15. *Federal Writers' Project: Slave Narrative Project, Vol. 14, South Carolina, Part 3, Abrams-Durant.*
16. *Federal Writers' Project: Slave Narrative Project, Vol. 14, South Carolina, Part 3, Abrams-Durant.*
17. Recently, a small group of scholars have interrogated the intertwined history of race and financial institutions in the United States, namely the Freedman's Bank. Theses scholars explore how the creation of a bank for the formerly enslaved influenced their lives postslavery. See Garrett-Scott, *Banking on Freedom*, 24–31; Levy, *Freaks of Fortune*, 104–149; Mehrsa Barandaran, *The Color of Money: Black Banks and the Racial Wealth Gap* (Cambridge, Mass.: Harvard University Press, 2017), 10–39.

SELECTED BIBLIOGRAPHY

MANUSCRIPT COLLECTIONS

LIBRARY OF CONGRESS, WASHINGTON, D.C.

Federal Writers' Project: Slave Narrative Project, Vol. 14, South Carolina, Part 1, Abrams-Durant. 1936. Manuscript/Mixed Material. https://www.loc.gov.item/mesn141/.
Federal Writers' Project: Slave Narrative Project, Vol. 14, South Carolina, Part 2, Eddington-Hunter. 1936. Manuscript/Mixed Material. https://www.loc.gov.item/mesn142/.
Federal Writers' Project: Slave Narrative Project, Vol. 14, South Carolina, Part 3, Jackson-Quattlebaum. 1936. Manuscript/Mixed Material. https://www.loc.gov.item/mesn143/.
Federal Writers' Project: Slave Narrative Project, Vol. 14, South Carolina, Part 4, Raines-Young. 1936. Manuscript/Mixed Material. https://www.loc.gov.item/mesn144/.
James Henry Hammond Papers
William Lowndes Papers

SOUTH CAROLINA HISTORICAL SOCIETY, CHARLESTON, S.C.

Pinckney Family Papers
Ravenel Family Papers

SOUTH CAROLINA DEPARTMENT OF ARCHIVES AND HISTORY, COLUMBIA, S.C.

Records of the Union District Criminal Court
Records of the General Assembly

Records of the Court of Magistrates and Freeholders
Anderson/Pendleton Districts
Greenville District
Kershaw District
Laurens District
Pickens District

SOUTHERN HISTORICAL COLLECTION, UNIVERSITY OF NORTH CAROLINA-CHAPEL HILL, CHAPEL HILL, N.C.

Bacot Family Papers
James Milling Papers
Perrin Family Papers
Ravenel Family Papers, 1790–1918
Ben Sparkman Plantation Journal, 1848–1859

UNIVERSITY OF SOUTH CAROLINA, COLUMBIA-SOUTH CAROLINIANA LIBRARY, COLUMBIA, S.C.

Hugh Kerr Aiken Papers
Peter Bacot Papers
Leach Carrigan Papers
Guignard Family Papers
Papers of the Glover and North families, 1732–1918
Davison McDowell Plantation Journal, 1815–1844
Mary Hart Means Cotton Book
Newberry Account Book, 1857–1859
Joseph Palmer Account Book
William Sims Reynolds plantation journal
Louisa McCord Smythe Recollections
John Willson Papers, 1839–1862

PRIMARY SOURCES

Ball, Charles. *Slavery in the United States: A Narrative of the Life and Adventures of Charles Ball, A Black Man.* New York: John S. Taylor, 1837. https://docsouth.unc.edu/neh/ballslavery/ball.html.

Bolzius, Johann Martin. "Reliable Answer to Some Submitted Questions Concerning the Land Carolina." *William and Mary Quarterly* 14, no. 2 (April 1957): 223–261.

Cooper, Thomas. *The Statutes at Large of South Carolina: Acts from 1682 to 1716*. Columbia, S.C.: A. S. Johnson, 1837.

Cooper, Thomas, and David J. McCord. *Statutes at Large of South Carolina: Acts, 1787–1814*. Columbia, S.C.: A. S. Johnson, 1839.

Cooper, Thomas, and David J. McCord. *Statutes at Large of South Carolina: Acts Relating to Charleston, Courts, Slaves, and Rivers*. Columbia, S.C.: A. S. Johnston, 1840.

Dayton, John. *A View of South Carolina, as Respects Her Natural and Civil Concerns*. Charleston, S.C., 1802.

DeBow, James. *The Interest in Slavery of the Southern Non-Slaveholder*. Charleston, S.C.: Evans & Cogswell, 1860.

DeSaussure, Henry W. *A Series of Numbers Addressed to the Public in the Subject of Slaves and Free People of Colour; First Published in the South Carolina State Gazette, in the Months of September and October 1822*. Columbia, S.C.: State Gazette Office, 1822.

Edwards, Adele Stanton. *Journals of the Privy Council, 1783–1789*. Columbia: South Carolina Department of Archives and History, 1971.

Gibbes, Robert Wilson. *Documentary History of the American Revolution Consisting of Letters and Papers Relating to the Contest for Liberty, Chiefly in South Carolina, From Originals in the Possession of the Editor, and Other Sources*. Vol. 2. New York: D. Appleton, 1853–1857.

Grimké, John F. *The South Carolina Justice of the Peace*. New York: T. & J. Swords, 1810.

Holland, Edwin C. *A Refutation of the Calumnies Circulated Against the Southern & Western States, Respecting the Institution and Existence of Slavery Among Them*. Charleston, S.C.: A. E. Miller, 1822.

Jackson, John Andrew. *Experience of a Slave in South Carolina*. Chapel Hill: University of North Carolina Press, 2011.

Jones, George Fenwick. "John Martin Boltzius' Trip to Charleston, October 1742." *South Carolina Historical Magazine* 82, no. 2 (April 1981): 87–110.

Laurens, Henry. *Correspondence of Henry Laurens: of South Carolina*. New York: Printed for the Zenger Club, 1861.

Martineau, Harriet. *Retrospect of Western Travel*. London: Saunders and Otley, 1838.

McCord, David J. *Statutes at Large of South Carolina: Containing the Acts Relating to Charleston, Courts, Slaves, and Rivers*. Columbia, S.C.: A. S. Johnson, 1840.

Olmstead, Frederick Law. *A Journey in the Seaboard States: With Remarks on Their Economy*. New York, 1861.

Pinckney, Thomas. *Reflections, Occasioned by the Late Disturbances in Charleston, by Achates*. Charleston, S.C.: A. E. Miller, 1822.

Schoepf, Johann David. "After the Revolution." In *The Travelers' Charleston: Accounts of Charleston and Lowcountry, South Carolina, 1666–1861*, ed. Jennie Holton Fant, 51. Columbia: University of South Carolina Press, 2016.

Seabrook, Whitemarsh. "An Essay on the Management of Slaves, and Especially, on their Religious Instruction: Read Before the Agricultural Society of St. John's Colleton." Charleston, S.C.: A. E. Miller, 1834.

CONTEMPORARY JOURNALS AND NEWSPAPERS

Camden Journal
Charleston City Gazette and Daily Advertiser
Charleston Evening Gazette
Charleston Mercury
City Gazette and Daily Advertiser
Columbian Herald
Edgefield Advertiser
South Carolina and American General Gazette
South Carolina Gazette
South Carolina Gazette and Country Journal
South Carolina Weekly Gazette
Southern Agriculturist and Register of Rural Affairs
Southern Cultivator

SECONDARY SOURCES

Anderson, James D. "Aunt Jemima in Dialectics: Genovese on Slave Culture." *Journal of African American History* 87 (Winter 2002): 26–42.

Ashton, Susana, ed. *I Belong to South Carolina: South Carolina Slave Narratives.* Columbia: University of South Carolina Press, 2010.

Ayers, Edward. *Vengeance and Justice: Crime and Punishment in the Nineteenth-Century American South.* New York: Oxford University Press, 1984.

Bailey, Anne E. *The Weeping Time: Memory and the Largest Slave Auction in American History.* New York: Cambridge University Press, 2017.

Baptist, Edward E. *The Half Has Never Been Told: Slavery and the Making of American Capitalism.* New York: Basic Books, 2014.

Baptist, Edward E. "Toxic Debt, Liar Loans, and Securitized Human Beings." *Common Place* 10 (April 2010), http://commonplace.online/article/toxic-debt-liar-loans.

Barandaran, Mehrsa. *The Color of Money: Black Banks and the Racial Wealth Gap.* Cambridge, Mass.: Harvard University Press, 2017.

Baumgarten, Linda. *What Clothes Reveal: The Language of Clothing in Colonial and Federal America.* New Haven, Conn.: Yale University Press, 2002.

Beckert, Sven. *Empire of Cotton: A Global History.* New York: Vintage Books, 2014.

Beckert, Sven, and Seth Rockman. eds. *Slavery's Capitalism: A New History of American Economic Development.* Philadelphia: University of Pennsylvania Press, 2016.

Beckles, Hilary McD. "An Economic Life of Their Own: Slaves as Commodity Producers and Distributors in Barbados." *Slavery & Abolition* 12, no. 1 (1991): 31–47.

Beckles, Hilary McD. *Natural Rebels: A Social History of Enslaved Women in Barbados.* New Brunswick, N.J.: Rutgers University Press, 1989.

Berlin, Ira. *Generations of Captivity: A History of African American Slaves*. Cambridge, Mass.: Harvard University Press, 2003.

Berlin, Ira. *Many Thousands Gone: The First Two Centuries of Slavery in North America*. Cambridge, Mass.: Belknap Press of Harvard University Press, 1998.

Berlin, Ira, and Herbert Gutman. "Natives and Immigrants, Free Men and Slaves: Urban Workingmen in the Antebellum American South." *American Historical Review* 88, no. 5 (1983): 1175–1200.

Berlin, Ira, and Philip D. Morgan, eds. *Cultivation and Culture: Labor and the Shaping of Slave Life in the Americas*. Charlottesville: University Press of Virginia, 1993.

Berlin, Ira, and Philip D. Morgan, eds. *The Slaves' Economy: Independent Production by Slaves in the Americas*. London: Frank Cass, 1991.

Berry, Daina Ramey. *The Price for Their Pound of Flesh: The Value of the Enslaved, from Womb to Grave, in the Building of a Nation*. Boston: Beacon Press, 2017.

Blassingame, John W. *The Slave Community: Plantation Life in the Antebellum South*. New York: Oxford University Press, 1979.

Bogin, Ruth. "Petitioning and the New Moral Economy in Post-Revolutionary America." *William and Mary Quarterly* 45, no. 3 (July 1998): 391–425.

Bolland, O. Nigel. "Proto-Proletarians? Slave Wages in the Americas." In *From Chattel Slaves to Wage Slaves: The Dynamics of Labour Bargaining in the Americas*, ed. Mary Turner, 123–146. London: James Currey; Bloomington: Indiana University Press, 1995.

Bolton, Charles C. *Poor Whites of the Antebellum South: Tenants and Laborers in Central North Carolina and Eastern Mississippi*. Durham, N.C.: Duke University Press, 1994.

Boyd, Robert L. "Survivalist Entrepreneurship Among Urban Blacks During the Great Depression: A Test of the Disadvantage Theory of Business Enterprise." *Social Science Quarterly* 81, no. 4 (2000): 972–984.

Breeden, James, ed. *Advice Among Masters: The Ideal in Plantation Management in the Old South*. Westport, Conn.: Greenwood Press, 1980.

Breen. Timothy. *The Marketplace of Revolution: How Consumer Politics Shaped American Independence*. New York: Oxford University Press, 2004.

Burnard, Trevor, and John Garrigus. *The Plantation Machine: Atlantic Capitalism in French Saint-Domingue and British Jamaica*. Philadelphia: University of Pennsylvania Press, 2016.

Bush, Barbara. *Slave Women in Caribbean Society, 1650–1838*. Kingston, Jamaica: Heinemann Caribbean; Bloomington: Indiana University Press, 1990.

Bush, Jonathan A. "Free to Enslave: The Foundation of Colonial American Slave Law." *Yale Journal of Law & the Humanities* 5, no. 2, (1993): 417–470.

Bushman, Richard. *The Refinement of America: Persons, Houses, Cities*. New York: Knopf, 1992.

Butler, Christina Rae. *Lowcountry at High Tide: A History of Flooding, Drainage, and Reclamation in Charleston, South Carolina*. Columbia: University of South Carolina Press, 2020.

Camp, Stephanie. *Closer to Freedom: Enslaved Women and Everyday Resistance in the Plantation South*. Chapel Hill: University of North Carolina Press, 2004.

Campbell, John. "As 'a Kind of Freeman'? Slaves' Market-Related Activities in the South Carolina Upcountry, 1800–1860." *Slavery & Abolition* 12, no. 1 (May 1991): 131–169.

Carney, Judith. *Black Rice: The African Origins of Rice Cultivation in the Americas.* Cambridge, Mass.: Harvard University Press, 2002.

Carruthers, Bruce G., and Wendy Nelson Espeland. "Accounting for Rationality: Double-Entry Bookkeeping and the Rhetoric of Rationality." *American Journal of Sociology* 97, no. 1 (1991): 31–69.

Channing, Steven A. *Crisis of Fear: Secession in South Carolina.* New York: Simon & Schuster, 1974.

Chaplin, Joyce E. *An Anxious Pursuit: Agricultural Innovation and Modernity in the Lower South, 1730–1815.* Chapel Hill: University of North Carolina Press, 1993.

Chaplin, Joyce E. "Creating a Cotton South in Georgia and South Carolina, 1760–1815." *Journal of Southern History* 57, no. 2 (May 1991): 171–200.

Chaplin, Joyce E. "Tidal Rice Cultivation and the Problem of Slavery in South Carolina and Georgia, 1760–1815." *William and Mary Quarterly* 49 (January 1992): 29–61.

Clark, Erskine. *Wrestlin' Jacob: A Portrait of Religion in Antebellum Georgia and the Carolina Lowcountry.* Tuscaloosa: University of Alabama Press, 2000.

Clark-Pujara, Christy. *Dark Work: The Business of Slavery in Rhode Island.* New York: NYU Press, 2016.

Cohen, Joanna. *Luxurious Citizens: The Politics of Consumption in Nineteenth-Century America.* Philadelphia: University of Pennsylvania Press, 2017.

Cottrol, Robert J. "Liberalism and Paternalism: Ideology, Economic Interest and the Business Law of Slavery." *American Journal of Legal History* 31, no. 4 (1987): 359–373.

Davis, Angela. "Reflections on the Black Woman's Role in the Community of Slaves." *Massachusetts Review* 13, no. 1/2 (Winter–Spring 1972): 81–100.

Davis, David Brion. *The Problem of Slavery in the Age of Revolution, 1770–1823.* Ithaca, N.Y.: Cornell University Press, 1975.

Diouf, Sylviane. *Slavery's Exiles: The Story of American Maroons.* New York: New York University Press, 2014.

Downey, Tom. *Planting a Capitalist South: Masters, Merchants, and Manufacturers in the Southern Interior, 1790–1860.* Baton Rouge: Louisiana State University Press, 2005.

Downs, Jim. *Sick from Freedom: African-American Illness and Suffering During the Civil War and Reconstruction.* New York: Oxford University Press, 2012.

Dubois, Laurent. *Avengers of the New World: The Story of the Haitian Revolution.* Cambridge, Mass.: Harvard University Press, 2009.

Dun, James Alexander. *Dangerous Neighbors: Making the Haitian Revolution in Early America.* Philadelphia: University of Pennsylvania Press, 2016.

Dunn, Richard S. *Sugar and Slaves: The Rise of the Planter Class in the English West Indies, 1624–1713.* Chapel Hill: University of North Carolina Press, 1972.

Dusinberre, William. *Them Dark Days: Slavery in the American Rice Swamps.* New York: Oxford University Press, 1996.

Duval, Lauren. "Mastering Charleston: Property and Patriarchy in British-Occupied Charleston, 1780–1782." *William and Mary Quarterly* 75, no. 4 (October 2018): 589–622.

Edelson, S. Max. "Affiliation Without Affinity: Skilled Slaves in Eighteenth Century South Carolina." In *Money, Trade, and Power: The Evolution of Colonial South Carolina's Plantation Society*, ed. Jack P. Greene, Rosemary Brana-Shute, and Randy J. Sparks, 217–255. Columbia: University of South Carolina Press, 2001.

Edelson, S. Max."Beyond 'Black Rice': Reconstructing Material and Cultural Contexts for Early Plantation Agriculture." *American Historical Review* 115, no. 1 (February 2010): 125–135.

Edelson, S. Max. *Plantation Enterprise in Colonial South Carolina*. Cambridge, Mass.: Harvard University Press, 2006.

Edgar, Walter. *South Carolina: A History*. Columbia: University of South Carolina Press, 1998.

Edwards, Laura F. "Enslaved Women and the Law: Paradoxes of Subordination in the Post-Revolutionary Carolinas." *Slavery & Abolition* 26, no. 2 (2005): 305–323.

Edwards, Laura F. "Status Without Rights: African Americans and the Tangled History of Law and Governance in the Nineteenth-Century U.S. South." *American Historical Review* 112, no. 2 (April 2007): 365–393.

Edwards, Laura F. *The People and Their Peace: Legal Culture and the Transformation of Inequality in the Post-Revolutionary South*. Chapel Hill: University of North Carolina Press, 2009.

Eelman, Bruce. *Entrepreneurs in the Southern Upcountry: Commercial Culture in Spartanburg, South Carolina, 1845–1880*. Athens: University of Georgia Press, 2008.

Egerton, Douglas. *Death or Liberty: African Americans and Revolutionary America*. New York: Oxford University Press, 2009.

Egerton, Douglas. *He Shall Go Out Free: The Lives of Denmark Vesey*. Madison: Madison House, 1999.

Egerton, Douglas. "Markets Without a Market Revolution: Southern Planters and Capitalism." *Journal of the Early Republic* 16, no. 2 (1996): 207–221.

Egerton, Douglas. "'Why They Did Not Preach Up This Thing': Denmark Vesey and Revolutionary Theology." *South Carolina Historical Magazine* 100, no. 4 (1999): 298–319.

Egerton, Douglas R., and Robert L. Paquette. *The Denmark Vesey Affair: A Documentary History*. Gainesville: University of Florida Press, 2017.

Eltis, David, Philip Morgan, and David Richardson. "Agency and Diaspora in Atlantic History: Reassessing the African Contribution to Rice Cultivation in the Americas." *American Historical Review* 112, no. 5 (December 2007): 1329–1358.

Faust, Drew Gilpin. *James Henry Hammond and the Old South: A Design for Mastery*. Baton Rouge: Louisiana State University Press, 1982.

Fede, Andrew. *People Without Rights: An Interpretation of the Fundamentals of the Law of Slavery in the U.S. South*. New York: Garland, 1992.

Fehrenbacher, Don E., and Ward McAfee. *The Slaveholding Republic: An Account of the United States Government's Relations to Slavery*. New York: Oxford University Press, 2002.

Feller, Daniel. *The Jacksonian Promise: America, 1815–1840*. Baltimore, Md.: Johns Hopkins University Press, 1995.

Fenn, Elizabeth A. *Pox Americana: The Great Smallpox Epidemic of 1775–82*. New York: Hill and Wang, 2001.

Ferman, Louis A., Stuart Henry, and Michele Hoyman. "Issues and Prospects for the Study of Informal Economies: Concepts, Research Strategies, and Policy." *Annals of the American Academy of Political and Social Science* 493 (1987): 154–172.

Finkelman, Paul, and Derrick Bell, eds. *Slavery and the Law.* Madison, Wis.: Madison House, 1998.

Fleishman, Richard K., David Oldroyd, and Thomas N. Tyson. "Accounting in Service to Racism: Monetizing Slave Property In the Antebellum South." *Critical Perspectives on Accounting* 15, no. 3 (Jan. 2004): 376–399.

Fleishman, Richard K., and Thomas N. Tyson "Plantation Accounting and Management Practices in the US and the British West Indies at the End of their Slavery Eras." *Economic History Review* 64, no. 3 (August 2011): 765–797.

Franklin, John Hope, and Loren Schweninger. *Runaway Slaves: Rebels on the Plantation.* New York: Oxford University Press, 1999.

Frederick, David A. "John Quincy Adams, Slavery, and the Right of Petition." *Law and History Review* 9, no. 1 (Spring 1999): 113–155.

Freehling, William W. *The Prelude to Civil War: The Nullification Controversy in South Carolina, 1816–1836.* New York: Oxford University Press, 1965.

Fogel, Robert, and Stanley Engerman. *Time on the Cross: The Economics of American Negro Slavery.* Boston: Little, Brown, 1974.

Ford, Lacy K. *Deliver Us From Evil: The Slavery Question in the Old South.* New York: Oxford University Press, 2009.

Ford, Lacy K. *Origins of Southern Radicalism: The South Carolina Upcountry, 1800–1860.* New York: Oxford University Press, 1988.

Ford, Lacy K. "Reconfiguring the Old South: 'Solving' the Problem of Slavery, 1787–1838." *Journal of American History* 95, no. 1 (June 2008): 95–122.

Ford, Lacy K. "Self-Sufficiency, Cotton, and Economic Development in the South Carolina Upcountry, 1800–1860." *Journal of Economic History* 45, no. 2 (1985): 261–267.

Forret, Jeff. *Race Relations at the Margins: Slaves and Poor Whites in the Antebellum Southern Countryside.* Baton Rouge: Louisiana State University Press, 2006.

Forret, Jeff. *Slave Against Slave: Plantation Violence in the Old South.* Baton Rouge: Louisiana State University Press, 2015.

Forret, Jeff. "Slaves, Poor Whites, and the Underground Economy of the Rural Carolinas." *Journal of Southern History* 70, no. 4 (November 2004): 783–824.

Fox-Genovese, Elizabeth, and Eugene Genovese. *Fatal Self-Deception: Slaveholding Paternalism in the Old South.* New York: Oxford University Press, 2011.

Fox-Genovese, Elizabeth, and Eugene Genovese. *The Mind of the Master Class: History and Faith in the Southern Slaveholders' Worldview.* New York: Oxford University Press, 2005.

Fox-Genovese, Elizabeth, and Eugene Genovese. "The Slave Economies in Political Perspective." *Journal of American History* 66, no. 1 (June 1979): 7–23.

Fox-Genovese, Elizabeth, and Eugene Genovese. *Slavery in White and Black: Class and Race in the Southern Slaveholders' New World Order.* New York: Oxford University Press, 2008.

Frey, Sylvia. *Water from the Rock: Black Resistance in a Revolutionary Age*. Princeton, N.J.: Princeton University Press, 1991.

Garrett-Scott, Shennette. *Banking on Freedom: Black Women in U.S. Finance Before the New Deal*. New York: Columbia University Press, 2019.

Genovese, Eugene D. *The Political Economy of Slavery: Studies in the Economy & Society of the Slave South*. New York: Pantheon Books, 1965.

Genovese, Eugene D. *Roll, Jordan, Roll: The World the Slaves Made*. New York: Pantheon Books, 1974.

Gilbert, Alan. *Black Patriots and Loyalists: Fighting for Emancipation in the War for Independence*. Chicago: University of Chicago Press, 2012.

Glymph, Thavolia. *Out of the House of Bondage: The Transformation of the Plantation Household*. Cambridge: Cambridge University Press, 2008.

Greenberg, Joshua R. *Banknotes and Shinplasters: The Rage for Paper Money in the Early Republic*. Philadelphia: University of Pennsylvania Press, 2020.

Goloboy, Jennifer L. *Charleston and the Emergence of Middle-Class Culture in the Revolutionary Era*. Athens: University of Georgia Press, 2016.

Goloboy, Jennifer L. "Strangers in the South: Charleston's Merchants and Middle-Class Values in the Early Republic." In *The Southern Middle Class in the Long Nineteenth Century*, ed. Jonathan Daniel Wells and Jennifer R. Green, 40–61. Baton Rouge: Louisiana State University Press, 2011.

Green, Jennifer R., and Jonathan Daniel Wells, eds. *The Southern Middle Class in the Long Nineteenth Century*. Baton Rouge: Lousiana State University Press, 2011.

Greene, Harlan, and Harry S. Hutchins Jr. *Slave Badges and the Slave-Hire System in Charleston, 1783–1865*. Jefferson, N.C.: McFarland & Company, 2004.

Greene, Jack P. "Colonial South Carolina and the Caribbean Connection." *South Carolina Historical Magazine* 88, no. 4 (October 1987): 192–210.

Gross, Ariela. *Double Character: Slavery and Mastery in the Antebellum Southern Courtroom*. Athens: University of Georgia Press, 2006.

Gutman, Herbert. *The Black Family in Slavery and Freedom, 1750–1925*. New York: Random House, 1976.

Hadden, Sally E. "The Fragmented Laws of Slavery in the Colonial and Revolutionary Eras." In *Cambridge History of Law in America*, ed. Christopher Tomlins and Michael Grossberg, 253–287. Cambridge: Cambridge University Press, 2008.

Hadden, Sally E. *Slave Patrols: Law and Violence in Virginia and the Carolinas*. Cambridge, Mass.: Harvard University Press, 2001.

Hadden, Sally E. "South Carolina's Grand Jury Presentments: The Eighteenth Century Experience." In *Signposts: New Directions in Southern Legal History*, ed. Sally Hadden and Patricia Hagler Minter, 89–110. Athens: University of Georgia Press, 2013.

Hammond, Bray. *Banks and Politics in America from the Revolution to the Civil War*. Princeton, N.J.: Princeton University Press, 1957.

Harris, LaShawn. *Sex Workers, Psychics, and Numbers Runners: Black Women in New York City's Underground Economy*. Urbana: University of Illinois Press, 2016.

Harrison, M. Leigh. "A Study of the Earliest Reported Decisions of the South Carolina Court of Law." *American Journal of Legal History* 16, no. 1 (January 1972): 51–70.

Hart, Emma. *Building Charleston: Town and Society in Eighteenth-Century British Atlantic World*. Charlottesville: University of Virginia Press, 2010.

Hart, Keith. "Informal Income Opportunities and Urban Employment in Ghana." *Journal of Modern African Studies* 11, no. 1 (March 1973): 61–89.

Hartigan-O'Connor, Ellen. *The Ties That Buy: Women and Commerce in Revolutionary America*. Philadelphia: University of Pennsylvania Press, 2009.

Haw, James. *John and Edward Rutledge of South Carolina*. Athens: University of Georgia Press, 1996.

Henry, H. M. "The Police Control of the Slave in South Carolina." PhD diss., Vanderbilt University, 1914.

Higginbotham, A. Leon. *In the Matter of Color: Race and the American Legal Process—The Colonial Period*. New York: Oxford University Press, 1978.

Hilliard, Kathleen. *Masters, Slaves, and Exchange: Power's Purchase in the Old South*. Cambridge: Cambridge University Press, 2014.

Hilliard, Sam Bowers. *Hog Meat and Hoecake: Food Supply in the Old South, 1840–1860*. Athens: University of Georgia Press, 2014.

Hindus, Michael S. "Black Justice Under White Law: Criminal Prosecutions of Blacks in Antebellum South Carolina." *Journal of American History* 63, no. 3 (December 1976): 575–599.

Hindus, Michael S. *Prison and Plantation: Crime, Justice, and Authority in Massachusetts and South Carolina, 1767–1878*. Chapel Hill: University of North Carolina Press, 1980.

Hoffer, Peter Charles. *Cry Liberty: The Great Stono River Slave Rebellion of 1739*. New York: Oxford University Press, 2010.

Hopwood, Anthony, and Peter Miller, eds. *Accounting as a Social and Institutional Practice*. Cambridge: Cambridge University Press, 1994.

Howe, Daniel Walker. *What Hath God Wrought: The Transformation of America*. New York: Oxford University Press, 2007.

Hudson, Larry E. *To Have and to Hold: Slave Work and Family Life in Antebellum South Carolina*. Athens: University of Georgia Press, 1997.

Hudson, Larry E, ed. *Working Toward Freedom: Slave Society and Domestic Economy in the Antebellum South*. Rochester, N.Y.: University of Rochester Press, 1994.

Hunter, Tera W. *Bound in Wedlock: Slave and Free Black Marriage in the Nineteenth Century*. Cambridge, Mass.: Harvard University Press, 2019.

Inabinet, L. Glen. "'The Fourth of July Incident' of 1816." In *South Carolina Legal History: Proceedings of the Reynolds Conference, University of South Carolina, December 2–3, 1977*, ed. Herbert A. Johnson, 209–221. Columbia: University of South Carolina Press, 1980.

Johnson, Michael P., and James Roark. *Black Masters: A Free Family of Color in the Old South*. New York: Norton, 1984.

Johnson, Michael P., and James Roark. "Denmark Vesey and His Co-Conspirators." *William and Mary Quarterly* 58, no. 4 (October 2001): 915–976.

Johnson, Michael P., and James Roark. "Telemaque's Pilgrimage? A Tale of Two Charleston Churches, Three Missionaries, and Four Ministers, 1783–1817." *South Carolina Historical Magazine* 118, no. 1 (January 2017): 4–36.

Johnson, Walter. "Clerks All! Or Slaves With Cash." *Journal of the Early Republic* 26, no. 4 (Winter 2006): 641–651.

Johnson, Walter. "On Agency." *Journal of Social History* 37, no. 1 (Autumn 2003): 113–124.

Johnson, Walter. *River of Dark Dreams: Slavery and Empire in the Cotton Kingdom*. Cambridge, Mass.: Harvard University Press, 2013.

Johnson, Walter. *Soul By Soul: Life Inside the Antebellum Slave Market*. Cambridge, Mass.: Harvard University Press, 1999.

Jones, George Fenwick. "John Martin Boltzius' Trip to Charleston, October 1742." *South Carolina Historical Magazine* 82, no. 2 (April 1981): 87–110.

Jones, Martha S. *Birthright Citizens: A History of Race and Rights in Antebellum America*. New York: Cambridge University Press, 2018.

Jones, Jacqueline, *Labor of Love, Labor of Sorrow: Black Women, Work, and the Family from Slavery to the Present*. New York: Basic Books, 1985.

Jones-Rogers, Stephanie. *They Were Her Property: White Women as Slaveholders in the American South*. New Haven, Conn.: Yale University Press, 2019.

Joyner, Charles. *Down by the Riverside: A South Carolina Slave Community*. Urbana: University of Illinois Press, 1984.

Karasch, Mary C. "Suppliers, Sellers, Servants, and Slaves." In *Cities and Societies in Colonial Latin America*, ed. Louisa S. Hoberman and Susan Socolow, 251–283. Albuquerque: University of New Mexico Press, 1986.

Kaplan, Edward. *The Bank of the United States and the American Economy*. Westport, Conn.: Greenwood Press, 1999.

Kaye, Anthony E. *Joining Places: Slave Neighborhoods in the Old South*. Chapel Hill: University of North Carolina Press, 2007.

Kennedy, Cynthia M. *Braided Relations, Entwined Lives: The Women's of Charleston's Urban Slave Society*. Bloomington: Indiana University Press, 2005.

King, Wilma. *Stolen Childhoods: Slave Youth in Nineteenth-Century America*. Bloomington: Indiana University Press, 1995.

Klein, Rachel. *Unification of a Slave State: The Rise of the Planter Class in the South Carolina Backcountry*. Chapel Hill: University of North Carolina Press, 1990.

Koger, Larry. *Black Slaveowners: Free Black Slave Masters in South Carolina, 1790–1860*. Jefferson, N.C.: McFarland, 1985.

Kulikoff, Allan. "The Transition to Rural Capitalism." *William and Mary Quarterly* 46, no. 1 (January 1989): 120–144.

Lakwete, Angela. *Inventing the Cotton Gin: Machine and Myth in Antebellum America*. Baltimore, Md.: Johns Hopkins University Press, 2003.

Lauer, Josh. *Creditworthy: A History of Consumer Surveillance and Financial Identity in America*. New York: Columbia University Press, 2017.

Lepler, Jessica. *The Many Panics of 1837: People, Politics, and the Creation of a Transatlantic Financial Crisis*. Cambridge: Cambridge University Press, 2013.

Lerner, Gerda. *The Grimké Sisters from South Carolina: Pioneers for Women's Rights and Abolition.* Chapel Hill: University of North Carolina Press, 2004.

Levine, Lawrence. *Black Culture, Black Consciousness: Afro-American Folk Thought from Slavery to Freedom.* New York: Oxford University Press, 1977.

Levy, Jonathan. *Freaks of Fortune: The Emerging World of Capitalism and Risk in America.* Cambridge, Mass.: Harvard University Press, 2012.

Lichtenstein, Alex. "'That Disposition to Theft, with Which They Have Been Branded': Moral Economy, Slave Management, and the Law." *Journal of Social History* 21, no. 3 (Spring 1988): 413–440.

Lipscomb, Terry W., and Theresa Jacobs, "The Magistrates and Freeholders Court." *South Carolina Historical Magazine* 77, no. 1 (January 1976): 62–65.

Little, Thomas J. "The South Carolina Slave Laws Reconsidered, 1670–1700." *South Carolina Historical Magazine* 94, no. 2 (April 1993): 86–101.

Littlefield, Daniel. *Rice and Slaves: Ethnicity and the Slave Trade in Colonial South Carolina.* Urbana: University of Illinois Press, 1991.

Lofton, John. *Denmark Vesey's Revolt: The Slave Plot That Lit a Fuse to Fort Sumter.* Kent, Ohio: Kent State University Press, 1983.

Lockley, Timothy J. *Lines in the Sand: Race and Class in Lowcountry Georgia, 1750–1860.* Athens: University of Georgia Press, 2001.

Lockley, Timothy J. *Maroon Communities in South Carolina: A Documentary Record.* Columbia: University of South Carolina Press, 2009.

Lockley, Timothy J. "Trading Encounters between Non-Elite Whites and African Americans in Savannah, 1790–1860." *Journal of Southern History* 66, no. 1 (February 2000): 25–48.

Lockley, Tim, and David Doddington. "Maroon and Slave Communities in South Carolina Before 1865." *South Carolina Historical Magazine* 113, no. 2 (April 2012): 125–145.

Mair, Lucille Mathurin. *A Historical Study of Women in Jamaica, 1655–1844.* Ed. Hilary McD. Beckles and Verene A. Shepherd. Kingston, Jamaica: University of the West Indies Press, 2006.

Mark, Gregory A. "The Vestigial Constitution: The History and Significance of the Right to Petition." *Fordham Law Review* 66, no. 6 (1998): 2153–2231.

Martin, Jonathan D. *Divided Mastery: Slave Hiring in the American South.* Cambridge, Mass.: Harvard University Press, 2004.

Matory, J. Lorand. "The Illusion of Isolation: The Gullah/Geechees and the Political Economy of African Culture in the Americas." *Comparative Studies in Society and History* 50, no. 4 (2008): 949–980.

McCurry, Stephanie. *Confederate Reckoning: Power and Politics in the Civil War South.* Cambridge, Mass.: Harvard University Press, 2011.

McCurry, Stephanie. *Masters of Small Worlds: Yeoman Households, Gender Relations, and the Political Culture of the Antebellum South Carolina Low Country.* New York: Oxford University Press, 1995.

McCurry, Stephanie. "The Two Faces of Republicanism: Gender and Proslavery Politics in Antebellum South Carolina." *Journal of American History* 78, no. 4 (March 1992): 1245–1264.

McDonald, Roderick A. *The Economy and Material Culture of Slaves: Goods and Chattels on the Sugar Plantations of Jamaica and Louisiana*. Baton Rouge: Louisiana State University Press, 1993.

McDonnell, Lawrence T. "Money Knows No Master: Market Relations and the American Slave Community." In *Developing Dixie: Modernization in a Traditional Society*, ed. Winfred B. Moore Jr., Joseph F. Tripp, and Lyon G. Tyler Jr. Westport, Conn.: Greenwood Press, 1988.

Megginson, W. J. *African American Life in South Carolina's Upper Piedmont, 1780–1900*. Columbia: University of South Carolina Press, 2006.

Menard, Russell R. *Sweet Negotiations: Sugar, Slavery, and Plantation Agriculture in Early Barbados*. Charlottesville: University of Virginia Press, 2006.

Mercantini, Jonathan. "The Great Carolina Hurricane of 1752." *South Carolina Historical Magazine* 102, no. 4 (October 2002): 351–365.

Merrill, Michael. "Putting 'Capitalism' in Its Place: A Review of Recent Literature." *William and Mary Quarterly* 52, no. 2 (April 1995): 315–326.

Merritt, Keri Leigh. *Masterless Men: Poor Whites and Slavery in the Antebellum South*. New York: Cambridge University Press, 2017.

Metzer, Jacob. "Rational Management, Modern Business Practices, and Economies of Scale in the Ante-Bellum Southern Plantations." *Explorations in Economic History* 12, no. 2 (April 1975): 123–150.

Meyers, Marvin. *The Jacksonian Persuasion: Politics and Belief*. Stanford, Calif.: Stanford University Press, 1957.

Mihm, Stephen. *A Nation of Counterfeiters: Capitalists, Con Men, and the Making of the United States*. Cambridge, Mass.: Harvard University Press, 2009.

Mintz, Sidney. "The Jamaican Internal Marketing System: Some Notes and Hypotheses." *Social and Economic Studies* 4, no. 1 (March 1955): 95–103.

Mintz, Sidney, and Douglas Hall. *The Origins of the Internal Marketing System*. New Haven, Conn.: Yale University Publications in Anthropology, 1960.

Moitt, Bernard. *Women and Slavery in the French Antilles, 1635–1848*. Bloomington: Indiana University Press, 2001.

Morgan, Jennifer. *Laboring Women: Reproduction and Gender in New World Slavery*. Philadelphia: University of Pennsylvania Press, 2004.

Morgan, Philip D. "The Ownership of Property by Slaves in the Mid-Nineteenth-Century Low Country." *Journal of Southern History* 49, no. 3 (August 1983): 399–420.

Morgan, Philip D. *Slave Counterpoint: Black Culture in the Eighteenth-Century Chesapeake and Lowcountry*. Chapel Hill: University of North Carolina Press, 1998.

Morgan, Philip D. "Work and Culture: The Task System and the World of Lowcountry Blacks, 1700–1880." *William and Mary Quarterly* 39, no. 4 (October 1982): 563–599.

Morris, Thomas D. *Southern Slavery and the Law, 1619–1860*. Chapel Hill: University of North Carolina Press, 1996.

Murphy, Sharon Ann. *Investing in Life: Insurance in Antebellum America*. Baltimore, Md.: Johns Hopkins University Press, 2010.

Murphy, Sharon Ann. *Other People's Money: How Banking Worked in the Early American Republic*. Baltimore, Md.: Johns Hopkins University Press, 2017.

Myers, Amrita Chakrabarti. *Forging Freedom: Black Women and the Pursuit of Liberty in Antebellum Charleston*. Chapel Hill: University of North Carolina Press, 2011.

Myers, Amrita Chakrabarti. "'Sisters in Arms': Slave Women's Resistance to Slavery in the United States." *Past Imperfect* 5 (1996): 141–176.

Navin, John J. *The Grim Years: Settling South Carolina, 1670–1720*. Columbia: University of South Carolina Press, 2019.

Nash, Gary. *The Unknown American Revolution: The Unruly Birth of Democracy and the Struggle to Create America*. New York: Viking, 2005.

Newman, Simon P. *A New World of Labor: The Development of Plantation Slavery in the British Atlantic*. Philadelphia: University of Pennsylvania Press, 2013.

Nicholson, Bradley J. "Legal Borrowing and the Origins of Slave Law in the British Colonies." *American Journal of Legal History* 38, no. 1 (January 1984): 38–54.

Novak, William J. *The People's Welfare: Law and Regulation in Nineteenth-Century America*. Chapel Hill: University of North Carolina Press, 1996.

Oakes, James. *The Ruling Race: A History of American Slaveholders*. New York: Norton, 1998.

Oakes, James. *Slavery and Freedom: An Interpretation of the Old South*. New York: Knopf, 1990.

Olwell, Robert. "'Domestick Enemies': Slavery and Political Independence in South Carolina, May 1775–March 1776." *Journal of Southern History* 55, no. 1 (Feb., 1989): 21–48.

Olwell, Robert. "'Loose, Idle and Disorderly': Slave Women in the Eighteenth-Century Charleston Marketplace." In *More Than Chattel: Black Women and Slavery in the Americas*, ed., David Barry Gaspar and Darlene Clark Hine, 97–110. Bloomington: Indiana University Press, 1996.

Olwell, Robert. *Masters, Slaves, and Subjects: The Culture of Power in the South Carolina Low Country, 1740–1790*. Ithaca, N.Y.: Cornell University Press, 1998.

O'Malley, Gregory. "Slavery's Converging Ground: Charleston's Slave Trade as the Black Heart of the Lowcountry." *William and Mary Quarterly* 74, no. 2 (April 2017): 271–302.

Patterson, Orlando. *Slavery and Social Death: A Comparative Study*. Cambridge, Mass.: Harvard University Press, 1982.

Pearson, Edward. *Designs Against Charleston: The Trial Record of the Denmark Vesey Slave Conspiracy of 1822*. Chapel Hill: University of North Carolina Press, 1999.

Penningroth, Dylan C. *The Claims of Kinfolk: African American Property and Community in the Nineteenth-Century South*. Chapel Hill: University of North Carolina Press, 2003.

Perkins, Edwin J. "Langdon Cheves and the Panic of 1819: A Reassessment." *Journal of Economic History* 44, no. 2 (June 1984): 455–461.

Peterson, David E. "Slavery, Slaves, and Cash in a Georgia Village, 1825–1865." *Journal of Southern History* 75, no. 4 (November 2009): 879–930.

Quarles, Benjamin. *The Negro in the American Revolution*. Chapel Hill: University of North Carolina Press, 1961.

Quintana, Ryan A. *Making a Slave State: Political Development in Early South Carolina*. Chapel Hill: University of North Carolina Press, 2018.

Rabateau, Albert. *Slave Religion: The "Invisible" Institution in the Antebellum South*. New York: Oxford University Press, 1978.

Rezneck, Samuel. "The Depression of 1819–1822, A Social History." *American Historical Review* 39, no. 1 (October 1933): 28–47.

Roberts, Alasdair. *America's First Great Depression: Economic Crisis and Political Disorder after the Panic of 1837*. Ithaca, N.Y.: Cornell University Press, 2012.

Robertson, David. *Denmark Vesey: The Buried History of America's Largest Slave Rebellion and the Man Who Led It*. New York: Knopf, 1999.

Rockman, Seth. "Negro Cloth: Mastering the Market for Slave Clothing in Antebellum America." In *American Capitalism: New Histories*, ed. Sven Beckert and Christine Desan, 170–194. New York: Columbia University Press, 2018.

Rockman, Seth. *Scraping By: Wage Labor, Slavery, and Survival in Early Baltimore*. Baltimore, Md.: Johns Hopkins University Press, 2009.

Roediger, David R. *The Wages of Whiteness: Race and the Making of the American Working Class*. London: Verso Books, 1991.

Rogers, George G., Jr., David R. Chestnutt, and Peggy J. Clark, eds. *The Papers of Henry Laurens, Volume 5: Sept. 1, 1765–July 31, 1768*. Columbia: University of South Carolina Press, 1968.

Rosengarten, Theodore. "The Southern Agriculturist in an Age of Reform." In *Intellectual Life in Antebellum Charleston*, ed. Michael O'Brien and David Moltke-Hansen, 279–281. Knoxville: University of Tennessee Press, 1986.

Rosenthal, Caitlin. *Accounting for Slavery: Masters and Management*. Cambridge, Mass.: Harvard University Press, 2018.

Rousseau, Peter. "Jacksonian Monetary Policy, Specie Flows, and the Panic of 1837." *Journal of Economic History* 62, no. 2 (June 2002): 457–488.

Rucker, Walter C. "'I Will Gather All Nations': Resistance, Culture, and Pan-African Collaboration in Denmark Vesey's South Carolina." *Journal of Negro History* 86, no. 2 (2001): 132–147.

Rugemer, Edward B. *Slave Law and the Politics of Resistance in the Early Atlantic World*. Cambridge, Mass.: Harvard University Press, 2018.

Salmon, Marylynn. *Women and the Law of Property in Early America*. Chapel Hill: University of North Carolina Press, 2016.

Schermerhorn, Calvin. *The Business of Slavery and the Rise of American Capitalism, 1815–1860*. New Haven, Conn.: Yale University Press, 2015.

Schlotterbeck, John T. "The Internal Economy of Slavery in Rural Piedmont Virginia." *Slavery & Abolition* 12, no. 1 (1991): 170–181.

Schoen, Brian. *Fragile Fabric of Union: Cotton, Federal Politics, and the Global Origins of the Civil War*. Baltimore, Md.: Johns Hopkins University Press, 2009.

Schweninger, Loren. *Appealing for Liberty: Freedom Suits in the South*. New York: Oxford University Press, 2018.

Schweninger, Loren. *Black Property Owners in the South, 1790–1915*. Urbana: University of Illinois Press, 1990.

Schweninger, Loren. "Slave Independence and Enterprise in South Carolina, 1782–1865." *South Carolina Historical Magazine* 93, no. 2 (April 1992): 101–125.

Schweninger, Loren. "The Underside of Slavery: The Internal Economy, Self-Hire, and Quasi-Freedom in Virginia, 1780–1865." *Slavery & Abolition* 12, no. 2 (Sept. 1991): 1–22.

Scott, Julius. *A Common Wind: Afro-American Organization in the Revolution Against Slavery*. London: Verso Books, 2018.

Sellers, Charles. *The Market Revolution: Jacksonian America, 1815–1846*. New York: Oxford University Press, 1991.

Sellick, Gary. "'Undistinguished Destruction': The Effects of Smallpox on British Emancipation Policy in the Revolutionary War." *Journal of American Studies* 51, no. 3 (August 2017): 865–885.

Senese, Donald J. "The Free Negro and the South Carolina Courts, 1790–1860." *South Carolina Historical Magazine* 63, no. 3 (July 1967): 140–153.

Shaw, Stephanie. "Using the WPA Ex-Slave Narratives to Study the Impact of the Great Depression." *Journal of Southern History* 69, no. 3 (2003): 623–658.

Sharples, Jason T. *The World That Fear Made: Slave Revolts and Conspiracy Scares in Early America*. Philadelphia: University of Pennsylvania Press, 2020.

Shuler, Jack. *Calling Out Liberty: The Stono Slave Rebellion and the Universal Struggle for Human Rights*. Jackson: University of Mississippi Press, 2009.

Sinha, Manisha. *Counterrevolution of Slavery: Politics and Ideology in Antebellum South Carolina*. Chapel Hill: University of North Carolina Press, 2000.

Sirmans, Eugene M. "The Legal Status of the Slave in South Carolina, 1670–1740." *Journal of Southern History* 28, no. 4 (November 1962): 462–473.

Smith, Alfred G. *The Economic Readjustment of an Old Cotton State: South Carolina, 1820–1860*. Columbia: University of South Carolina Press, 1958.

Smith, Hayden R. *Carolina's Golden Fields: Inland Rice Cultivation in the South Carolina Lowcountry, 1670–1860*. New York: Cambridge University Press, 2020.

Smith, Mark M. *Debating Slavery: Economy and Society in the Antebellum American South*. Cambridge: Cambridge University Press, 1998.

Smith, Mark M. "Remembering Mary, Shaping Revolt: Reconsidering the Stono Rebellion." *Journal of Southern History* 67, no. 3 (August 2001): 513–534.

Spady, James O'Neil. "Power and Confession: On the Credibility of the Earliest Reports of the Denmark Vesey Slave Conspiracy." *William and Mary Quarterly* 68, no. 2 (April 2011): 287–304.

Stamp, Kenneth. *The Peculiar Institution: Slavery in the Ante-Bellum South*. New York: Knopf, 1956.

Steffen, Charles G. "In Search of the Good Overseer: The Failure of the Agricultural Reform Movement in Lowcountry South Carolina, 1821–1834." *Journal of Southern History* 63, no. 4 (November 1997): 753–802.

Stewart, Catherine A. *Long Past Slavery: Representing Race in the Federal Writers' Project*. Chapel Hill: University of North Carolina Press, 2016.

Stewart, Louis J. "A Contingency Theory Perspective on Management Control Systems Design Among U.S. Ante-bellum Slave Plantations." *Accounting Historians Journal* 25 (June 2010): 91–120.

Stoesen, Alexander R. "The British Occupation of Charleston." *South Carolina Historical Magazine* 63, no. 2 (April 1962): 71–82.

Stoll, Steven. *Larding the Lean Earth: Soil and Society in Nineteenth-Century America*. New York: Hill & Wang, 2002.

Stubbs, Tristan. *Masters of Violence: The Plantation Overseers of Eighteenth-Century Virginia, South Carolina, and Georgia*. Columbia: University of South Carolina Press, 2018.

Sweeney, Shauna. "Market Marronage: Fugitive Women and the Internal Marketing System in Jamaica, 1781–1834." *William and Mary Quarterly* 76, no. 2 (April 2019): 197–222.

Taylor, Alan. *American Revolutions: A Continental History, 1750–1804*. New York: Norton, 2017.

Temin, Peter. *The Jacksonian Economy*. New York: Norton, 1969.

Thompson, Michael D. "'Some Rascally Business': Thieving Slaves, Unscrupulous Whites, and Charleston's Illicit Waterfront Trade." In *Capitalism by Gaslight: Illuminating the Economy of Nineteenth-Century America*, ed. Brian P. Luskey and Wendy A. Woloson, 150–167. Philadelphia: University of Pennsylvania Press, 2015.

Thompson, Michael D. *Working on the Dock of the Bay: Labor and Enterprise in an Antebellum Southern Port*. Columbia: University of South Carolina Press, 2015.

Thornton, John K. "African Dimensions of the Stono Rebellion." *American Historical Review* 96, no. 4 (October 1991): 1101–1113.

Timberlake, Jr., Richard H. "The Specie Circular and the Distribution of Surplus." *Journal of Political Economy* 68 (April 1960): 109–117.

Trouillot, Michel-Rolph. *Silencing the Past: Power and the Production of History*. Boston: Beacon Press, 2005.

Van Cleve, George. *A Slaveholders' Union: Slavery, Politics, and the Constitution in the Early American Republic*. Chicago: University of Chicago Press, 2010.

Venkatesh, Sudhir Alladi. *Off the Books: The Underground Economy of the Urban Poor*. Cambridge, Mass.: Harvard University Press, 2009.

Waldstreitcher, David. *Slavery's Constitution: From Revolution to Ratification*. New York: Hill and Wang, 2009.

Walsh, Richard. "The Charleston Mechanics: A Brief Study, 1760–1776." *South Carolina Historical Magazine* 60, no. 3 (July 1959): 123–144.

Walker, Juliet E. K. *The History of Black Business in America: Capitalism, Race, Entrepreneurship*. 2nd ed. Chapel Hill: University of North Carolina Press, 2009.

Walker, Juliet E. K. "Racism, Slavery, and Free Enterprise: Black Entrepreneurship in the United States before the Civil War." *Business History Review* 60, no. 3 (1986): 343–382.

Webber, Mabel L. "Presentment of the Grand Jury, March 1733/34." *South Carolina Historical and Genealogical Magazine* 25, no. 4 (October 1924): 193–195.

Wells, Jonathan Daniel. *The Origins of the Southern Middle Class, 1800–1861*. Chapel Hill: University of North Carolina Press, 2004.

Welsh, Kimberly M. *Black Litigants in the Antebellum American South*. Chapel Hill: University of North Carolina Press, 2018.

West, Emily. *Chains of Love: Slave Couples in Antebellum South Carolina*. Urbana: University of Illinois Press, 2004.

White, Ashli. *Encountering Revolution: Haiti and the Making of the Early American Republic.* Baltimore, Md.: Johns Hopkins University Press, 2010.

White, Deborah Gray. *Ar'n't I a Woman: Female Slaves in the Plantation South.* New York: Norton, 1985.

Williams, Eric. *Capitalism and Slavery.* Chapel Hill: University of North Carolina Press, 1944.

Williams, Heather Andrea. *Help Me Find My People: The African American Search for Family Lost in Slavery.* Chapel Hill: University of North Carolina Press, 2012.

Wilentz, Sean. *Rise of American Democracy: Jefferson to Lincoln.* New York: Norton, 2005.

Wood, Betty. "'White Society' and the 'Informal' Slave Economies of Lowcountry Georgia, c. 1730–1830." *Slavery & Abolition* 11, no. 3 (December 1990): 313–331.

Wood, Betty. *Women's Work, Men's Work: The Informal Slave Economies of Lowcountry Georgia.* Athens: University of Georgia Press, 1995.

Wood, Peter. *Black Majority: Negroes in Colonial South Carolina from 1670 Through the Stono Rebellion.* New York: Norton, 1974.

Young, Jeffrey Robert. *Domesticating Slavery: The Master Class in Georgia and South Carolina, 1670–1837.* Chapel Hill: University of North Carolina Press, 1999.

Zaborney, John V. *Slaves for Hire: Renting Enslaved Laborers in Antebellum Virginia.* Baton Rouge: Louisiana State University Press, 2012.

INDEX

COLUMBIA STUDIES IN THE HISTORY OF U.S. CAPITALISM

Series Editors: Devin Fergus, Louis Hyman, Bethany Moreton, and Julia Ott

Capital of Capital: Money, Banking, and Power in New York City, 1784–2012, by Steven H. Jaffe and Jessica Lautin

From Head Shops to Whole Foods: The Rise and Fall of Activist Entrepreneurs, by Joshua Clark Davis

Creditworthy: A History of Consumer Surveillance and Financial Identity in America, by Josh Lauer

American Capitalism: New Histories, edited by Sven Beckert and Christine Desan

Buying Gay: How Physique Entrepreneurs Sparked a Movement, by David K. Johnson

City of Workers, City of Struggle: How Labor Movements Changed New York, edited by Joshua B. Freeman

Banking on Freedom: Black Women in U.S. Finance Before the New Deal, by Shennette Garrett-Scott

Threatening Property: Race, Class, and Campaigns to Legislate Jim Crow Neighborhoods, by Elizabeth A. Herbin-Triant

How the Suburbs Were Segregated: Developers and the Business of Exclusionary Housing, 1890–1960, by Paige Glotzer

Brain Magnet: Research Triangle Park and the Idea of the Idea Economy, by Alex Sayf Cummings

Histories of Racial Capitalism, edited by Destin Jenkins and Justin Leroy